Text Genres and Registers: The Computation of Linguistic Features

Alex Chengyu Fang • Jing Cao

Text Genres and Registers: The Computation of Linguistic Features

 Springer

Alex Chengyu Fang
Linguistics and Translation
City University of Hong Kong
Hong Kong
China

Jing Cao
Zhongnan University of Economics
and Law
Wuhan
China

ISBN 978-3-662-45099-4   ISBN 978-3-662-45100-7 (eBook)
DOI 10.1007/978-3-662-45100-7

Library of Congress Control Number: 2014952898

Springer Berlin Heidelberg New York Dordrecht London

Printed on acid-free paper

Springer is part of Springer Science+Business Media (www.springer.com)

In loving memory of my father, Sui-fu Fang 方綏撫, *and my mother, Jiu-qiong He* 賀玖瓊

Preface and Acknowledgements

This book and the research that it describes would not have been completed without the full support received from the family and friends of the two authors.

The research described in this book was supported in part by grants received from the General Research Fund of the University Grant Council of the Hong Kong Special Administrative Region, China (Project no. CityU 142711), Humanities and Social Sciences Research Fund of the Education Department of Hubei Province (Project no. 2012G409), City University of Hong Kong (Project nos. 6354005, 7004091, 9610283, 7002793, 9610226, 9041694, and 9610188), Zhongnan University of Economics and Law (Project no. 32511102006) and the Fundamental Research Funds for the Central Universities (Project no. 31541110215). The authors would also like to acknowledge supports received from the Dialogue Systems Group, Department of Linguistics and Translation, and the Halliday Centre for Intelligent Applications of Language Studies, City University of Hong Kong.

Heartfelt thanks also goes to Ms. Rebecca Zhu for her support and assistance throughout the preparation of the book.

Hong Kong   Alex Chengyu Fang
July 2014   Jing Cao

Contents

About the Authors

Dr. Alex Chengyu Fang is an Associate Professor at City University of Hong Kong, where he directs the Dialogue Systems Group based at the Department of Linguistics and Translation. He is Adjunct Professor at the Beijing University of Aeronautics and Astronautics. He received his PhD (2006) from University College London. He has also taught or researched at University of Sussex, University College London and the Guangzhou Institute of Foreign Languages. His research interests include corpus linguistics, computational linguistics, dialogue systems and information retrieval. National Expert representing China in Technical Committee 37 in International Organisation for Standardisation, he is also an expert member of the China National Technical Committee on Terminology for Standardisation. He was Deputy Director of Survey of English Usage, University College London from 1995 to 1996.

Dr. Jing Cao is an Associate Professor at Zhongnan University of Economics and Law. She received her PhD (2011) from City University of Hong Kong. Her research interests include corpus linguistics and dialogue act analysis.

Chapter 1
Introduction

This book is about the identification of linguistic features that can be applied to the automatic detection and classification of texts according to different criteria, including modes of production such as speech and writing, genres such as academic writing and newspaper articles and registers such as formal and informal discourse. To a large extent, the discussions in this book are different from other approaches to the similar end. While many other studies focus on the computational aspects, the various chapters here address different linguistic aspects related to the syntactic structure and empirically demonstrate their usefulness for the identified application tasks.

The research described in this book originated from a fundamental interest in literary stylistics when C. A. Fang was reading English language and literature as a university undergraduate in Guangzhou, south of China, in the early 1980s, where he developed a keen interest in T. S. Eliot and his poems. Specific questions there and then include 'What exactly in his poems that marks them out as composed by the poet?', 'Is it his diction, his use of imageries, or his preference for unusual grammatical devices?', 'Is it possible to pinpoint his literary fingerprints such that would separate him out from the other contemporary poets?'. After graduation, he was offered a position in the same department as a lecturer and was soon introduced to what was then a rather unknown area called corpus linguistics by Prof Gui Shichun, who had just returned from a visit to the University of Lancaster, UK, with a book entitled *The Computational Analysis of English: A Corpus-Based Approach* edited by Roger Garside, Geoffrey Leech and Geoffrey Sampson in 1987. The book triggered a series of investigations that C.A. Fang was to pursue, which has included the construction of linguistic corpora (including the very first albeit small corpus of poems by T. S. Eliot), grammatical tagging, syntactic parsing and computational modelling of linguistic variations across different registers, genres, subject domains and authors. So, in a nutshell, this book is a descriptive account of such investigations aimed at the identification of characteristic features as 'fingerprints' and the application of such features to identify a specific genre, register or author. More specifically, through his association during 1990s with the Survey of

© Springer-Verlag Berlin Heidelberg 2015
A. C. Fang, J. Cao, *Text Genres and Registers: The Computation of Linguistic Features,*
DOI 10.1007/978-3-662-45100-7_1

English Usage, University College London, he was deeply influenced by the work of Professor Sidney Greenbaum, who was at the time busy managing the syntactic annotation of the International Corpus of English-Great Britain (ICE-GB) corpus and writing his Oxford English Grammar , and has since been focusing on the grammatical aspects of language. This volume therefore has demonstrated some preference for the grammatical and syntactic properties of language as a potentially rich repertoire to yield characteristic features. At the same time, however, this volume also intends to provide a balanced view of the different approaches through the additional inclusion of research experiments that involved the use of lexical and semantic properties.

1.1   The Corpus as a Model of Linguistic Use

Looking back at the rather short course of development since the completion of the Brown University Corpus of Edited Present-Day American English in 1964 as the first computerised corpus, one cannot but agree that corpus linguistics is seen today as perhaps one of the most important approaches to linguistic studies. Based on a systematic collection of authentic texts either written or transcribed from natural speech, corpus linguistics has revolutionised people's view on language as a complex system that cannot be adequately described by a set of rewrite rules handcrafted according to intuitive knowledge. It has engendered a research methodology that, in addition to our a priori understanding about language, relies on empirical observations as the ultimate informant. It has as a result revolutionised natural language processing systems that can now robustly handle unforeseen phenomena in language through the employment of transitional probabilities regarding words, grammatical entities and syntactic constructions. It has extended the notion of linguistics as a scientific study of language to one that affords a powerful instrument underlying most of the commercial systems that handle man–machine interactions either through the use of the keyboard or via voice. It is in this sense that corpus linguistics has penetrated the barrier of linguistics as removed from the populace and established closest links with people's everyday lives.

Although a good part of the use of linguistic corpora has been devoted to lexical studies, starting from Edward Thorndike (Thorndike and Lorge 1944) and J.B. Carroll (Carroll et al. 1971) to John Sinclair (Sinclair 1991) for their monumental effort to use corpus evidence for the selection of lexical items, an equally important part is devoted to the grammatical aspects of language, which took place even before the Brown Corpus. In 1959, Randolph Quirk started the project of Survey of English Usage, which aimed to provide documented resources, both spoken and written, for accurate descriptions of grammatical uses by educated British nationals. This work is ground-breaking in that its corpus was designed according to a range of registerial differences, which included speech and writing as the two basic modes of production. In speech, the texts are grouped according to different social scenarios such as dialogues and monologues. The written texts are also categorized such that they further demonstrate a range of different topics in different contexts, reflecting different degrees of formality and intimacy. The corpus hence serves as a miniature model of language production that demonstrates special preferences for grammatical constructions defined in terms of social contexts. The same tradition was carried forth by Sidney Greenbaum, who pushed further the notion of parameterized grammatical studies to different varieties of English through the International Corpus of English, which he first proposed in 1988 (Greenbaum 1988). Upon the completion of the British component, he published an edited volume entitled *Comparing English Worldwide: The International Corpus of English* (Greenbaum 1996a) and shortly afterwards a grammar entitled *The Oxford English Grammar* (Greenbaum 1996b). This work is monumental. It sees the corpus as a carefully structured collections of texts selected to represent a systematic range of text production contexts that entail registerial changes. A study of grammar on the basis of the corpus is a study of parameterized grammatical preferences and conventions which, once held to be representative, can be used to categorise unseen texts not included in the corpus.

We thus see in ICE a classic use of corpus evidence: observation of the same linguistic phenomenon within different contexts and the validation of the observations through a process that is often referred to nowadays as prediction, that is, the prediction of a text about its genre and/or register according to the previously observed linguistic preferences or features. Central to this model of investigation is the corpus itself, which embodies an internal and an external dimension.

1.2   The Internal and External Dimensions in the Corpus

Here, the internal dimension of language refers to the linguistic constituents within the language architecture that speakers employ to express their intended meaning. In Halliday's terms, such constituents can be described as phonological, graphological and lexicogrammatical (Halliday and Matthiessen 2004, pp. 3–10). Alternatively, this dimension includes lexis, grammar and syntax and can be further extended to semantics, pragmatics and discourse. The external dimension is defined through the various contexts within which elements of the internal dimension are used. Obviously, this dimension can be defined in a multitude of ways, for example according to modes of production such as speech and writing, genders such as male and female and age groups such as toddler and adult. An important notion here is the observation about the internal dimension from the perspective of the external dimension. More importantly, the investigation is usefully focused on changes in the internal dimension along with the changes in the external dimension. In another word, such a model provides us with the insight into 'language use' which glosses together linguistic variations appropriate for a certain context. Figurre 1.1 is a graphical representation of such a model.

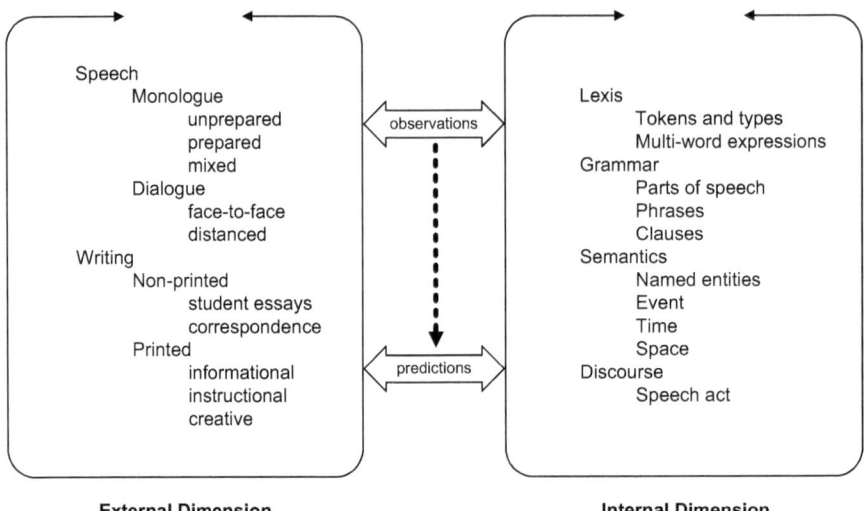

Fig. 1.1 A model of corpus-based investigation of language use

From Fig. 1.1, we see that the internal dimension includes lexis, grammar, semantics and discourse as well as some of the subsumed areas of investigation such as multiword expressions, parts of speech and speech act. The external dimension is defined according to speech and writing, where speech is subdivided into monologues and dialogues and writing into nonprinted and printed, which generally demonstrate varying degrees of formality and hence different register. Such a model allows for interactions between the two dimensions: a change in the external dimension will result in some corresponding change in the internal dimension. Conversely, a change in the internal dimension in terms of the use of words and choice of grammatical construction will lead to the perception that such a use is appropriate for a certain external dimension. For instance, the spoken genre will generally refer to an internal dimension with a higher frequency of personal pronouns such as *you* and *I* as far as lexis is concerned. Grammatically speaking, the spoken genre commonly entails a preferred use of active voices and the present tense. This is a perspective oriented towards the genre or the type of text. Alternatively, from a perspective focused on the internal dimension, we tend to associate a text with a higher concentration of passive constructions and the past tense with the written genre that is generally more formal and informative than speech. It is thus as if there was an interaction between the two dimensions: A type in the external dimension, such as speech, opts for a designated set of features in the internal dimension; conversely, the choice of a subset of features from the internal dimension will point towards a linguistic mode of production or a specific genre. The double-headed arrow marked *observations* is an attempt to reflect this interaction. It is exactly this kind of interaction that we are interested in finding out about which defines the predictive power of the corpus as a model of language use.

1.3   The Predictive Power of the Corpus

Following the dotted arrow leading from *observations* in Fig. 1.1, our attention is now focused on the double-headed arrow named *predictions*. First of all, we say that a powerful use of the corpus has to do with its ability to generalize from empirical observations.[1] Second and more importantly, such generalisations can be validated, again in empirical terms to the extent where one can substantiate such generalisations according to their success rate as well as contexts of use, something that simply cannot be adequately achieved through any approach to language other than corpus linguistics. The ability to generalize about linguistic phenomena beyond the corpus is afforded for by the representativeness of the corpus, which is achieved through two major considerations. The first concerns the informed selection of a range of representative genres of texts for inclusion in the corpus. This has to do with the careful planning or designing of the corpus composition which should address the fundamental purpose of the corpus. If the primary objective is to represent general English, then the corpus composition should comprise a range of genres and text types that commonly come across in everyday use of the language. The design of the Brown Corpus of Edited American English is a classic example, which aims to model the major genres of writing that an average American is exposed to, therefore necessitating the inclusion of informative and imaginative genres comprising newspaper reports, academic articles, science fiction and western stories, etc. Additionally, the relative degrees of importance amongst the text categories should also be decided. In the Brown Corpus, this is done through the actual number of samples or texts assigned to each category. The more important categories get assigned more samples. The Survey of English Usage Corpus, as another example, assigns more samples to the spoken category which eventually accounted for 60 % of the overall corpus size, reflecting its chosen emphasis on the spoken genres. This step of corpus design ensures that the genres and text categories chosen for inclusion in the corpus will be maximally reusable once the corpus is completed. The next consideration to ensure representativeness of the corpus is to scientifically select the component texts. This typically is achieved through random or equidistant sampling. This step continues until the predefined number of samples is reached.

The two steps above ensure that the corpus is maximally representative of the language. Observations based thereon are theoretically generalisable to unseen texts. If we observe a higher use of demonstrative pronouns in the spoken genre, we can generalize and *predict* that an unseen spoken text not included in the corpus should similarly exhibit a higher use of such pronouns. This is the predictive power of the corpus, which is usefully defined in terms of probabilities of success when extended to unseen texts. Even more usefully, such probabilities of success with unseen texts are additionally defined in terms of scenarios. Consider the written genre, which is observed to yield a higher frequency, and hence probability, of

---

[1] Here, corpus linguists tend to differentiate between the 'corpus-based' method and the 'corpus-driven' method, which is outside the scope of this book and hence not discussed. The authors' view is that there is no real difference between the two.

occurrence of the passive construction. On the basis of the component categories with the written genre, we may further observe that between news reports and academic exposition, the latter is more likely to make use of this construction. This fact suggests that there are different degrees of granularity associated with corpus-based prediction: the more fine-grained the component categories and text types, the more fine-grained the prediction will be. Similarly, the predictive power of the corpus also largely rests with its linguistic annotations. Generally speaking, the more fine-grained the annotation is, the more likely the corpus is to produce useful features that can be utilised at a later stage to help with prediction. For example, a coarsely designed tagset noting the major parts of speech such as nouns, verbs and adjectives will not be as informative as a linguistically rich tagset that, for the class of verbs, distinguishes between different types of transitivities. As yet another example to demonstrate the usefulness of fine-grained linguistic analysis, a canonical parse tree showing the NP–VP structure will not be able to compete with a fine analysis that explicitly indicates the clausal functions of syntactic categories, such as the adverbial use of the PP and the PP as NP postmodification. We thus see an advanced state of corpus-based approach to linguistic investigations that eventually feed into applications in the areas of information processing, which requires a carefully designed repertoire of text categories in terms of genres and registers and also an annotation framework with detailed linguistic analyses.

A paradigm of past research indiscriminately made use of collections of texts and applied linguistic analyses that were either ill chosen or plainly inappropriate. It was not uncommon to read conclusions from some of the past studies that the use of additional linguistic information for the task of information processing led to poorer results. This book is therefore intended to be a radical departure from this research paradigm and aims to illustrate the importance of insightful linguistic understanding that feeds into the proper choice of training texts and the appropriate selection of linguistic annotation for characteristic features. It will aim to demonstrate that, through the various empirical results to be reported here, fine linguistic models can be constructed and useful features extracted which will eventually contribute towards high-performance NLP systems.

1.4   Genres and Registers

By and large in the past 50 years, the representative function of the corpus has been thoroughly understood and appreciated. Most of the corpora constructed and available nowadays are scientifically sampled to maximally facilitate statistical inferences. At the same time, many have additionally aimed to be linguistically balanced with a variety of different text categories, mostly following the good practices laid out in the Brown corpus. A more recent interest has been placed in the design and construction of corpora that include both spoken and written texts, following the pioneering work of the Survey of English Usage Corpus and also the British component of the International Corpus of English, both of which contain a larger portion of transcribed speech than writing. As mentioned earlier, in this book, linguistic features will be investigated within the parameters from the external dimension. Therefore, it is necessary to discuss our understanding of text typology, especially 'genre' and 'register', notions that have been considered as most problematic (Lee 2001) .

There are, nevertheless, well-recognized definitions for both terms. Genre is no longer restricted to literary studies. Swales (1990), for example, considered genre as 'a class of communicative events, the members of which share some set of communicative purposes' (Swales 1990, p. 58). Martin (2001, p. 155) defined genre as 'a staged, goal-oriented, purposeful social activity in which speakers engage as members of our culture'. The term 'register', suggested by Reid (1956), was referred to the capacity of human language to adapt itself to different social situation (as cited in Moreno 2006, p. 92). The problematic nature of the two terms result in two different schools of thought: some use the two terms interchangeably, while others prefer a distinction between genre and register.

Douglas Biber represents the first group by defining both genre and register with the same criteria such as purpose and topic. Biber (1988) asserted that '[g]enre categories are determined on the basis of external criteria relating to the speaker's purpose and topic; they are assigned on the basis of use rather than on the basis of form' (p. 170). Later, Biber et al. (1998) pointed out that registers are varieties of texts defined by external criteria based on situational characteristics, including their 'purpose, topic, setting, interactiveness, mode, etc.' (p. 135).

The second group including Couture (1986), Lee (2001), and Martin (2001) distinguished register from genre. According to Couture (1986, p. 82), the differentiation between register and genre is described as follows:

> While registers impose explicitness constraints at the level of vocabulary and syntax, genres impose additional explicitness constraints at the discourse level.

Lee (2001) asserted that 'registers and genre are in essence two different ways of looking at the same object' (p. 46). To be more specific,

> Register is used when we view a text as language: as the instantiation of a conventionalized, functional configuration of language tied to certain broad societal situations, that is, variety according to use (Lee 2001, p. 46).

> Genre is used when we view the text as a member of a category: a culturally recognized artefact, a grouping of text according to some conventionally recognized criteria, a grouping according to purposive goals, culturally defined (Lee 2001, p. 46).

Martin (2001) believes that genre is associated with culture while register with situation. The relation between register and genre can be illustrated in a model of language called 'co-tangential circles' (Martin 2001, p. 156) see (Fig. 1.2). The model shows that 'language functions as the phonology of register, and register (and thus language) function as the phonology of genre' (Martin 2009, p. 22).

In this book, we treat register and genre as two distinctive aspects of a text, which can be viewed from the two dimensions in the model proposed earlier in

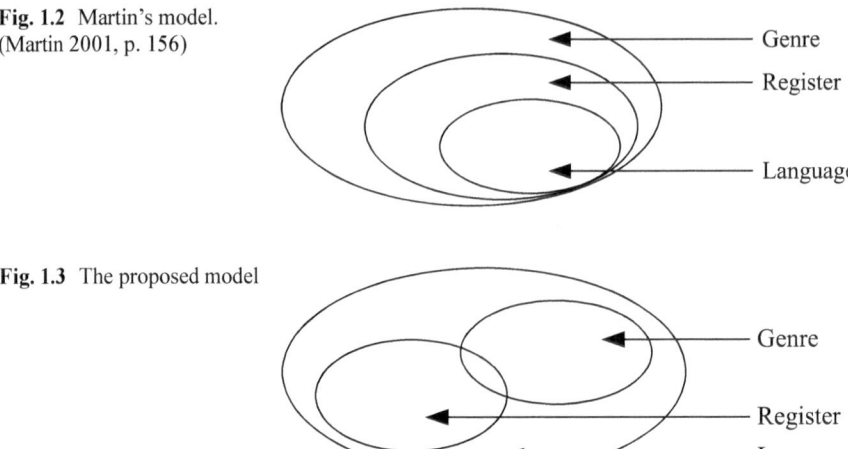

Fig. 1.2 Martin's model.
(Martin 2001, p. 156)

Fig. 1.3 The proposed model

Sect. 1.2. For example, we may say that a public speech is more likely to be in a higher register than daily conversation in terms of linguistic features such as lexical choice and syntactic structure. In this sense, register can be viewed from the internal dimensions. Therefore, through the use of language, we would understand register as the degree of formality. Meanwhile, from the external dimensions, genre corresponds to text categories such as fiction, newspaper and academic prose. Although register and genre are separate aspects, there is a natural affinity between them. For example, it is also quite natural that even among the same genre, some texts may be more formal than some others. More interestingly, because of the long established linguistic conventions regarding form and meaning, we say that a certain genre is seen to designate a certain degree of formality, and vice versa. For instance, academic prose is commonly seen to be more formal than fictional writing. As another example, the genre of interactive speech is generally less formal than monologues. This is where register and genre may overlap. According to our model of the two dimensions, the relation between the register and the genre can be presented as in Fig. 1.3.

According the figure above, Language encapsulates both Genre and Register, suggesting the internal (the register) and the external (the genre) aspects as the two intrinsic dimensions of language. The overlapping between genre and register has a twofold implication. First, when reading texts from the same genre, we can tell the difference in the degree of formality in terms of language use. For example, within the genre of academic prose, when employing more uses of the passive voice, texts from Science tend to be more formal than those from Arts. Second, different genres are observed to have different degree of formality. For example, texts from academic prose, when treated as a whole, are often considered more formal than those from newspapers.

1.5   Linguistic Variation across Genres and Registers

With the availability of corpora and their applications in language studies, it is
well recognized that corpus-based observations of language use inevitably illustrate 'different preferences for language use under different conditions' (Yamazaki
and Sigley 2013, p. 17). The different conditions have usually resulted from the
metadata in the chosen corpus or corpora, which are often referred to factors such
as gender, time and text categories. When the parameter of conditions is chosen,
the language preference is then observed from a particular linguistic aspect or
at different levels such as lexical, syntactic and grammatical levels. Therefore,
corpus-based studies into language variation have productive research potentials.
As a matter of fact, considerable research has been devoted to corpus-based investigations of language variations, with subsequent publications in various forms
such as papers, books and conference proceedings. For example, *Approaching
Language Variation through Corpora* edited by Shunji Yamazaki and Robert
Sigley (2013), *English Corpus Linguistics: Variation in Time, Space and Genre
(Selected papers from ICAME 32)* edited by Andersen and Bech (2013), the International Conference on Genre- and Register-Related Text and Discourse Features
in Multilingual Corpora held in Brussels in January 2013, to name just a few most
recent ones. While studies have contributed significantly to various fields such
as linguistic theories, sociolinguistics and second language acquisition, this book
will investigate empirically the linguistic variation across genres and registers
based on the proposed two-dimensional model.

When it comes to linguistic variation across genres and registers, substantial
studies have also been done. *Variation across Speech and Writing* (Biber 1988) has
been considered as a classic work. The study investigated a variety of linguistic features (i.e. 67 linguistic features) and employed a multidimensional analytical model
that has been well recognized and applied (e.g. Biber et al. 2002; Biber and Kurjian
2006; Van Rooy and Terblanche 2009; Grieve et al. 2010). More recently, further
efforts have been continued in the direction of lexical studies (e.g. hapax legomena,
Renouf 2013; signalling nouns, Flowerdew and Flowerdew 2013), grammatical and
syntactic studies (e.g. adjectival complementation, Kaatari 2013; clause fragments,
Bowie and Aarts 2013; light verb constructions, Ronan and Schneider 2013) and
pragmatic studies (e.g. general extender, Federica 2013).

According to our two-dimensional model, studies reported in this book will also
observe linguistic features from the internal dimension, covering lexical, grammatical, syntactic, semantic and pragmatic features. Instead of conflating the chosen
features, we intend to examine closely the distributional tendency of each individual
feature across genres or registers represented in the corpora. More importantly, we
also attempt to investigate these features from the computational perspective. In
other words, experiments are carried out to see how or to what extent the distributional pattern of the observed linguistic features could contribute to the field of
natural language processing, especially in the area of automatic genre analysis and
text classification.

Chapter 2
Language Resources

As for corpus-based studies, the research questions, observations and findings are largely dependent on the language resources. General corpora usually provide a diverse range of genres and registers, whereas specialised corpora have an exclusive focus. It is also worth noting that language resources are not restricted to different types of corpora, either as the target corpus or as the reference corpus. Very often, corpus-based investigations would turn to lexical resources for further analysis of the data obtained from the chosen corpus or corpora. In this chapter we are going to briefly review some of the well-known language resources, among which some are used in our studies (e.g. BNC, ICE) while some (e.g. PubMed, WordNet) are commonly used in the computation of language features. We should admit that it would be difficult to provide a comphrehensive list of all the important resources or to mention all the studies that have been done on the basis of the resources. Therefore, the overview of language resources in this chapter will be focused on the design of the selected resources, their intended purposes and major application.

2.1 General Corpora

2.1.1 The Brown Corpus and the Brown Family

The Brown Corpus It would be safe to say that no introduction to corpora would fail to mention the Brown Corpus, the first publicly available computerised, general corpus. Better known as the Brown Corpus, the Standard Corpus of Present-Day Edited American English was compiled by W. Nelson Francis and Henry Kučera and first released in 1964. The manual available at http://icame.uib.no/brown/bcm. html reveals the following features of the corpus:

1. The corpus consists of edited English prose printed in the USA during 1961.
2. A rough count of 2000 words was made for each sample.
3. Five hundred samples were chosen for their representative quality.

© Springer-Verlag Berlin Heidelberg 2015
A. C. Fang, J. Cao, *Text Genres and Registers: The Computation of Linguistic Features*,
DOI 10.1007/978-3-662-45100-7_2

4. The samples represent 15 different categories of prose.
5. The corpus will be used for comparative studies.

See Table 2.1 for the composition of the Brown Corpus.

The Brown Family The Brown Corpus is well recognised not only because it is the first computerised general corpus but also because the structure of the Brown composition has been cloned in a set of corpora that are often referred to as the 'Brown Family', which includes the four core members (i.e. Brown, LOB, Frown and FLOB) and the extended family members as well. See Table 2.2 for a summary, where the corpora are arranged according to the date of their first release. The members of the Brown family not only copied the composition of the Brown Corpus and the size of the sample text (about 2000 words each), and they are also samples of printed materials, or written English.

Application

a. Linguistic Studies

As McEnery et al. (2006) pointed out, 'lexical and grammatical studies are probably the areas that have benefited most from corpus data' (p. 145). With the availability of the Brown family, substantial studies have been made on various aspects both intra-corpus and inter-corpora.

In terms of intra-corpus studies[1], the most typical study would be frequency investigation (e.g. Zettersten and Kučera 1978; Francis and Kučera 1982; Nakamura 1989, 2002), and substantial studies have also been made in linguistics, including lexical and grammatical studies (e.g. Johansson 1978; Ellegård 1978; Kjellmer 1979, 1980), semantic studies (e.g. Hermerén 1978; Warren 1978), and also studies on collocations (e.g. Backlund 1981; Kjellmer 1982).

Inter-corpora studies have been firstly focus on the comparison between American and British English since for a long time the Brown and LOB corpora have been the only available comparable language resources. Again, the studies consist of frequency investigation (e.g. Johansson 1980; Hofland and Johansson 1982; Krogvig and Johansson 1984), lexical and grammatical analysis (e.g. Krogvig and Johansson 1981; Johansson and Norheim 1988; Collins 1996), and syntax and semantic analysis (e.g. Coates and Leech 1980; Coates 1983; Johansson and Oksefjell 1996). With the availability of the Brown family, comparative studies start to cover more variations of English, for instance, a comparison between American, British and Indian English (e.g. Leitner 1994).

In addition to the aforementioned synchronic studies, diachronic comparison has also been made across the four core members of the Brown family (i.e. Brown, LOB, Frown, and FLOB), such as historical syntactic investigation in general (Rissanen 2012), and more specifically on English adverbial subordinators (Rissanen 2011).

---

[1] http://www.helsinki.fi/varieng/CoRD/corpora/BROWN/bibliography.html.

Table 2.1 Composition of the Brown Corpus

Writing (100 %)				
Informative prose			Imaginative prose	
A: Press: Reportage	Political	14	K: General fiction	
	Sports	7	Novels	20
	Society	3	Short stories	9
	Spot news	9		
	Financial	4	L: Mystery and detective fiction	
	Cultural	7	Novels	20
B: Press: Editorial	Institutional	10	Short stories	4
	Personal	10		
	Letters to the editor	7	M: Science fiction	
C: Press: Reviews		17	Novels	3
D: Religion	Books	7	Short stories	3
	Periodicals	6		
	Tracts	4	N: Adventure and western fiction	
E: Skills and hobbies	Books	2	Novels	15
	Periodicals	34	Short stories	14
F: Popular lore	Books	23		
	Periodicals	25	P: Romance and love story	
G: Belles-lettres, etc.	Books	38	Novels	14
	Periodicals	37	Short stories	15
H: Miscellaneous	Government documents	24		
	Foundation reports	2	R: Humour	
	Industry reports	2	Novels	3
	College catalogue	1	Essays, etc.	6
	Industry house organ	1		
J: Learned	Natural sciences	12		
	Medicine	5		
	Mathematics	4		
	Social and behavioural sciences	14		
	Polit, law, education	15		
	Humanities	18		
	Technology and engineering	12		

Table 2.2 Corpora of the Brown family

Corpus	First release	Language	Data period
Brown Corpus	1964	American English	1961
Lancaster-Oslo-Bergen (LOB)[a]	1976	British English	1961
The Kolhapur Corpus of Indian English[b]	1986	Indian English	1978
The Australian Corpus of English (ACE)[c]	1987	Australian English	1986
The Wellington Corpus of Written New Zealand English (WWC)[d]	1993	New Zealand English	1986–1990
Freiburg Update of the Brown Corpus (Frown)[e]	1999	American English	1992
Freiburg-LOB Corpus of British English (FLOB)[f]	1999	British English	1991
CROWN[g]	2012	American English	2009
CLOB[g]	2012	British English	2009/± 1 year

[a] Manual: http://khnt.hit.uib.no/icame/manuals/lob/INDEX.HTM
[b] Manual: http://khnt.hit.uib.no/icame/manuals/kolhapur/index.htm
[c] Manual: http://khnt.hit.uib.no/icame/manuals/ace/INDEX.HTM
[d] Manual: http://icame.uib.no/wellman/well.htm
[e] Manual: http://khnt.aksis.uib.no/icame/manuals/frown/INDEX.HTM#pre
[f] Manual: http://khnt.aksis.uib.no/icame/manuals/flob/INDEX.HTM
[g] http://www.fleric.org.cn/crown/

b. Dictionary Compilation

The Brown Corpus has also been used as the resource for the compilation of dictionaries. *American Heritage Dictionary* (1969), employing linguistic information (e.g. frequency counts) from the Brown Corpus, can be considered as the first corpus-based dictionary during the computerised corpus era. Later in 1994, *A Dictionary of English Collocations: based on the Brown Corpus* (1994), written by Kjellmer, was published by the Clarendon Press.

2.1.2 The International Corpus of English (ICE) Family

The International Corpus of English (ICE), first proposed by Sidney Greenbaum in 1988, was designed to serve as the language resource for comparative studies of English worldwide. Here *English* refers to the English language used in 24 nations or regions, where it is the first language or an official additional language. Due to the main goal of such a corpus, a general design[2] is expected to be followed by all the corpora in the ICE family:

[2] http://ice-corpora.net/ice/manuals.htm.

1. The overall size of each corpus is one million words of English produced after 1989.
2. Each corpus consists of 500 texts of about 2000 words each.
3. Each corpus covers 300 spoken and 200 written English texts.

See Table 2.3 for the general structure[3] (table quoted from Fang 2007, p. 29).

The ICE launched in 1990, and so far the following 12 subsets of the ICE family are available commercially or free under license:

1. Canada (ICE-CAN)
2. East Africa (ICE-EA)
3. Great Britain (ICE-GB)
4. Hong Kong (ICE-HK)
5. India (ICE-IND)
6. Ireland (ICE-IRE)
7. Jamaica (ICE-JA)
8. New Zealand (ICE-NZ)
9. Singapore (ICE-SIN)
10. Sri Lanka (ICE-SL)
11. The Philippines (ICE-PHI)
12. The USA (written) (ICE-USA)

ICAME Journal No 34 (2010) discusses the creation of new members of the ICE family, including Fiji, Bahamas, Malta and Nigeria. In addition, according to the ICE website (February 2013) , '[t]he tagging of all currently available ICE corpora with CLAWS7 and the USAS semantic tagger is now complete'. Among them, the ICE-GB is tagged and parsed, and manually validated. Tagging and parsing will be discussed later in Chap. 3.

Application

a. Linguistic Studies

The primary goal of ICE project is to facilitate the intercorpus studies between different varieties of Englishes. This section will mainly introduce special volumes devoted to the ICE project.

In 2004, a special issue of *World Englishes* reported the first series of ICE-based studies. The comparisons are made between inner circle varieties (e.g. British or New Zealand English) and outside circle varieties (e.g. Hong Kong, Indian and Singapore English). Linguistic features include multi-word verbs (Schneider 2004), negation of lexical *have* (Nelson 2004) and article use (Sand 2004).

A most recent book *Mapping Unity and Diversity Worldwide: Corpus-based Studies of New Englishes* edited by Hundt and Gut (2012)[4] can be considered a second series of the ICE-based studies. Again, varieties from the outside circle are compared with those from the inner circle, and language use has been examined from various

---

[3] http://ice-corpora.net/ice/design.htm.

[4] http://benjamins.com/#catalog/books/veaw.g43/main.

Table 2.3 Composition of ICE-GB

Speech (60%)

		Code	Category	
Dialogue	*Private*			
		S1A1	Direct conversations	90
		S1A2	Distanced conversations	10
	Public			
		S1B1	Class lessons	20
		S1B2	Broadcast discussions	20
		S1B3	Broadcast interviews	10
		S1B4	Parliamentary debates	10
		S1B5	Legal cross-examinations	10
		S1B6	Business transactions	10
Monologue	*Unscripted*			
		S2A1	Spontaneous commentaries	20
		S2A2	Unscripted speeches	30
		S2A3	Demonstrations	10
		S2A4	Legal presentations	10
	Mixed			
		S2B1	Broadcast news	20
	Scripted			
		S2B2	Broadcast talks	20
		S2B3	Nonbroadcast talks	10

Writing (40%)

		Code	Category	
Nonprinted	*Student writing*			
		W1A1	Untimed essays	10
		W1A2	Timed essays	10
	Correspondence			
		W1B1	Social letters	15
		W1B2	Business letters	15
Printed	*Informational*			
		W2A1	Learned: humanities	10
		W2A2	Learned: social sciences	10
		W2A3	Learned: natural sciences	10
		W2A4	Learned: technology	10
		W2B1	Popular: humanities	10
		W2B2	Popular: social sciences	10
		W2B3	Popular: natural sciences	10
		W2B4	Popular: technology	10
		W2C1	Press news reports	20
	Instructional			
		W2D1	Administrative writing	10
		W2D2	Skills and hobbies	10
	Persuasive			
		W2E1	Press editorials	10
	Creative			
		W2F1	Fiction	20

aspects, including verbs (Nelson and Ren 2012; Schilk et al. 2012; Schneider and Hundt 2012; Zipp and Bernaisch 2012), modals (Auwera et al. 2012; Collins and Yao 2012; Deuber et al. 2012), progressives (Hilert and Krug 2012), relativization strategies (Gut and Coronel 2012), infinitives (Mair and Winkle 2012) and quotatives (Höhn 2012).

In addition, as pointed out at the ICE website[5], 'for most participating countries, the ICE project is stimulating the first systematic investigation of the national variety'. Therefore, empirical studies have also contributed to our understanding of 'New' Englishes, such as Indian (e.g. Lange 2012), African (e.g. Jeffery and Van Rooy 2004; Nelson and Ren 2012) and Asian Englishes (e.g. Auwera et al. 2012).

b. Grammar Book Compilation

Another most important outcome from the ICE family is the production of grammar books, namely,

> *Oxford English Grammar* (Greenbaum 1996)
> *An Introduction to English Grammar* (3rd ed.) (Greenbaum and Nelson 2009)
> *Oxford Modern English Grammar* (Aarts 2011)

2.1.3 BNC and ANC

2.1.3.1 The British National Corpus (BNC)

The British National Corpus (BNC), a financially available corpus, was built on the efforts of an academic-industrial consortium, including Oxford University Press, Longman Group Ltd, Chambers Harrap, Oxford University Computing Services, Lancaster University and British Library Research and Development Department. The BNC is a 100-million-word corpus designed to represent contemporary English, and the main features can be summarised as follows:

1. It consists of both written (90 %) and spoken (10 %) samples.
2. The texts are mainly from the period of 1985 to 1994.
3. Written texts are selected from newspapers, periodicals, journals, books, student essays, letters and other sources.
4. Spoken texts are collected in different contexts with speakers from a balanced demographic background.

These features have categorised the BNC as a large, balanced, general corpus. Till now, there are three versions available as listed in Table 2.4.

More importantly, in the planning of the compilation of the BNC, quite a few applications have been laid out, as listed in the *BNC User Reference Guide*[6]:

---

[5] http://ice-corpora.net/ice/index.htm.

[6] http://www.natcorp.ox.ac.uk/docs/URG/BNCdes.html.

Table 2.4 BNC versions

Versions	First release	Distribution	Features
BNC 1.0	1995	European researchers	
BNC World	2001	Worldwide	Tagged
BNC XML	2007	Worldwide	Tagged, XML

- Reference book publishing
- Academic linguistic research
- Language teaching
- Artificial intelligence
- Natural language processing
- Speech processing
- Information retrieval

According to the *BNC User Reference Guide*, the BNC contains eight different text categories based on the categorizations by Lee (2001). Table 2.5 summarises the composition of the BNC.

Application

a. Linguistic Studies

The major contribution of the BNC is the application in linguistic studies, including investigations into morphological features (e.g. Plag et al. 1999), syntactic features (e.g. Kerz and Haas 2009; Choi 2012), pragmatic features (e.g. Deutschmann 2003; Jucker et al. 2008; Cheng 2010), register variations (e.g. Takahashi 2006) and also sociolinguistic studies (e.g. Xiao and Tao 2007).

With 100 million words, the BNC has been used to create frequency lists (e.g. Rayson and Garside 2000; Leech et al. 2001;Wang 2005); being a general corpus, the BNC has also been used as a reference corpus (e.g. Louwerse et al. 2008).

b. English Education

The BNC has been used in language teaching in mainly two ways: direct and indirectly. Texts from the BNC have been directly used as the material for English learners with the goal to improve their English proficiency (e.g. Aston 1998; Miangah 2011). Indirectly, the BNC has been used as the native English corpus to evaluate the English of non-native speakers (e.g. Chujo 2004; Liu et al. 2008; Mukundan and Roslim 2009; Philip et al. 2012; Sonbul and Schmitt 2013).

c. Artificial Intelligence and Natural Language Processing

The BNC has been contributed in the field of artificial intelligence by providing extensive data. It has been serving as the test bed for a variety of experiments, such as automatic acquisition of topic signatures (e.g. Cuadros et al. 2006), text semantic similarity (e.g. Mihalcea et al. 2006), nontopical classification of documents (e.g. Bekkerman et al. 2006) and automatic extraction of concept–feature triples (e.g. Kelly et al. 2010).

Table 2.5 Composition of BNC. (Adapted from http://www.natcorp.ox.ac.uk/docs/URG/codes. html#classcodes)

Speech (10%)			Writing (90%)		
Broadcasting	Discussion	53	*Academic prose*	Humanities_arts	87
	Documentary	10		Medicine	24
	News	12		Nat_science	43
				Polit_law_edu	186
Classroom		58		Soc_science	142
				Tech_engin	23
Consultations		128	*Admin*		12
			Advertisements		59
Conversations		153	*Biography*		100
			Commerce		112
Courtroom		13	*Email*		7
			Essays	School	7
Demonstrations		6		University	3
			Fiction	Drama	2
Interviews		13		Poetry	30
				Prose	431
Interview oral history		119	*Hansard*		4
			Institute doc		43
Lectures	Commerce	3	*Instructional*		15
	Humanities_arts	4	*Letters*	Personal	6
	Nat_science	4		Professional	11
	Polit_law_edu	7	*Miscellaneous*		503
	Soc_science	13	*News script*		32
			Newsp_brd-sht_nat	Arts	51
Meeting		132		Commerce	44
				Editorial	12
Parliamentary		6		Miscellaneous	95
				Report	49
Pub_debate		16		Science	29
				Social	36
Sermon		16		Sports	24

Table 2.5 (continued)

Speech (10%)	Writing (90%)		
	Newsp_other	Arts	15
		Commerce	17
		Report	39
		Science	23
		Social	37
		Sports	9
	Newsp_tabloid		6
	Nonacademic	Humanities_arts	110
		Medicine	17
		Nat_science	62
		Polit_law_edu	93
		Soc_science	123
		Tech_engin	123
	Pop_lore		211
	Religion		35

The BNC has also been used in the field of natural language processing for evaluations of models, such as text genre detection (e.g. Stamatatos et al. 2000), automatic term extraction (e.g. Kit and Liu 2008), *n*-grams for search engine (e.g. Keller and Lapata 2003), semantic graph (e.g. Widdows et al. 2002), speech recognition (e.g. Goyoh and Renals 1999; Athanaselis et al. 2005).

2.1.3.2   The American National Corpus (ANC)[7]

The ANC project began in 1988 for the goal of creating an American counterpart of the BNC, at least 100 million words of contemporary American English represented in a spectrum of genres. Similar to the BNC, the ANC consists of both spoken and written texts. The unique features of the ANC are as follows:

1. Sample texts are from the year of 1990 onward.
2. Each sample text is at least 1000 words.
3. All data are marked up with multi-layer annotations, including structural markup, sentence boundaries, part-of-speech (POS) tags, noun chunks, verb chunks and named entities.
4. All the data and annotations are free.

The ANC was designed to serve for the purposes of education, linguistic research and technology development.

---

[7] http://www.americannationalcorpus.org/index.html.

Table 2.6 Composition of OANC

Speech (22%)		Writing (78%)	
Face to face	93	Government, technical	6441
Telephone	2307	Travel guides	179
		Technical	1089
		Fiction	1
		Letters	245
		Nonfiction	45
		Journal	4563

Carrying out their goal of free resources, the ANC project now has been focusing on two sets of data. One is the Open American National Corpus (OANC)[8], which contains about 15 million words. See Table 2.6 for the composition.

The other is the Manually Annotated Sub-Corpus (MASC)[9], which is a subset of the OANC. Although it only consists of about 500,000 words, the MASC has both written and spoken data and are marked up with sentence boundaries, token, lemma and POS; noun and verb chunks; named entities; syntactic annotation; and coreference (Table 2.7).

Application So far the application of the ANC has been largely focused in the field of natural language processing, including word sense annotation (Passonneau et al. 2011; de Melo et al. 2012), annotator analysis (e.g. Bhardwaj et al. 2010; Passonneau et al. 2010) and multi-layer annotation (e.g. Ide and Suderman 2006).

Table 2.7 Composition of MASC

Speech (17%)		Writing (83%)	
Court transcript	2	Email	78
Debate transcript	2	Essay	7
Spoken	11	Fiction	5
		Government documents	5
		Journal	10
		Letters	40
		Newspaper	41
		Nonfiction	4
		Technical	8
		Travel guides	7
		Twitter	2
		Blog	21
		Ficlets	5
		Movie script	2
		Spam	110
		Jokes	16

[8] http://www.anc.org/data/oanc/.

[9] http://www.anc.org/data/masc/.

2.2 Specialised Collections

2.2.1 Wall Street Journal

The Wall Street Journal (WJS), published since July 8, 1889, has been considered as the largest newspaper in the USA by circulation. This daily newspaper, with a special emphasis on business and economic news, has been a valuable language resource for linguistic research and most of the WJS-based collections have been released through Linguistic Data Consortium.

1. WSJ collection from 1987 to 1989 was first released in 1993 as part of the ACL Data Collection[10] provided by Dow Jones, Inc. It contains 98,732 stories.
2. Paul and Baker (1991) reported the design for the WSJ-based corpus, named WJS CSR Corpus. The first two CSR Corpora, known as WSJ0 LDC93S6A, released in 1993) and WSJ1 (LDC94S13A, released in1994), consist of read speech with texts drawn from a machine-readable corpus of WSJ news text.
3. In 1995, Treebank-2 (LDC1999T42) released the raw text of 2499 stories from the 3-year WSJ, within which 1 million words of 1989 WSJ material was hand-parsed in Treebank-2 style.
4. In 1999, the same 2499 stories in Treebank-2 was syntactically parsed and released in Treebank-3 (LDC1999T42).
5. The Rhetorical Structure Theory (RST) Discourse Treebank (LDC2002T07) was released in 2002. The dataset contains a selection of 385 WSJ articles from the Penn Treebank, which have been annotated with discourse structure in the RST framework.
6. The Proposition Bank I (LDC2004T14) was released in 2004. This time the WSJ section of Treebank-2 was semantically annotated, 'each verb occurring in the Treebank has been treated as a semantic predicate and the surrounding text has been annotated for arguments and adjuncts of the predicate'.[11]

Application WSJ1 and WSJ2 have been widely used to develop spoken language technology. Some early studies can be found in the *Proceedings of the Spoken Language Technology Workshop* (Advanced Research Project Agency 1994). The dataset has also been used to train ASR (e.g. Vertanen 2006; Hurmalainen et al. 2013). Penn Treebank data has been extensively used in the testing of data annotations, including POS tagging (e.g. Brill 1995; Renshaw et al. 2014) and parsing (e.g. Socher et al. 2011; Vadas and Curran 2011; Flickinger et al. 2012). Other WJS-based collections such as DeepBank have also been used in linguistic studies. For example, Kordoni (2013) examined the English compound units in the DeepBank.

---

[10] https://catalog.ldc.upenn.edu/LDC93T1.

[11] https://catalog.ldc.upenn.edu/LDC99T42.

2.2.2   *PubMed*

PubMed is a well-known search engine in the biomedicine provided by The National Centre for Biotechnology Information (NCBI) and contains specialised collections such as MEDLINE, Medical Subject Headings (MeSH) and PubMed Central (PMC).

MEDLINE[12] MEDLINE, the NLM's premier citation database, is the largest component of PubMed. It was started in the 1960s and now provides over 20 million references to biomedical and life sciences journal articles back to 1946. The subject scope of MEDLINE is biomedicine and health, involving areas such as the life sciences, behavioral sciences, chemical sciences and bioengineering.

MeSH Database[13] MeSH is the US National Library of Medicine's controlled vocabulary for indexing articles for MEDLINE/PubMed. Use the MeSH database to find MeSH terms, including subheadings, publication types, supplementary concepts and pharmacological actions. MeSH terminology provides a consistent way to retrieve information that may use different terminology for the same concepts.

PMC[14] PMC launched in 2000 as a free archive for full-text biomedical and life sciences journal articles. As an archive, PMC is designed to provide permanent access to all of its content, even as technology evolves and current digital literature formats potentially become obsolete. In addition to its role as an archive, the value of PMC lies in its capacity to store and cross-reference data from diverse sources using a common format within a single repository. With PMC, a user can quickly search the entire collection of full-text articles and locate all relevant material. PMC also allows for the integration of its literature with a variety of other information resources that can enhance the research and knowledge fields of scientists, clinicians and others.

Application The specialised collections in PubMed have been used in areas such as information retrieval (e.g. Kayaalp et al. 2003; Díaz-Galiano et al. 2009; Pestana 2009; Jalali and Borujerdi 2011; Yeganova et al. 2011; Darmoni et al. 2012) and word sense disambiguation (e.g. Jimeno-Yepes et al. 2011; Chen et al. 2013).

---

[12] http://www.nlm.nih.gov/databases/journal.html.

[13] http://www.nlm.nih.gov/mesh/meshhome.html.

[14] http://www.ncbi.nlm.nih.gov/pmc/about/intro/.

2.3   Lexical Sources

2.3.1   WordNet[15]

WordNet (Miller 1995) is a large lexical database of English where words are grouped according to meaning. Different from ordinary collections of words such as a thesaurus, the WordNet has the following unique features:

1. Words are linked by specific senses.
2. Words are linked by conceptual-semantic and lexical relations.
3. The database only contains nouns, verbs, adjectives and adverbs.

Although the latest online-version of WordNet is 3.1 (announced on June 2011), the latest released version is still the version 3.0 (released on December 2006), which contains 155,287 words organised in 117,659 synsets for a total of 206,941 word-sense pairs[16].

Synsets are sets of cognitive synonyms that are intertwined with conceptual-semantic and lexical relations. The main relations include the super-subordinate relation and the part-whole relation, and the majority of the WordNet's relations connect words from the same POS, with few cross-POS pointers.

Application[17] The compilation of such a database has led to in-depth linguistic research, such as studies on semantic network (Fellbaum 1990, 1996), antonyms (Fellbaum 1995), semantic annotation (Fellbaum et al. 1998, 2001), metaphors (Fellbaum 2004). In addition, the unique structure of the WordNet has made it a useful tool for research in various fields, including:

1. Information retrieval (e.g. Flank 2000; Magnini and Strapparava 2001, Mihalcea and Moldovan 2001).
2. Word sense disambiguation (e.g. Banerjee and Pedersen 2002, 2003; Fellbaum et al. 2001; Kwong 2001).
3. Text analysis (e.g. Elberrichi et al. 2008; Li et al. 2009; Bawakid and Oussalah 2010).
4. Machine translation (e.g. Moon and Kim 1995; Rigau et al. 1995; Dorr 1997).

2.3.2   FrameNet

Another well-recognised lexical database is FrameNet (Baker et al. 1998), which contains more than 10,000 word senses interlinked according to frame semantics. In addition, the word senses are also presented in annotated examples, among which

---

[15] http://wordnet.princeton.edu/.

[16] http://wordnet.princeton.edu/wordnet/man/wnstats.7WN.html.

[17] http://wordnet.princeton.edu/wordnet/publications/.

are 170,000 manually annotated sentences. For instance, e.g. …[Cook the boys] … GRILL [Food their catches] [Heating_Instrument on an open fire].

Since the frames are mainly semantic that are often similar across languages, several projects are underway to build parallel FrameNets for languages around the world, including:

- Spanish FrameNet, http://sfn.uab.es:8080/SFN
- German FrameNet, http://www.laits.utexas.edu/gframenet/
- Japanese FrameNet, http://jfn.st.hc.keio.ac.jp/
- Swedish FrameNet, http://spraakbanken.gu.se/eng/swefn
- FrameNet Brasil, http://www.ufjf.br/framenetbr/
- Chinese FrameNet, http://115.24.12.8:8080/cfn/.

Application[18] The FrameNet has contributed substantially in natural language processing. For example, semantic frames sampled in the FrameNet have been used widely in automatic semantic role labelling (e.g. Gildea and Jurafsky 2000, 2001, 2002; Thompson et al. 2003; Kwon et al. 2004). It has also been widely used in applications such as information extraction (e.g. Baker and Sato 2003; Chow and Webster 2007; Ben Aharon et al. 2010), sentiment analysis (e.g. Ruppenhofer and Rehbein 2012), question answering (e.g. Fliedner 2004; Shen and Lapata 2007), machine translation (e.g. Boas 2002; Fung and Chen 2006).

It is worth noticing that frame-semantic analysis has been made in specialised domains such as biomedicine (e.g. Dolbey et al. 2006; Dolbey 2009), legal domain (e.g. Venturi et al. 2009) and soccer (e.g. Schmidt 2006).

Still other contributions of FrameNet have been made to the fields such as lexicography (e.g. Atkins et al. 2003; Fillmore and Petruck 2003), phraseology (e.g. Coyne and Rambow 2009) and collocation (e.g. Ruppenhofer et al. 2002).

---

[18] https://framenet.icsi.berkeley.edu/fndrupal/fnbibliography.

Chapter 3
Corpus Annotation and Usable Linguistic Features

Over the past 50 years of corpus linguistics since the Brown Corpus, the development of corpus annotation can be described as a process of gradual sophistication, one that is facilitated by the rapid development of computer technologies and also, more importantly, one that is propelled by the need for increasingly fine granularity of linguistic analysis for better descriptive insight into language. The need for fine-grained analysis at the same time is largely driven by the popularity of ubiquitous computing and intelligent computer software that attempts to model human intelligence and mimic human behaviour based on useful features made available by annotation of different types. Man–machine dialogue systems, as an example, perform at a high level of linguistic sophistication that draws from annotations on the basis of lexis, grammar, semantics and speech processing. Having said this, in corpus linguistics, there remains a debate over the necessity of corpus annotation. While some scholars believe that corpus annotation provides added value to linguistic corpora, others believe that corpus annotation can be harmful to linguistic insight. When talking about part of speech (POS) tagging, John Sinclair suggested that the tags would restrict the view of a linguist to what had already been annotated; in this sense, the text annotation would be equivalent to 'text contamination' (Sinclair 2004, p. 191). In this book, we take the view that corpus annotation is a process that implements what we have already understood about language and that the consolidated knowledge embodied in annotation will serve as an instrument to enable the discovery of new knowledge. In this view, there is no real confrontational conflict between corpus annotation and the enabling power of linguistic corpora but that they complement and lift each other to higher levels of development.

Despite the annotation versus non-annotation debate, a quick look-back at the course of development of corpus linguistics reveals a progress from raw to annotated corpora. As a matter of fact, one required condition nowadays for a corpus of any importance is whether or not it is annotated in any way or according to any specific analytical framework. A major reason for this implicit requirement is the fact that annotated corpora have come to be regarded as an important source of knowledge which, aided by sophisticated computing power and methods, can be extracted and modelled according to specific applications. These applications have extended from

© Springer-Verlag Berlin Heidelberg 2015

A. C. Fang, J. Cao, *Text Genres and Registers: The Computation of Linguistic Features,*
DOI 10.1007/978-3-662-45100-7_3

pure linguistic research into the area of knowledge engineering to facilitate, for instance, ubiquitous software systems for question answering. The emphasis on annotation and the subsequent proliferation of annotation schemes have triggered the need for standardization in order to ensure interoperability of language resources that have been annotated differently according to different annotation schemes. The International Organization for Standardization (ISO), as an example, has a sub-committee within its Technical Committee 37 that is devoted to the proposal and drafting of standards for various types of linguistic annotations. These standards have greatly helped to maximise the reusability and interoperability of annotated linguistic sources. This topic would be rediscussed later towards the end of chapter.

We identify the following levels of annotation that are commonly applied to linguistic corpora: textual annotation, grammatical annotation, syntactic annotation and semantico-pragmatic annotation. They will be discussed in the following sections.

3.1 Textual Annotation

Textual annotation refers to the inclusion or insertion of information that serves to explain the production background of the text. In this sense, it refers to any additional information about the original text layout on the printed page such as chapter names and end-of-line hyphenation. It also refers to the in-text inclusion of information regarding the publication of the text such as year of publication, source of publication, name of author, age of author at the time of publication and sometimes even the gender of the author. Textual annotation therefore touches the demographic aspect of the text. An excellent example for the textual annotation of the corpus can be found in the British National Corpus (BNC), which allows for user access to the following textual information:

- The boundary and part of speech of each word
- The sentence structure identified by CLAWS
- Paragraphs, sections, headings and similar features in written texts
- Speech turns, pausing, and paralinguistic features such as laughter in spoken texts
- Meta-textual information about the source or encoding of individual texts

Corpora of spoken texts are generally more complex in terms of textual annotation than their written counterparts. The spoken section of the BNC, for instance, requires the annotation of the utterance, paralinguistic phenomena and the alignment of overlapping speech. More specialised spoken corpora, such as the Survey of English Usage Corpus, require prosodic annotations of the tone unit including the onset and the nuclear. Strictly speaking, textual annotation is a nontrivial issue. While the annotation of spoken texts often entails a good deal of speech analysis, the annotation of written texts involves tokenisation, which can be rather problematic with languages such as Chinese where there are no explicit word boundaries. Therefore, textual annotation requires considerable manual validation and tends to be expensive in terms of time and cost.

3.2 Grammatical Annotation

The grammatical annotation of a corpus refers to the indication of the part of speech for the component word tokens in a text, a process that is often called part of speech (POS) tagging. Unlike textual annotation, POS tagging is largely performed automatically and, depending on projects, manual validation is performed to ensure maximum accuracy. Tagging schemes, also known as tagsets, are project-specific systems that set out the scope and content of analyses. While grammarians differ in terms of the number of word classes, a consensus has shown that the following classes form the core set:

- Adjective
- Adverb
- Conjunction
- Determiner
- Noun
- Preposition
- Pronoun
- Verb

We may fairly safely say that the half a dozen or so tagging schemes widely publicised today are all based on the above classes. They include those designed for the following projects: the Brown Corpus of Present-Day American English (Greene and Rubin 1971), the London-Lund Corpus of Spoken English (Svartvik and Eeg-Olofsson 1982), the Lancaster-Oslo/Bergen Corpus of Present-Day British English (LOB; Johansson et al. 1986), the Penn Treebank (Santorini 1990), the British National Corpus (Leech et al. 1994), the International Corpus of English (ICE; Greenbaum 1995) and the American National Corpus (Ide and Suderman 2004). Such a core set allows for comparisons between different tagsets for the same language such as English. It also additionally allows for comparisons across different languages; in the Translearn project, it was necessary to design such a core set to be applied to the 11 languages of the EU member states for purposes of multilingual text alignment (Campbell and Fang 1995) .

The differences between these schemes mainly exist in terms of subcategorisation, i.e. additional information regarding a specific word class such as the indications of proper nouns, past-tense verbs and intensifying adverbs. Broadly speaking, the more the subcategorisation information, the more likely it will be to identify characteristic features. To illustrate the different levels of subcategorisation, we shall describe the LOB and the ICE tagsets.

3.2.1 The LOB Tagset

Adapted from the tagset for the Brown Corpus of American English, the LOB tagset
was designed to tag the LOB Corpus, whereby each word and punctuation mark is
accompanied by a tag. The tags consist of 'one to five characters, usually mnemonic
labels forming groups with a transparent, partially hierarchical structure' (Johansson et al. 1986, p. 10). It is also the basis of the tagset for the British National Corpus
(Burnard and Aston 1998). In all, the LOB tagset can be classified by 23 base tags:

1.	**A...**	determiner/pronoun
2.	**BE...**	be (lexical verb or auxiliary)
3.	**CC**	coordinating conjunction
4.	**CD...**	cardinal numeral
5.	**CS**	subordinating conjunction
6.	**DO...**	do (lexical verb or auxiliary)
7.	**DT...**	determiner/pronoun
8.	**EX**	existential *there*
9.	**HV...**	have (lexical verb or auxiliary)
10.	**IN**	preposition
11.	**J...**	adjective
12.	**MD**	modal auxiliary
13.	**N...**	noun
14.	**OD...**	ordinal numeral
15.	**P...**	pronoun
16.	**QL...**	qualifier
17.	**R...**	adverb
18.	**TO**	infinitival *to*
19.	**UH**	interjection
20.	**VB...**	lexical verb
21.	**W...**	wh-word
22.	**XNOT**	not
23.	**ZZ**	letter

These expand into a total of 134 different tags when followed by suffixes marking
subclasses and inflections. For example, the adjective class has the following five
subclasses:

JJ	adjective
JJB	attributive-only adjective (*chief, entire, main*, etc.)
JJR	comparative adjective
JJT	superlative adjective
JNP	adjective with word-initial capital (*English, German*, etc.)

The expansion is achieved by appending J, JB, JR, JT, and NP suffixes to the
base tag J. These suffixes provide extra information regarding the word's lexical

characteristics (attributive-only adjective and adjective with word-initial capital) as well as its inflectional forms (comparative and superlative).

As another example, the noun class is expanded into 29 subclasses according to different considerations.

NC	cited word
NN	singular common noun
NN$	singular common noun + genitive
NNP	singular common noun with word-initial capital (*Englishman, German*, etc.)
NNP$	singular common noun with word-initial capital + genitive
NNPS	plural common noun with word-initial capital
NNPS$	plural common noun with word-initial capital + genitive
NNS	plural common noun
NNS$	plural common noun + genitive
NNU	abbreviated unit of measurement unmarked for number *hr, lb*, etc.)
NNU$	possessive abbreviated neutral unit of measurement: e.g. *cwt's*
NNUS	abbreviated plural unit of measurement (*gns, yds*, etc.)
NNUS$	possessive abbreviated plural unit of measurement: e.g. *c.c.s'*
NP	singular proper noun
NP$	singular proper noun + genitive
NPL	singular locative noun with word-initial capital (*Abbey, Bridge*, etc.)
NPL$	singular locativ noun with word-initial capital + genitivee
NPLS	plural locative noun with word-initial capital
NPLS$	plural locative noun with word-initial capital + genitive
NPS	plural proper noun
NPS$	plural proper noun + genitive
NPT	singular titular noun with word-initial capital (*Archbishop, Captain*, etc.)
NPT$	singular titular noun with word-initial capital + genitive
NPTS	plural titular noun with word-initial capital
NPTS$	plural titular noun with word-initial capital + genitive
NR	singular adverbial noun (*January, Sunday, east, today, downtown, home*)
NR$	singular adverbial noun + genitive
NRS	plural adverbial noun
NRS$	plural adverbial noun + genitive

The LOB tagset not only aims at a general classification of English words according to their grammatical categories but also introduces classes according to lexical forms. Special tags are assigned to various inflected forms of verbs: be (BE), do (DO), and have (HV) as well as existential *there* (EX), infinitival *to* (TO) and not (XNOT). No distinction, in the case of the three verbs, is made between uses as auxiliaries and as lexical verbs, except for *done* and *doing* which are always used as lexical verbs and are therefore tagged as VBN and VBG respectively. See Appendix B for a full list of LOB tags.

In short, the LOB tagset may be summarised as one that has a fairly comprehensive coverage of the major English word classes. Its main strength lies in the notation of the lexical characteristics of words and major shortcoming is the inability to provide detailed information for certain verbs that are equally frequently used as lexical verbs and auxiliaries. The reason for this is that the LOB tagset was initially designed for the study of lexical properties of English words and therefore pertains primarily to the morpho-syntactic features. As will be demonstrated in the following section, there is another tagset that is predominantly syntactically oriented and captures longer distance relations between words.

3.2.2   The ICE Tagset

The ICE tagset covers the following 22 basic classes:

ADJ	adjective
ADV	adverb
ANTIT	anticipatory *it*
ART	article
AUX	auxiliary
CLEFTIT	cleft *it*
CONJUNC	conjunction
CONNEC	connective
EXTHERE	existential *there*
FRM	formulaic expression
GENM	genitive marker
INTERJEC	interjection
NADJ	nominal adjective
N	noun
NUM	numeral
PRTCL	particle
PREP	preposition
PROFM	proform
PRON	pronoun
REACT	reaction signal
V	verb

Except for ANTIT, CLEFTIT, EXTHERE, and GENM, each of the above classes are subcategorised by a set of features describing both the word's grammatical characteristics and its inflectional changes. There are a total of 270 grammatically possible tag-feature combinations. See Appendix A for a complete list of ICE tag-feature combinations.

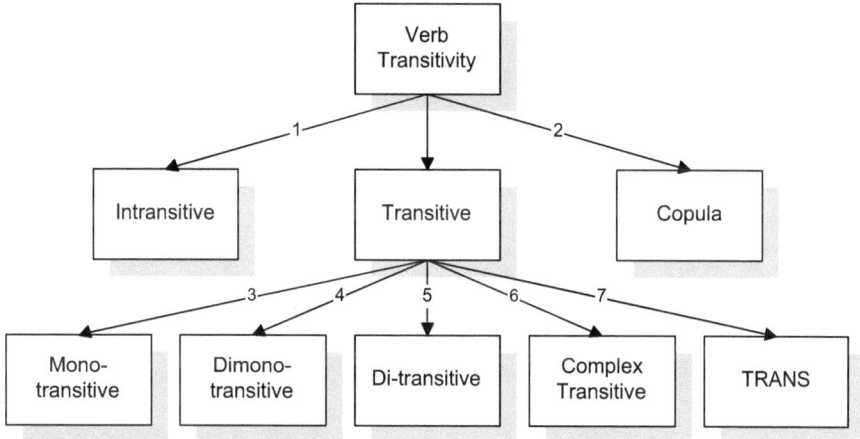

Fig. 3.1 The transitivity types in ICE

To illustrate the tag-feature hierarchy, the verb class is not only described for possible forms, such as past and present tenses, infinitival and past and present participles, but also subcategorised into seven transitivity types as illustrated in Fig. 3.1. Here are some examples to demonstrate these transitivity types.

Type 1: Intransitive (Subject + Verb) This type refers to verbs that do not possess any complement. Syntactically speaking, it results in a simple SV construction, as illustrated in [1] below:

[1]   *As an actor, I had <u>appeared</u> in innumerable schools broadcasts, in Sat-urday Night Theatre and in The Dales.*

Type 2: Copular (Subject + Verb + Subject Complement) This type is alternatively called link verbs, which are typically followed by adjective phrases and noun phrases analysable as subject complements, resulting in a SVC construction. See [2] below for an example, which involves the prototypical copular verb *be*.

[2]   *Of all my broadcasting, the Monday morning spot <u>was</u> perhaps the best fun.*

Type 3: Monotransitive (Subject + Verb + Direct Object) Monotransitive verbs are complemented by a direct object, the function of which is typically performed by a noun phrase or a clause.

[3]   *The programme had a biggish audience (in radio terms) because it <u>fol-lowed</u> the Today programme, and because people listened to it in their cars on the way to work.*

Type 4: Ditransitive (Subject + Verb + Indirect Object + Direct Object) Ditransitive verbs have two complements: indirect object and direct object. While the indirect object is invariably a noun phrase, the direct object can be either an NP or a clause.

[4]   *His parents were then recommended to stop comforting him as they were*
       giving him positive reinforcement for undesirable behaviour.

Type 5: Dimonotransitive (Subject + Verb + Indirect Object) The analysis of Type 5 involves a Type 4 verb except that the direct object is missing.

[5]   *The pen though, as Shakespeare will tell you, is more Mighty than the*
       sword.

Type 6: Complex Transitive (Subject + Verb + Direct Object + Object Complement) A verb is complex transitive if it commands both a direct object and an object complement. The object complement is obligatory, removal of which results in either an incomplete sentence or the change of meaning, as [6] below illustrates:

[6]   *If television was going to be bloody-minded, radio would keep me busy.*

Type 7: Trans (Subject + Verb + Nonfinite Clause with Overt Subject) The notation of Type 7, *TRANS* here, is used in the ICE project to tag transitive verbs followed by a noun phrase that may be the subject of the following nonfinite clause. They are so tagged in order to avoid making a decision on their transitivity types[1] (cf. Greenbaum 1993). This verb type is best demonstrated by the following sentences:

[7]   *Just before Christmas, the producer of Going Places, Irene Mallis, had*
       asked me to make a documentary on 'warm-up men'.
[8]   *They make others feel guilty and isolate them.*
[9]   *I can buy batteries for the tape - but I can see myself spending a fortune!*
[10]   *The person who booked me in had his eyebrows shaved and replaced by*
       straight black painted lines and he had earrings, not only in his ears but
       through his nose and lip!

In the above examples, *asked, make* and *had* are all complemented by nonfinite clauses with overt subjects, the main verbs of these nonfinite clauses being infinitive, present participle and past participle.

---

[1] This type of verb can be analysed differently according to various tests into, for instance, monotransitives, ditransitives and complex transitives (cf. Quirk et al. 1972, Chap. 15, 1985; Mair 1990) . Accordingly, to avoid arbitrary decisions, the complementing nonfinite clause is assigned a catchall term 'transitive complement' in parsing.

The need of syntactic information to apply ICE tags correctly can be addition-ally illustrated by the treatment of two different uses of pronoun *it*, namely the anticipatory use and the cleft use. 'Anticipatory *it* is used when a clause (generally one that might have functioned as subject) is postponed to provide a more balanced sentence, a sentence where what precedes the verb is shorter than what follows it' (Greenbaum 1996, p. 174), as exemplified by [11]:

[11]   *Before trying to answer the question it is worthwhile highlighting briefly some of the differences between current historians.*

'Cleft *it* serves as subject of a cleft sentence or cleft clause. The sentence is split to put the focus on some part of it. The cleft sentence is introduced by cleft *it* followed by a verb phrase whose main verb is a copular verb, generally *be*. The focused part comes next, followed by the rest of the sentence introduced by a relative item' (Greenbaum 1996, p. 175), as illustrated by [12]:

[12]   *It is from this point onwards that Roman Britain ceases to exist and the history of sub-Roman Britain begins.*

3.2.3   A Comparison of LOB and ICE

At a first glance, the two sets are similar enough. Both cover such major grammati-cal categories as articles, adjectives, adverbs, auxiliaries, nouns and verbs. Both assign compound tags (ditto tags) to a multi-word sequence, which functions as a single grammatical unit. A closer look, however, soon reveals many differences.

Some differences are minor. The LOB set, for instance, notes distinctions in case form for personal pronouns whereas ICE does not, assuming that the informa-tion can be easily retrieved through word forms. LOB treats *be*, *have*, *do*, *not* and existential *there* separately while ICE does so only for existential *there* and *it*. The infinitival *to* is assigned the tag TO in LOB. ICE, on the other hand, assigns to it PRTCL (particle), which covers not only infinitival *to* but also *for* (when introduc-ing the subject of an infinitival clause)and *with* and *without* (when introducing the subject of nonfinite clauses) . The treatment of particles in ICE can be demonstrated by the following examples, in which both the LOB and ICE tags are shown:

LOB	ICE	Example
TO	PRTCL(to)	*Do you want to see me?*
IN	PRTCL(for)	*It's for you to decide.*
IN	PRTCL(with)	*We can't have a party with a dead body lying on the doorstep.*

With prepositions, LOB assigns IN whereas ICE differentiates general preposi-tions PREP(ge) from those combining with verbs to form prepositional verbs PREP(phras). Here is an example:

LOB	ICE	Example
IN	PREP(ge)	*It rained <u>from</u> morning <u>till</u> night.*
IN	PREP(phras)	*He looked <u>at</u> the object and was puzzled.*

ICE has a more detailed subcategorisation for adverbs (ADV). This subclassification indicates features both semantic (intensifiers, particularisersand additives) and syntactic (phrasal adverbsand *wh*-adverbs). In LOB, they are generally tagged as RB. RP is applied to adverbs that typically pattern with verbs; this being more or less identical with ADV(phras) in ICE. Consider the following examples.

LOB	ICE	Example
RB	ADV(add)	*We <u>likewise</u> were invited to the reception.*
RB	ADV(excl)	*I was <u>merely</u> trying to get rid of it.*
RB	ADV(inten)	*It took us an <u>incredibly</u> long time to get home.*
RP	ADV(phras)	*He's making the story <u>up</u>.*
RB	ADV(ge)	*He stepped into the cave <u>carefully</u>.*

In the case of nouns, the LOB tags were found to be more detailed with 14 subclasses excluding the genitive marker $ whereas ICE has only four. Noting number distinctions and common and proper nouns as ICE does, LOB also tags nouns differently as locative (NPL), titular (NPT) and adverbial (NR)—features not found in ICE. Mostly for the benefit of parsing, the ICE system applies compound or 'ditto' tags to every sequence of two or more nouns with a noun as head that constitutes a unit (cf. Greenbaum 1992). In such a unit, every member is tagged according to the head. The following are a few examples to illustrate compound nouns in the ICE annotation scheme:

LOB	ICE	Example
NN	N(com,sing):1/2	*railway*
NN	N(com,sing):2/2	*station*
NN	N(com,plu):1/2	*potato*
NNS	N(com,plu):2/2	*crisps*
JNP	N(com,sing):1/3	*English*
NNP	N(com,sing):2/3	*Department*
NN	N(com,sing):3/3	*office*
JNP	N(com,plu):1/4	*European*
NNP	N(com,plu):2/4	*Community*
NN	N(com,plu):3/4	*finance*
NNS	N(com,plu):4/4	*ministers*

As can be seen from the examples above, the ICE scheme is not particularly well suited for single word extraction when it comes to noun compounds. Less they are considered as a whole unit; it is odd to see *potato* tagged as a plural noun and *European* tagged as a plural common noun, for instance. The LOB scheme does better in this regard. Further, LOB distinguishes between proper nouns (NP) and common nouns with word-initial capitals (NNP) whereas ICE does not, tagging as proper any noun with a word-initial capital, except words at the beginnings of sentences. With adjectives and *-ed/-ing* forms in nominal positions, on the other hand, ICE has a more explicit treatment by assigning NADJ with features indicating both plurality and form. Following are the examples:

LOB	ICE	Example
NNPS	NADJ(prop)	*The French are our allies.*
JJ	NADJ(plu)	*The careless suffer most.*
JJ	NADJ(sing)	*a glimpse of the obvious*
JJT	NADJ(sup,sing)	*at my best*
JJ	NADJ(edp,plu)	*The wounded were carried away.*
JJ	NADJ(ingp,plu)	*Judgement is left to the discerning.*

A greater difference can be found in the tagging of auxiliaries. LOB assigns MD to modal auxiliaries, but the ambiguous *be*, *have* and *do* are tagged in LOB respectively BE, HV and DO, with suffixes to indicate their tense and plurality, irrespective, however of whether they are auxiliaries or lexical words. ICE, in contrast, has a much more delicate treatment of auxiliaries, with features indicating the following different uses of auxiliaries:

AUX(do)	*do*
AUX(let)	*let*
AUX(modal)	modal
AUX(pass)	passive
AUX(perf)	perfect
AUX(prog)	progressive
AUX(semi)	semi-auxiliary
AUX(semip)	semi-auxiliary followed by *-ing* participle

The examples below indicate the extent of the differences between LOB and ICE tagging of auxiliaries.

LOB	ICE	Example
DOD	AUX(do,past)	*You didn't say that, did you?*
VB	AUX(let,imp)	*Let's play some jazz.*
MD	AUX(modal,past)	*He could not find it.*
BEN	AUX(pass,edp)	*You should have been told.*
HVZ	AUX(perf,pres)	*She has passed the examination.*
BEN	AUX(prog,edp)	*I have been using the computer all morning.*
VBZ	AUX(semi,pres)	*The secretary appears to have already paid the workers.*
VBD	AUX(semip,past)	*The children kept on chasing my cat.*

Information on different uses of *it* is covered in ICE but is missing in LOB. LOB invariably tags it as third person singular pronoun (PP3) whereas it can be given three different tags in ICE according to its functions in context. The four tags are ANTIT, CLEFTIT, and PRON(pers,sing). Consider the following examples:

LOB	ICE	Example
PP3	**ANTIT**	*It would be a shade awkward for the police to know about the incident.*
PP3	**CLEFTIT**	*It was in Rome that he first met his girlfriend.*
PP3	**PRON(pers,sing)**	*He hasn't seen the film yet. But he is going to see it.*

The biggest difference between LOB and ICE lies in their treatment of lexical verbs. In LOB, lexical verbs are tagged for tense and number with the following symbols:

VB	base form
VBD	past tense
VBG	*-ing* participle
VBN	*-ed* participle
VBZ	third person singular

In ICE, the following verb forms are distinguished that separate verbs into two groups: finite and nonfinite. The finite group comprises past tense, present tense, imperative and subjunctive. The nonfinite group includes past participle, present participle and infinitive.

edp	*-ed* participle
ingp	*-ing* participle
infin	infinitive
imp	imperative
past	past
pres	present
subjun	subjunctive

Note that VB in LOB does not indicate whether the verb is finite or nonfinite. In the following examples, LOB tags *give* as VB irrespective of its actual functions whereas ICE tags this verb variously.

LOB	ICE	Example
VB	V(ditr,pres)	*They very often give him some help.*
VB	V(ditr,imp)	*'Give me my book!', she shouted angrily.*
VB	V(montr,infin)	*People were anxious to know if he would give his support.*
VB	V(ditr,subjun)	*I insist that he give us some help.*

Apart from the features relating to form, ICE more importantly distinguishes the following transitivity features:

`intr`	intransitive
`cop`	copular
`montr`	monotransitive
`dimontr`	dimonotransitive
`ditr`	ditransitive
`cxtr`	complex transitive
`cxditr`	complex ditransitive
`trans`	transitive

These subclasses and features combine to give 78 possible tags for verbs in ICE. Undoubtedly, this imposes extra work on the tagger (and on the tag selector) but also greatly enriches the annotation of the corpus in terms of the use and behaviour of verbs. Most important of all, it will make any subsequent parsing of the corpus far more accurate and efficient. For discussions of the transitivity features of verbs in ICE, see Greenbaum (1992) and Greenbaum and Ni (1996).

The examination of two tagsets showed that while sharing similarities in broad grammatical categories, LOB and ICE present great differences in subcategorisation. The LOB tags are, so to speak, more lexically oriented whereas those used in ICE contribute more to syntactic analysis. The treatment of some of the word classes in ICE is complex—auxiliaries and lexical verbs, for example—but there are rather exhaustive lists available in the ICE lexicon for these special cases.

3.3   Syntactic Annotation

Syntax as a study of the principles and rules for the sentence structure provides a formal mechanism to combine small feature units such as words into larger and more complex units such as phrases and clauses. There are very good intuitive reasons to believe that more complex units are more likely to yield features characteristic of a certain genre, register or text type, which serve as a major rationale for many of the experiments described in this book that investigated the correlation between granularities of linguistic analysis and the resulting system performance in terms of accuracy. The development of computational linguistics has seen many different syntactic frameworks that aim to describe the syntactic structure of the sentence. Simplistically speaking, we identify a functional approach that relies on word dependencies to produce a sentence structure (Tesnière 1959) as well as a structuralist approach that makes use of constituent structures to formulate a sentence hierarchy (Harris 1951). While the functional approach is vastly interesting in many different perspectives such as cognition and sociolinguistics, the structural approach has

Fig. 3.2 The structural hierarchy of a sentence

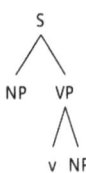

been more popular in terms of computational implementations. As is obvious from a cursory look, while all attempt to produce a hierarchical tree representing the syntactic structure of the sentence such as one shown in Fig. 3.2, they nonetheless exhibit different degrees of linguistic granularity.

Some frameworks provide only a skeletal description of the syntactic structure while others aim at a more detailed analysis. The former typically focuses on the overall sentence structure composed of phrases as the basic constituent while leaving out the syntactic functions of the constituents and their internal analysis. The latter explicitly describes the syntactic functions of the constituents and aims to provide a detailed analysis of their internal structures. In this section, we shall use the Penn Treebank scheme to illustrate the former and the ICE scheme to illustrate the latter.

3.3.1   The Penn Treebank Scheme

The Penn Treebank is a project to annotate naturally occurring text, most notably, Wall Street Journal, according to a skeletal parse scheme showing rough syntactic and semantic information. The scheme includes POS tagging and syntactic parsing. The POS tags are based on the Brown Tagset but modified to remove those tags that are unique to a particular lexical item. For example, the original tag group HV (HV, HVZ, HVD, HVN and HVG) for the verb *have* is removed for the project and replaced by a more generic VB group. This reduction process was applied to verbs *be* and *do*, based on the principle of lexical recoverability. The sample principle was similarly applied to reduce the original distinctions for prequalifiers and prequantifiers to the tag PDT (predeterminer). Reflexive pronouns, both singular and plural, were collapsed with personal pronouns (PRP). A most significant departure from the original scheme is the conflation of subordinating conjunctions and prepositions such that both classes are now tagged as IN, namely, preposition. The exact motivation for this treatment is not very clear although Taylor et al. (2003) claim that 'subordinating conjunctions can be recovered as those instances of IN that precede clauses, whereas prepositions are those instances of IN that precede noun phrases or prepositional phrases'. See Appendix C for a complete list of the Penn Treebank tags.

The Penn Treebank project employed two different styles of parsing. The skeletal parsing applies context-free bracketing 'with limited empty categories and no indication of noncontiguous structures and dependencies' (Taylor et al. 2003, p. 7).

ADJP	Adjective phrase
ADVP	Adverb phrase
NP	Noun phrase
PP	Prepositional phrase
S	Simple declarative clause
SBAR	Subordinate clause
SBARQ	Direct question introduced by *wh*-element
SINV	Declarative sentence with subject-aux inversion
SQ	Yes/no questions and subconstituent of SBARQ excluding *wh*-element
VP	Verb phrase
WHADVP	Wh-adverb phrase
WHNP	Wh-noun phrase
WHPP	Wh-prepositional phrase
X	Constituent of unknown or uncertain category
*****	'Understood' subject of infinitive or imperative
0	Zero variant of *that* in subordinate clauses
T	Trace of wh-Constituent

Consider [13][2] as an example.

[13]   *Martin Marietta Corp. was given a $29.9 million Air Force contract for low-altitude navigation and targeting equipment.*

The sentence receives the following skeletal bracketing:

```
( (S
        (NP Martin Marietta Corp.)
        was
        (VP given
                (NP a
                $ 29.9
                million Air Force contract
                (PP for
                        (NP low-altitude navigation
                        and
                        targeting equipment)))))
.)
```

The bracketing above is equivalent to the syntactic tree below (Fig. 3.3).

As can be seen from the graphic representation of the syntactic analysis by Penn Treebank scheme, the constituent structure is provided with each labelled for constituent type such as S, NP and VP. However, the broad analysis does not provide a detailed enough analysis for the phrase-internal structure. For example, low-altitude

---

[2] Example taken from Taylor et al. (2003, p. 7).

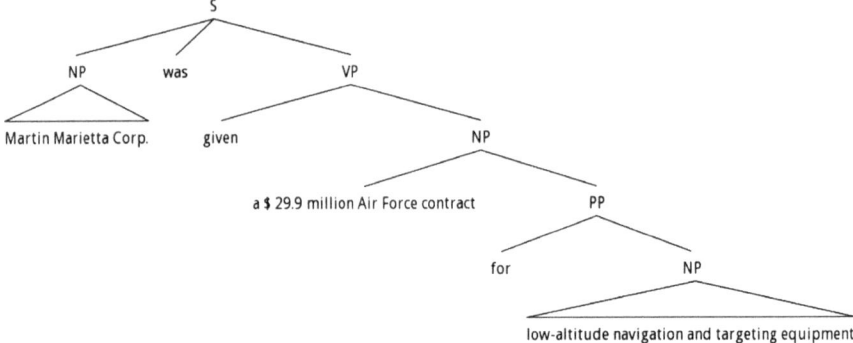

Fig. 3.3 A Penn Treebank syntactic tree for [13]

Fig. 3.4 NP coordination

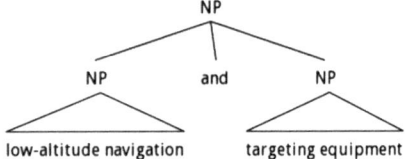

navigation and targeting equipment are analysed as a single NP without the explicit indication of a coordinated structure such as the following (Fig. 3.4).

In addition, as is the case for most of the syntactic parsers, the Penn Treebank scheme does not explicitly indicate the syntactic functions of the constituents such that the pre-VP NP is indicated as the subject and the NP in post-VP position as direct object while the PP is ideally labelled as NP postmodifier. In this regard, the ICE parsing scheme provides a very fine-grained framework of analysis, described in the following section.

3.3.2   The ICE Parsing Scheme

With its 270-strong POS tags (see Appendix A) as labels for terminal nodes and a set of parsing symbols for both categories and functions (see Appendix D), the ICE parsing scheme is perhaps the most detailed scheme that has been empirically tested and applied to a large corpus of over a million word tokens. And, unlike most other parsing schemes, it has been extensively tested with transcribed speech since the ICE-GB corpus comprises spoken data that accounts for 60 % of the total corpus size. The Survey Parser was specially developed to apply the annotation scheme fully automatically to the corpus, which produces either a full parse or a partial

Fig. 3.5 The ICE NP structure

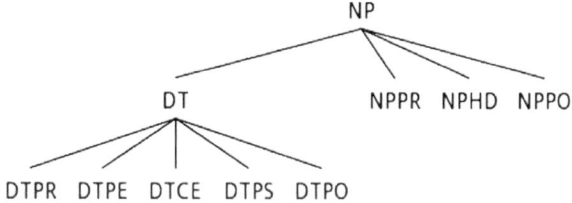

parse (Fang 1994, 1996a, b, 2000) . The parser is capable of parsing naturally occurring sentences with an *F*-score of about 86 % (Fang 2006a).

The ICE parsing scheme recognises five basic syntactic phrases: adjective phrase (AJP), adverb phrase (AVP), noun phrase (NP), prepositional phrase (PP) and verb phrase (VP). The scheme also provides a detailed account of the internal structure of the phrase. The noun phrase, as an example, maximally comprises the following (Fig. 3.5):

where, in addition to the NP head (NPHD), the premodifier (NPPR) and postmodifier (NPPO) are explicitly marked. We also see a detailed analysis for the determiner (DT), which comprises an international structure formed of DTPR (determiner premodifier), DTPE (predeterminer), DTCE (central determiner), DTPS (postdeterminer) and DTPO (determiner postmodifier), demonstrating a linguistically fine-grained scheme that is unparalleled by most other parsing schemes. Consider [14] as an example illustrating the ICE analysis of an NP:

[14]   *no fewer than six schemes for building deep-water ports*

The ICE phrasal scheme for the NP would produce the following tree structure, where the NP is seen to comprise a determiner (DT), NP head (NPHD) and NP postmodifier (NPPO). The DT additionally comprises a determiner premodifier (DTPR), a postdeterminer (DTPS) and a determiner postmodifier (DTPO). As is obvious from this example, the extraction of specific information can be enabled through the explicit labelling of the internal structure of the NP for functions as well as categories (Fig. 3.6).

Externally in the sentential hierarchy, these phrases as the basic syntactic building blocks are explicitly labelled for an array of syntactic functions.[3] Thus, according to the ICE scheme, each syntactic tree is represented as a functionally labelled hierarchy, with features describing the characteristics of phrases, clauses and the sentence. Each constituent node contains information about the function and the category. Attributes are additionally provided for each constituent with supplementary information.

To illustrate the ICE analysis of the sentence, consider [15] as an example, which receives a tree structure as in Fig. 3.7.

---

[3] See Appendix D for a complete listing and explanation.

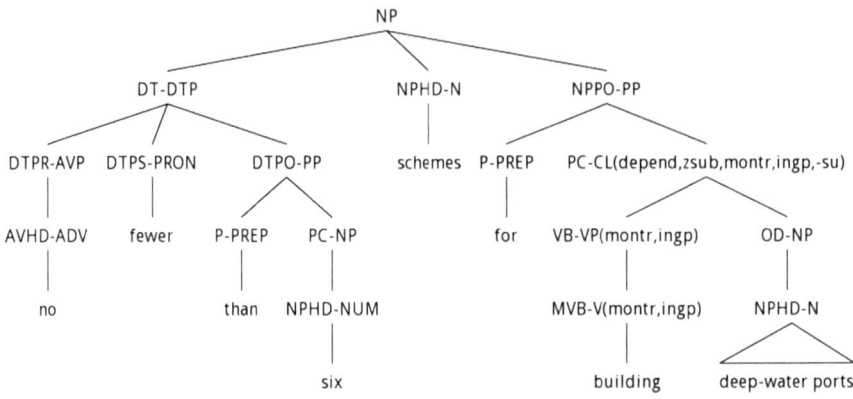

Fig. 3.6 The ICE analysis of [14]

[15]   *The decisions he takes in the next few weeks will define his place in the*
        history books.

As can be seen, each node is indicated for its syntactic category and syntactic function. SU-NP, for instance, includes an NP node that functions as the subject of the
clause. NPPO-PP as another example indicates a PP functioning as the noun phrase
postmodifier. While most of the node attributes are missing from the graph, some
attributes are retained for the clause. The clause *he takes in the next few weeks* is
analysed as `NPPO-L(depend, zrel, montr, preod)`, namely, a noun postmodifying dependent clause with zero relative pronoun and a preposed direct object.

3.3.3   Summary

We have seen that while most parsers are based on a structuralist view of the sentence that can be analysed into a hierarchy of constituent structures, different parsing schemes demonstrate a different granularity of analysis. While the choice of
which parsing scheme to adopt is largely based on the specific type of application,
generally speaking, the more detailed analysis provides for a better linguistic strati-
fication that affords a wider spectrum of linguistic features for modelling purposes.

3.4   Dialogue Act Annotation

Semantic and pragmatic annotation is largely propelled by the increasing need
for content analysis, which primarily serves a multitude of practical applications.
Examples of practical applications include word sense disambiguation, sentiment
analysis, domain identification, term extraction, spatio-temporal annotation, event

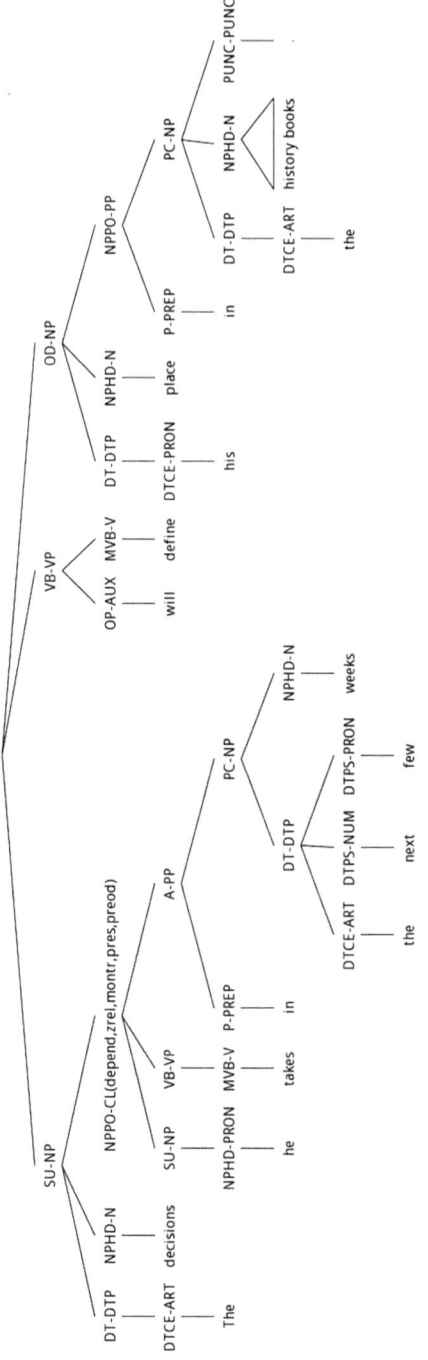

Fig. 3.7 A graphical representation of the syntactic tree for [15]

recognition and dialogue act analysis. In this section, we shall focus on dialogue act annotation.

Dialogue act (DA), a notion often considered to be derived from speech acts (Traum 1999) is proposed, most notably in Bunt (1994), to describe the characteristics of utterances at the function level (Rosset et al. 2008). DAs are believed to play a key role in the interpretation of the communicative behaviour of dialogue participants and offer valuable insight into the design of human–machine dialogue systems (Bunt et al. 2010) . According to the newly developed ISO 24617-2 standard (2012), dialogue acts are defined as the

> communicative activity of a participant in dialogue interpreted as having a certain communicative function and semantic content (p. 2).

The semantic content specifies the objects, relations, events, etc. that the dialogue act is about; the communicative function can be viewed as a specification of the way an addressee uses the semantic content to update his or her information state when he or she understands the corresponding stretch of dialogue.

To define a dialogue act in the conversation is not an easy job in that '[g]enerally speaking, there is no unique mapping between dialog act tags and words' (Rosset et al. 2008, p. 1). Generally speaking, there are two distinctive features of dialogue acts. First, utterances often express more than one dialogue act (e.g. Bunt 2009, 2011).

[16]   a.   A: *Um, are you working right now?*
                  B: *Yes.*

         b.   A: *Well, it's been interesting that we,*
                  B: *Extremely expensive, though.*
                  A: *Yes.*

In this set of examples, the single word 'yes' functions as an answer to a question in [16a] and as an agreement to an opinion in [16b].

Second, a dialog act is very often realized by different utterances.

[17]   a.   A: *So it's fairly safe.*
                  B: *Yeah.*

         b.   A: *That's not always possible.*
                  B: *That's true.*

As can be seen in both [16a] and [17], utterances such as 'yes', 'yeah' and 'that's true' can all function as agreement.

Still, an utterance in dialogue typically serves several functions.

[18]   A: *Well, Michael, what do you think about, uh, funding for AIDS research? Do you…*
         B: *Well, uh, uh, that's something I've thought a lot about.*

In example [18], A performs two dialogue acts: he (a) assigns the next turn to the participant Michael and (b) formulates an open question. B, in his response, (a) accepts the turn, (b) stalls for time and (c) answers the question by making a statement. Such a phenomenon is often regarded as the multifunctionality of utterances.

As a result, DA tags are often expected to be defined precisely and clearly enough for a good degree of applicability measured in terms of acceptable inter-annotator agreement and, at the same time, to be generic enough in order to be repurposeful. Thus, these DA taxonomies are often pragmatic systems in themselves as a product of reasonable compromises between practical and generic considerations. As Popescu-Belis (2004) put it:

> The general goal behind DA sets is therefore to reliably extract some useful information from dialogs, where the information is not at the level of syntax or semantics, but at a higher level, which is related to the dialog structure and to the intentions of the speakers, falling thus broadly under the scope of pragmatics (p. 3).

3.4.1   Notable DA Schemes

Up till now, different DA taxonomies have been proposed in different projects (e.g. Klein and Soria 1998; Quarteroni et al. 2008). For example, Klein and Soria (1998) reviewed 27 different DA schemes. Among them, the well-recognized schemes include the Dialogue Act Markup in Several Layers (DAMSL; Core and Allen 1997), the Switchboard SWBD-DAMSL (Jurafsky et al. 1997), the ICSI MRDA scheme (Shriberg et al. 2004), the Verbmobil-2 DA scheme (Alexandersson et al. 1998), the HCRC Map Task DA scheme (Carletta et al. 1996) and the AMI DA scheme (Becker and Wilson 2012). The following are examples from the above-mentioned schemes (DA tags are in the font of Courier New for emphasis.).

1. Dialogue Act Markup in Several Layers (DAMSL; Core and Allen 1997)

[19]   `Open-option`   utt1: s: *we can unload them and then reuse the boxcars on the way to Corning*
          `Accept(utt1)`   utt2: u: *alright*

2. Switchboard SWBD-DAMSL (Jurafsky et al. 1997)

[20]   `sd`   A.12 utt2 : *[I, + {F uh, } two months ago I] went to Massachusetts -- /*
          (`sd` = statement-non-opinion)

3. ICSI MRDA scheme (Shriberg et al. 2004)

[21]   Time   Chan   DA   AP   Transcript
        442.938-447.028   c3   s   25b.26a *it's ics- - uh icsi has a format for*
                                                  frame-level representation of
                                                  features.
        447.808-448.338   cB   s^bk   26b   *o_k .*

(Chan = channel (speaker); DA = DA tag, ^ links multiple tags; AP = adjacency pairs)
(s = statement; s^bk = statement + acknowledgment)

4. Verbmobil-2 DA scheme (Alexandersson et al. 1998)

[22]   (CDROM13, R423C)
        ANV001: <Schmatzen> <#klicken> <A> <#Klicken> how 'bout <;comma>
        <#klicken> <#klicken> at <;comma> three on <;comma> <A> Februray third
        <;quest> <A> <;seos> @(SUGGEST) (#Rascheln) would that be okay <;quest>
        <#> <#klicken> <#> <#> <;seos> @(REQUEST_COMMENT)

5. HCRC Map Task DA scheme (Carletta et al. 1996)

[23]   *E 1 IG instruct
        Start at the extinct volcano
        *M instruct
        and go down round the tribal settlement.
        *M instruct
        And then
        *M instruct

        *E 2 IF query-w em
        Whereabouts is the tribal settlement?
        *M reply-w

(IG = instruction giver; IF = instruction follower; M = moves; em = embedded)

6. AMI DA scheme (Becker and Wilson 2012)

[24]   D: So they w all work actually function together but I have different
            remote controls for each of them.
        B: MM-HMM (backchannel)
        D: So it's sort of ironic...

It is also worth pointing out that the number of DA types also varies in different DA schemes, ranging from 5 (e.g. Ang et al. 2005)[4] to more than 1000 (e.g. Shriberg et al. 2004).

3.4.2 ISO DA Scheme

Given the current situation, the ISO has published ISO 24617-2 (2012), which is a new standard for DA annotation, in an attempt to identify a core set of DA types and to implement consistent interpretations of the DA types and to promote interoperability. A basic premise of the ISO standard for dialogue act annotation (ISO 24617-2) is that utterances in dialogue are often multifunctional; hence the standard supports so-called 'multidimensional tagging', i.e. the tagging of utterances with multiple DA tags. It does so in two ways. First of all, it defines nine dimensions to which a dialogue act can belong:

- Task
- Auto-feedback
- Allo-feedback
- Turn management
- Time management
- Discourse structuring
- Social obligations management
- Own communication management
- Partner communication management

Second, as a unit in dialogue to be tagged with DA information, it takes the so-called 'functional segment', defined as a 'minimal stretch of communicative behaviour that has one or more communicative functions' (ISO 24617-2, 2012, p. 3). A functional segment is allowed to be discontinuous and to overlap with or be included in another functional segment. A functional segment may be tagged with at most one DA tag for each dimension. Another important feature is that an ISO DA tag consists not only of a communicative function encoding but also of a dimension indication, with optional attributes for representing certainty, conditionality, sentiment and links to other dialogue units expressing semantic, rhetorical and feedback relations (Table 3.1).

Theoretically, utterances will be annotated in all the possible dimensions. Take Example [20] from the Switchboard Dialogue Act Corpus. Instead of annotating as a statement, which equals to Inform in the ISO standard, the utterance will be annotated from the following three dimensions.

---

[4] The five DA categories in Ang et al. (2005) are *Statement, Disruption, Backchannel, Filler* and *Question.*

Table 3.1 Dialogue acts in the ISO standard

Dimensions		Dialogue act
Task	Information-seeking	Question; propositionalQuestion; setQuestion; checkQuestion; choiceQuestion
	Information-providing	Inform; agreement; disagreement; correction; answer; confirm; disconfirm
	Commissive	Promise; offer; addressRequest; acceptRequest; declineRequest; addressSuggest; acceptSuggest; declineSuggest
	Directive	Request; instruct; addressOffer; suggest; acceptOffer; declineOffer
Auto-feedback	Feedback	AutoPositive; autoNegative
Allo-feedback	Feedback	AlloPositive; alloNegative
Turn management		TurnAccept; turnAssign; turnGrab; turnKeep; turnRelease; turnTake
Time management		Stalling; pausing
Discourse structuring		InteractionStructuring; opening
Social obligations management		InitialGreeting; returnGreeting; initialSelfIntroduction; returnSelfIntroduction; apology; acceptApology
Own and partner communication management		Completion; correctMisspeaking; signalSpeakingError; retraction; selfCorrection
Qualifier	Certainty	Certain; uncertain
	Conditionality	Conditional; unconditional
	Partiality	Partial; full
	Sentiment	Sentiment

```
communicativeFunction = "inform"
dimension = "task"

communicativeFunction = "stalling"
dimension = "timeManagement"

communicativeFunction = "self-correction"
dimension = "ownCommManagement"
```

As a matter of fact, attempts have been made to map the existing DA schemes to the ISO standard, such as the ongoing project of mapping the SWBD-DAMSL scheme to the new ISO standard (e.g. Fang et al. 2011, 2012; Bunt et al. 2013) .

3.5   Machine Learning and Linguistic Features

The first four sections of this chapter are devoted to different linguistic annotations that prove beneficial to linguistic research, and this section will talk about machine learning techniques that have been drawn upon to utilise various linguistic features for better understanding of genres and registers.

The relation between linguistic variations and genres has been examined from two perspectives: (1) linguistic features have been extracted and examined across different text types; and (2) observable linguistic variations have been used to identify and classify texts automatically (Fig. 3.8).

From the first perspective, statistical analyses are often employed to calculate the most salient features of a targeted genre. For example, factor analysis has been employed by Biber (1988) to build the multidimensional model, which has been widely used in the research not only on different genres in English, such as conversation (e.g. Biber 2004), academic writing (e.g. Gray 2013; Nesi 2009), newspaper editorials (e.g. Westin and Geisler 2002), blogs (e.g. Grieve et al. 2010), Google subject categories (e.g. Biber and Kurjian 2006), and also on other languages, such as crosslinguistic patterns (e.g. Biber 1995), Spanish (e.g. Biber et al. 2006) and Brazilian Portuguese (e.g. Berber-Sardinha 2011).

As for the second perspective, observable linguistic variations across the genres are often taken as feature sets to train a model which in turn is used to label and classify new texts. Although an earlier study by Karlgren and Cutting (1994) uses discriminant analysis, the analysis methods have been shifted to machine learning techniques in the field of Artificial Intelligence (AI). Thus, this second perspective has successfully carried forward the corpus-based linguistic studies to the practical application in natural language processing. Due to its unique contribution, this chapter is devoted to a brief introduction of machine learning, including its nature and also its application in text classification. In addition, considering the computing aspect of machine learning, we will then introduce a free machine learning tool (i.e. Weka).

3.5.1   Machine Learning and Text Classification

Originally, machine learning is 'concerned with the development of algorithms that learn or improve their performance from experience or previous encounters with

Fig. 3.8 Relation between linguistic features and texts

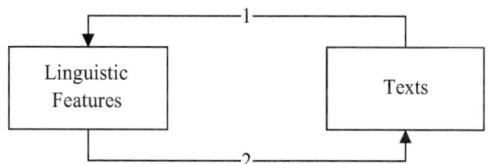

data' (Pustejovsky and Stubbs 2012, p. 21). A machine learning system usually 'learns' by generalizing patterns from the existing or stored data and then performs the designed task.

Classification has been considered as 'the most mature and widely used' type of machine learning (Domingos 2012, p. 79), and it refers to 'the task of identifying the labelling for a single entity from a set of data' (Pustejovsky and Stubbs 2012, p. 22). An often quoted example of classification tasks is to separate spam mails from non-spam mails (e.g. Alpaydin 2010; Pustejovsky and Stubbs 2012). In particular, linguistic features observed in the spam mails will be used by a classifier to train a model which will then be used to identify the spam mails as opposed to non-spam mails.

Quite a few learning algorithms are commonly used in classification tasks, such as support vector machine (SVM), K-nearest neighbour, naïve Bayes and decision trees. Books specialized in machine learning (e.g. Nilsson 1996; Alpaydin 2010; Pustejovsky and Stubbs 2012) provide detailed introduction to different algorithms, and the literature has also thoroughly reviewed the machine learning techniques used in automatic text categorization or classification (e.g. Kessler et al. 1997; Sebastiani 2002; Kehagias et al. 2003; Ikonomakis et al. 2005; Sharoff 2007).

By definition, machine learning is often regarded as a technique in the field of AI, and yet it is similar to statistical analyses, in that both are techniques for data analysis (Witten and Frank 2005). More importantly, 'the two perspectives have converged' (Witten and Frank 2005, p. 29) because statistical techniques are also widely employed in the test and evaluation of learning algorithms. Therefore, this section will not go into details of the specific techniques, and rather we briefly introduce the process that different techniques would share, including the training, testing and evaluation.

Training and Testing In the area of corpus-based machine learning, algorithms of the classifiers are often trained on predefined text categories and then tested on new dataset. The rational would be that after the training on the training dataset, a certain algorithm would be tested on the testing data to see if the performance would be confident on unseen dataset. A common practice is to divide a corpus into two parts (i.e. training and testing sets). There is no strict rule about the split ratio, and 'it is common to hold out one-third of the data for testing and use the remaining two-thirds for training' (Witten and Frank 2005, p. 149). However, such a simple split of the dataset still carries a risk of bias to the representativeness of the data.

'A more general way to mitigate any bias … is to repeat the whole process, training and testing, several times with different random samples' (Witten and Frank 2005, p. 149). With due consideration of data size and to minimize the bias in the data, it is recommended that the experimental results are obtained from stratified tenfold cross validation. In other words, 'the data is divided randomly into ten parts in which the class is represented in approximately the same proportions as in the full dataset. Each part is held out in turn and the learning scheme trained on the remaining nine-tenths' (Witten and Frank 2005, p. 150). The standard practice is to repeat the above-mentioned procedure ten times.

Evaluation As mentioned earlier, the purpose of training and testing is to see if the classifier is competent in categorizing the new dataset, and another process is the evaluation of the classification results. The simplest way is to count the number of correct instances and calculate the accuracy; or to count the number of incorrect instances and calculate the error rate. Nevertheless, a well-received method is a statistical measure called *F*-score (F_1), where the results of the classification performance are evaluated in terms of precision (*P*), recall (*R*) and *F*-score (*F*), which are defined as:

$$precision: P = \frac{TP}{TP + FP} \tag{3.1}$$

$$recall: R = \frac{TP}{TP + FN} \tag{3.2}$$

$$F-score: F = \frac{2PR}{P + R} \tag{3.3}$$

where TP = true positives, FP = false positives, FN = false negatives.

3.5.2   *Weka*

This subsection introduces a general purpose machine learning software package provided by the University of Waikato, New Zealand[5], which is Waikato Environment for Knowledge Analysis, better known as Weka (Hall et al. 2009). Two noticeable characteristics of such a software package are: (1) it is open source software; and (2) it is a collection of machine learning algorithms and offers tools for classification.

Classifiers In the Weka toolkit, classifiers are grouped into seven categories:

- Bayes
- Functions
- Lazy
- Meta
- Misc
- Rules
- Trees

Within these categories, the following classifiers (see Table 3.2) are more commonly used in text identification and classification.

---

[5] http://www.cs.waikato.ac.nz/ml/weka/index.html.

Table 3.2 Commonly used classifiers in Weka categories

Categories	Classifiers
Bayes	NaiveBayes; NaiveBayesMultinomial
Functions	LibSVM; Logistic (regression)
Lazy	IBK (K-Nearest Neighbours)
Trees	J48 (decision trees)

Training and Testing

Test options

○ Use training set

○ Supplied test set   [Set...   ]

◉ Cross-validation   Folds   [10]

○ Percentage split   %   [66]

[More options...   ]

There are four options for the training and testing of learning algorithms:

- To train and test with the same dataset
- To test on a test dataset loaded separately
- To employ cross validation with a free choice of the number of folds
- To split the dataset with a free choice of the split ratio

Output A typical output of a classifier includes the following aspects:

- The training set model
- Error on the training data
- Detailed accuracy of the training set
- Confusion matrix of the training set
- Stratified cross validation
- Detailed accuracy of the test set
- Confusion matrix of the test set

Among these aspects, the detailed accuracy section reports the values of precision, recall and *F*-score.

Chapter 4
Etymological Features across Genres and Registers

The English language, 'a conglomerate of many different origins' (Hoffmann 2009), has borrowed extensively from other languages such as Latin, Greek and French. The borrowing includes both scholarly and everyday words (Stockwell and Minkova 2001) and many text types and subject domains are characterised by their extensive use of such words. The study reported here is a survey of Latinate, Greek and French words (henceforth referred to as borrowed words) and their use in contemporary British English. The survey has the objective to chart the distribution of borrowed words across a set of different text types and subject domains. We report their frequencies of use and present a quantitative description of their distribution in different text categories (such as writing vs. speech and academic prose vs. non-academic prose) and different domains (such as medicine and social sciences). The survey is significant in that it makes use of a large corpus of contemporary British English totalling 100 million words. To our knowledge, no similar survey has ever been performed on such a scale. It is also significant in that it measures the use of borrowed words both across different text types as an important stylistic feature and across a set of different domains as a subject-specific differentia. As our results show, such a study not only lends itself to our understanding of the impact of borrowed words on contemporary English lexicon but will also contribute to text typology in general and automatic text classification and genre detection in particular.

4.1 Research Background

Previous studies have shown that borrowed words occur frequently in English texts, and that they tend to characterise the texts in certain domains. Gramley and Paetzold (1992, p. 251), for instance, regard Greek and Latinate lexical items as important

An earlier version of this chapter was previously published as Fang, A. C. and J. Cao. 2010. A corpus-based quantitative survey of the etymological composition of contemporary British English: The case of Latin, Greek and French. *Glottotheory* 3(1):49–64.

© Springer-Verlag Berlin Heidelberg 2015
A. C. Fang, J. Cao, *Text Genres and Registers: The Computation of Linguistic Features*,
DOI 10.1007/978-3-662-45100-7_4

characteristics of the vocabulary of the English for science and technology. Roberts (1965) reports the composite nature of borrowed words in American English albeit based on a vocabulary list of borrowed words and hence not relating to their actual frequency of occurrence in natural texts. Culpeper and Clapham (1996) study the overall proportions of borrowed words based on the Oxford English Dictionary, and yet the investigation is based on types rather than tokens of actual occurrence in authentic texts.

Still, other studies have focused on certain specific foreign origin, for example, Latin. Laar (1998) reports a high proportion of Latin components in English medical texts, which contributes to the distinction between medical texts and texts of other kinds. De Forest and Johnson (2001) analyse the density of Latinate words in the speeches and letters of Jane Austen's characters, showing that a higher density of Latinate words indicates a higher social status and education of the speaker and that a lower density indicates lesser intelligence or humble birth. A more recent study can be found in Márquez (2007), which, as a study of the core vocabulary of British English, has shown that Latin is 'not only a supplier of technical vocabulary' (Márquez 2007, p. 712) but contributes in a significant way to the top 1000 most frequent words in English. Bar-Ilan and Berman (2007) investigate the Latinate elements of the English lexicon as a more formal, literate level of language use than words of a Germanic origin. A corpus was created that contains samples produced by 20 subjects from four age groups (9–10, 12–13, 16–17 and graduate-level university students). After a short video, each subject was asked to produce an oral and written narration of the event in the video as well as an oral and written exposition of the same event. Their results indicate that 'the Latinate-Germanic divide is a valid diagnostic of register level in English' and that the Latinate elements of the English lexicon can be taken as 'diagnostic of linguistic register across the variables of age and text type' (Bar-Ilan and Berman 2007, p. 1).

Although important in their own right, the past studies quoted above are nonetheless limited in terms of their scope of analysis as well as sample size. For instance, Bar-Ilan and Berman (2007) use a small data set for analytical results and conclusions. The actual size of the corpus is not given but it expectedly contains 80 samples (20 subjects × 2 narrations × 2 expositions) of an unknown size. Assuming a higher estimate of 1000 word tokens per sample, written or transcribed, the corpus contains 80,000 word tokens only. Laar (1998), as another example, is limited to medical texts only. Such limitations have suggested the necessity to perform systematic studies according to predefined linguistic settings so that the use of such words and, indeed, the variations in the use of such words can be investigated along with types of text categories. It is also desirable to study these words quantitatively based on empirical observations from a much larger corpus of authentic texts than what has been used in past studies.

4.2   Resources

In this study, we are concerned with the following specific research issues regarding the use of borrowed words: whether there is a systematic variation in relation to the chosen text types, whether different subject domains also demonstrate a pattern of variation and how the three individual sources (i.e. Latin, Greek and French) differ from each other across the two settings. Therefore, two language resources are needed: (1) a large corpus of samples of contemporary English that is already encoded for text categories and subject domains, and (2) a large lexicon of contemporary English that provides etymological information. The two chosen resources are described in the following sections.

4.2.1   Corpus Resource

The British National Corpus (BNC, XML Edition 2007) was chosen as the basis of our study. Different from the composition described in Sect. 2.1.3, we followed the text categories proposed by Lee (2001). Table 4.1 summarises the text categories with corresponding tokens.

As shown , while most of the category names are self-explanatory, other published writing (OTHERPUB) and unpublished writing (UNPUB) need some explanation. OTHERPUB is a category that contains a mixture of administrative and regulatory instructions, advertisements and biographies. UNPUB is mainly a category that lumps together letters, emails, school and university essays and other miscellaneous written material.

Intuitively speaking, the eight categories in Table 4.1 have different degrees of formality. It is possible to plot the text categories along a continuum of changing degrees of formality, starting from the informal (conversation and other speech), to the less formal (fiction and news), and then finally to the formal (prose of an academic

Table 4.1 The text composition of the British National Corpus (BNC)

Text category		Text code	Token	Total	%
Spoken	Conversation	CONVRSN	4,233,962	10,409,858	10.58
	Other speech	OTHERSP	6,175,896		
Written	Academic prose	ACPROSE	15,781,859	87,953,849	89.42
	Fiction	FICTION	16,143,913		
	Newspapers	NEWS	9,412,174		
	Nonacademic prose	NONAC	24,179,010		
	Other published writing	OTHERPUB	17,970,212		
	Unpublished writing	UNPUB	4,466,681		
Total			98,363,707	98,363,707	100.00

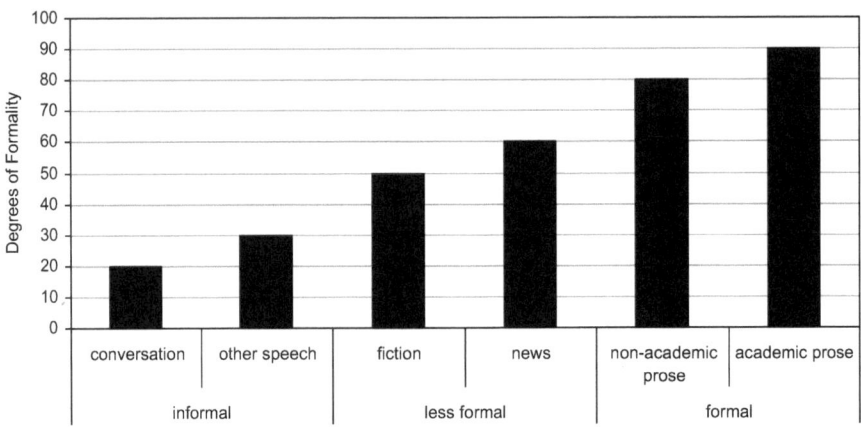

Fig. 4.1 A hypothetical plot relating text categories to formality degrees

content for academic and nonacademic purposes). See Fig. 4.1 for a hypothetical, notional plot of the relationship between categories and formality degrees.

As a matter of fact, the relation between text categories and formality degrees has been explored in various ways. For example, Heylighen and Dewaele (1999) study the correlation between formality scores and text types in Dutch and Italian texts. Frequencies in percent of parts of speech (such as nouns, verbs and adverbs) were used for the calculation of formality scores expressed as the F-measure:

$$F = \frac{\left[\sum freq(\text{n., adj., prep., art.}) - \sum freq(\text{pron., v., adv., interj.})\right] + 100}{2}, \quad (4.1)$$

where F is normalised to 100 and varies from 0 to 100 %. As can be seen from the equation above, F measure is based on two polarities: noun-oriented and verb-oriented, which produce a continuum indicating a higher formality degree if noun-related properties such as adjectives and articles outweigh verb-related properties such as pronouns and adverbs.

The focus of our study here is different. Our objective is to see whether borrowed words would also correlate with degrees of formality of different text categories and whether there is also a correlation between the use of borrowed words and subject domains.

4.2.2   Lexical Resource

The Collins English Dictionary (CED) is chosen as a source of etymological information. It is available from the Linguistic Data Consortium (LDC), in two different forms: typographical and parsed. The parsed form was used in our investigation, which contains explicitly labelled data fields indicating the headword's pronunciation, part of speech, definition and etymology, among others.

Table 4.2 Subdivisions of Latin, Greek and French

	Number of subdivisions	Freq.	%
Latin	9	17,943	36.93
Greek	6	2156	4.44
French	12	11,886	24.46

The CED has 249,331 entries, among which 28,526 (or 11.4 %) contain explicit etymological information, i.e. entries marked with the label ety. Implicit etymological information was recovered for an additional 20,066 entries via the label head that links the derived entries to their corresponding root that has an explicit etymology indication ety. For example, the entry abandonment does not have an explicit etymology indication. However, this entry has a head field linking the entry to abandon, which has an explicit indication of its Latin origin. The entry abandonment is thus counted as a Latinate word. By so doing, the total number of entries with etymological information, both explicit and implicit, is up to 48,593, accounting for 19.5 % of the CED entries. Altogether, 247 different language origins are identified.

In addition, subdivisions of etymological origin were also observed. For example, there are nine different types of Latin origin, namely, Latin, New Latin, Late Latin, Medieval Latin, Anglo-Latin, Old Latin, Ecclesiastical Latin, Modern Latin and Vulgar Latin. In this study, the subdivisions of etymological origin were conflated. Table 4.2 summarises detailed conflation information for Latin, Greek and French.

As can be noted from Table 4.2, Latin is the largest singular foreign language that accounts for 36.93 % of the entries with etymological information. French represents the second largest contribution with 11,886 entries in the CED, constituting 24.46 % of the borrowed words. In comparison, Greek has a much smaller number of entries, 2156 only, taking up only 4.44 %. Discounting English, however, Greek represents the third largest borrowing source.

4.2.3   Reference Lists

In order to recognise borrowed words in the BNC, a reference list was generated from the CED containing all the headword entries with a Latinate, French or Greek origin. Then, three reference lists of Latin, Greek and French were generated, respectively, from the CED for the identification of foreign words in the BNC. It is worth noting that the three lists were then filtered with a stoplist of 2000 most frequent word types extracted from the BNC. All word types covered by the BNC stoplist were excluded from the three reference lists. We believe that the 2000 most frequent words can be regarded as part of the core vocabulary for English and that the words of a foreign origin in the stoplist tend to have attained the characteristics of 'nativeness' and therefore can be excluded.

4.3   Investigation of Text Categories

To investigate in the setting of text categories, a sub-corpus was created with samples randomly selected from the eight text categories in the BNC (Table 4.1). A total of 3 million word tokens' worth of texts were randomly selected for each category, resulting in a sub-corpus of over 24 million word tokens. Table 4.3 presents the actual number of word tokens sampled for each category.

Of this sub-corpus, 80 % is used as the training set (of about 19 million word tokens), and the remaining 20 % retained as the test set (of just over 5 million word tokens). Our primary data come from the training set. In the event of any significant findings, we use the test set as secondary data to verify them.

4.3.1   Descriptive Statistics

From the training set of the sub-corpus, we extracted all the lemmatised word tokens or the headwords in BNC terms, which were subsequently matched with the reference lists of Latinate, Greek and French words generated from the CED. Table 4.4 presents the final statistics for such words in terms of type, token and type-token ratio. As is shown, the text categories are arranged alphabetically according to the text code.

As shown in Table 4.4, Latin has the largest number of occurrences in the training set with 417,167 tokens and 6733 types, resulting in a type-token ratio of 1.61 %. As many as 394,945 French word tokens were identified with 5298 unique types, resulting in a TTR of 1.34 %. In comparison, Greek has the smallest number of occurrences, with 12,139 word tokens and only 465 word types, resulting in a higher TTR of 3.83 %. This initial observation seems to indicate Latin and French as the two most important sources of borrowed language. It also yields the initial suggestion that although both Latin and Greek have been conventionally described as the source of vocabulary for science and technology, the use of Greek is really marginal compared with Latin and French.

Table 4.3 Composition of the sub-corpus

Text code		Token
Spoken	CONVRSN	3,017,930
	OTHERSP	3,019,043
Written	ACPROSE	3,124,550
	FICTION	3,026,196
	NEWS	3,018,301
	NONAC	3,083,486
	OTHERPUB	3,013,586
	UNPUB	3,001,746
Total		24,304,838

Table 4.4 Basic statistics for Latin, Greek and French in the training set

Text Code	Latin			Greek			French		
	Token	Type	TTR	Token	Type	TTR	Token	Type	TTR
ACPROSE	103,112	4190	4.06	3148	273	8.67	55,883	2665	4.77
CONVRSN	11,343	1455	12.83	711	48	6.75	25,967	1769	6.81
FICTION	39,863	3446	8.64	791	126	15.93	57,856	3248	5.61
NEWS	45,198	3033	6.71	965	124	12.85	59,578	2978	5.00
NONAC	80,823	4145	5.13	3121	255	8.17	56,338	3039	5.39
OTHERPUB	55,153	3642	6.60	1189	156	13.12	61,020	3312	5.43
OTHERSP	28,825	2487	8.63	595	95	15.97	28,273	2247	8.63
UNPUB	52,850	2965	5.61	1619	116	7.16	50,030	2681	5.36
Total	417,167	6733	1.61	12,139	465	3.83	394,945	5298	1.34

More clearly from Fig. 4.2, which is a graphical representation of Table 4.4, we see that Latin excels in academic informative writing (ACPROSE) and popular informative writing (NONAC), both covering a range of subject domains from arts and humanities to medicine and natural sciences. In contrast, French is preferred to Latin in the categories of conversation (CONVRSN), fiction (FICTION) and news (NEWS). Take conversation as an example. The positions of Latin and French are reversed, with French taking the lead (25,967 occurrences) compared with Latin's 11,343 occurrences. This suggests that French is preferred to Latin in daily, casual or less formal communication. The leading position of French in the news category, as another example, confirms its role on a social level in everyday communication. Again, the use of Greek is expectedly minimal here.

4.3.2 Borrowed Words and Text Categories

The distribution of borrowed words (D) is computed by, respectively, the proportion of Latin, Greek and French word tokens amongst the total number of word tokens in each text category:

$$D = \frac{\text{number of Latinate, Greek or French word tokens}}{\text{number of total word tokens}} \times 100. \qquad (4.2)$$

In other words, D represents the number of word tokens of a foreign language per 100 word tokens. Table 4.5 lists the respective Ds for Latin, Greek and French. The column *Combined* lists the sum of all the word tokens from the three languages. The eight BNC text categories are sorted according to the combined D in ascending order.

As can be seen from the row marked *Total*, borrowed word tokens from the three languages jointly account for 4.30 % of the total occurrence of word tokens in the

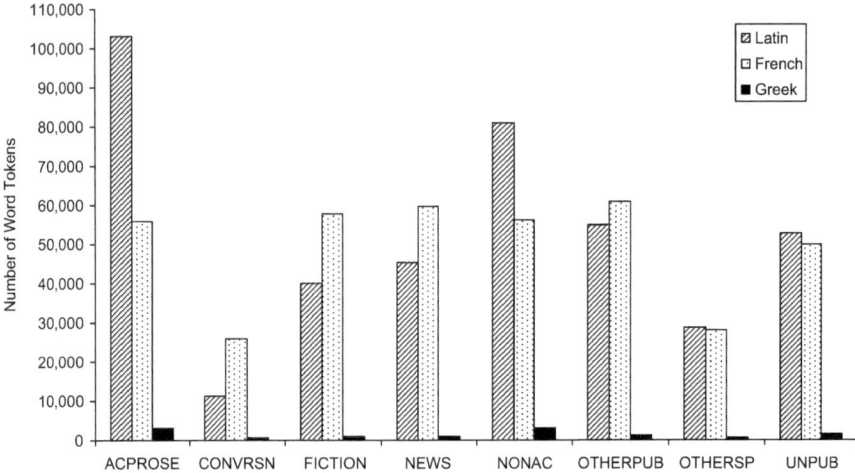

Fig. 4.2   Distribution across categories in word tokens

training set. Among the three, Latin and French have a similar proportion, i.e. 2.18 and 2.06 %. This finding is contrary to the claim by Culpeper and Clapham (1996, p. 215) that Latin has a much greater impact than French. Greek is observed to have a minimal presence of only 0.06 %. Empirical data have thus established Latin and French as the two most important sources of borrowing in contemporary English. The use of Greek is marginal, an observation emphasised by Fig. 4.3, which is a graphical representation of Table 4.5.

Considering the ranking of the text categories according to the combined D, one striking feature comes from the observation that D seems to yield a pattern where texts are polarised into two groups: formal, informative text of an academic nature on the one hand (such as ACPROSE and NONAC), and less formal, transcribed speech on the other (such as CONVRSN and OTHERSP), with NEWS, UNPUB and FICTION in the middle. It is apparent from Fig. 4.3 that the formality of the text categories increases along with the increase of combined D, which suggests that the more formal the category, the greater the proportion of borrowed words. A sharp increase can be observed between the spoken categories and the written ones, suggesting D as a good differentiator between speech and writing. More specifically, ACPROSE has the highest D of borrowed words (6.57 %) whereas CONVRSN has the lowest D of 1.61 %. From the perspective of speech and writing, it can be observed that writings generally have a higher proportion of foreign words than speech; the written texts are grouped together on top of the scale and the spoken ones are clustered together towards the bottom of the scale. In other words, D may be regarded as a distinguishing factor between speech and writing. Moreover, within the six written categories, ACPROSE has a higher D than NONAC. Published writing, such as ACPROSE, NONAC and OTHERPUB, has a higher D than unpublished writing UNPUB. Fiction has the lowest D among the written texts, bordering on the spoken texts on the scale represented in Table 4.5.

Table 4.5 Distribution of borrowed words (D) across text categories

Rank	Text code	Combined		Latin		French		Greek	
		#	D	#	D	#	D	#	D
1	CONVRSN	38,021	1.61	11,343	0.48	25,967	1.10	711	0.03
2	OTHERSP	57,693	2.42	28,825	1.21	28,273	1.19	595	0.02
3	FICTION	98,510	4.13	39,863	1.67	57,856	2.43	791	0.03
5	UNPUB	104,499	4.36	52,850	2.21	50,030	2.09	1619	0.07
4	NEWS	105,741	4.48	45,198	1.91	59,578	2.52	965	0.04
6	OTHERPUB	17,362	4.98	55,153	2.34	61,020	2.59	1189	0.05
7	NONAC	40,282	5.72	80,823	3.30	56,338	2.30	3121	0.13
8	ACPROSE	62,143	6.57	103,112	4.18	55,883	2.26	3148	0.13
Total		824,251	4.30	417,167	2.18	394,945	2.06	12,139	0.06

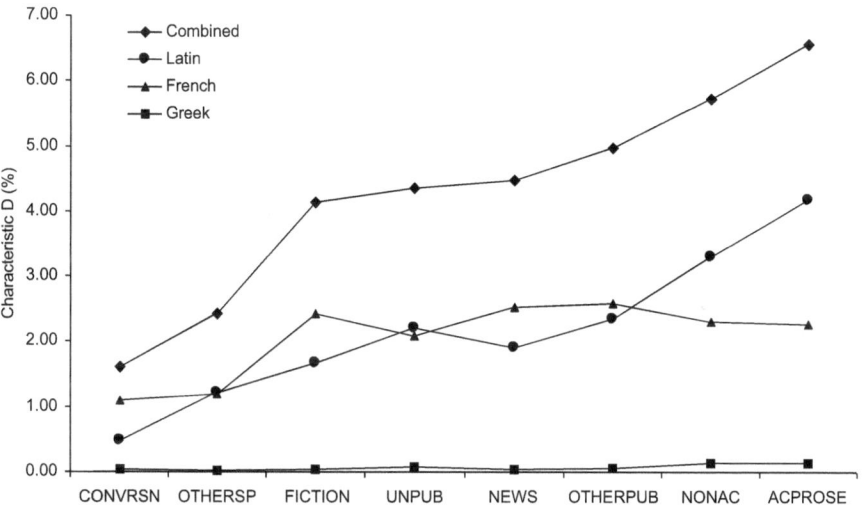

Fig. 4.3 Text categories arranged according to the combined D in ascending order

We next turn to the variations in the use of the individual sources of borrowed words. An interesting phenomenon can be observed here. Latin and French seem to be polarised: a higher D for Latin is typically accompanied by a lower D for French, and vice versa. This is clear evidence, which suggests that different categories have different preferences for different sources of borrowing. Take conversation (CONVRSN) as an example. The higher D for French indicates a greater use of French than Latin. Academic prose, on the other hand, prefers Latin to French. Altogether, we have conversation, fiction, and news as categories where French is favoured. In contrast, nonacademic and academic writing prefers Latin. The exceptional junctures of Latin and French occur at OTEHRSP, UNPUB and OTHERPUB, which

Table 4.6 Correlation between D and text categories

	r	r^2
French	0.725	0.526
Greek	0.842	0.709
Latin	0.956	0.913
Combined	0.968	0.936

are mixtures of miscellaneous writings and spoken material less clearly defined than the other categories. The evidence here supports the plausible hypothesis that in contemporary English, writing and speech for social purposes seem to exhibit a greater use of French while writing for academic purposes exhibits a heavier use of Latin. This hypothesis may be partially supported by the observation that academic writing tends to have a higher concentration of terminologies (see, for example, Fang et al. 2009), which, in the areas of natural science and medicine, are largely derived from Latin and Greek (see Gramley and Paezold 1992; Laar 1998).

In short, the observations suggest a correspondence between the ranking according to D and the ranking of the same categories according to degrees of formality associated with such categories. A linear regression analysis was performed to examine the relation between combined D and text categories.

Figure 4.4 shows that the points follow a linear pattern with a positive slop. Then the linear correlation coefficient (r) was computed, and the value of r is 0.968 ($p < 0.01$), suggesting a strong positive linear relationship between the combined D and degrees of text formality. The coefficient of determination (r^2) is 0.936, indicating that about 93.6 % of the variation in the D value can be explained by the degree of text formality. Table 4.6 is a summary of the correlation between text formality and the three borrowing origins concerned in the study.

4.3.3   Summary

We examined the use of Latin, French and Greek word tokens across a set of eight text categories, where the categories include samples of speech and writing that represent a continuum of degrees of formality. The following observations were made based on empirical evidence.

- Latin and French are the two major sources of borrowing in contemporary British English. Greek, which has traditionally been regarded as a supplier of vocabulary for science and technology, has a minimal use.
- Informal categories tend to have a lower proportion of borrowed words while formal categories are characterised by a higher distribution of such word tokens.
- Latin and French are polarised in terms of use in different categories. French is favoured in speech and writing for social purposes and Latin is preferred in informative, academic texts. In this regard, Greek is predominantly used in academic texts despite its marginal occurrence compared with the other two languages.

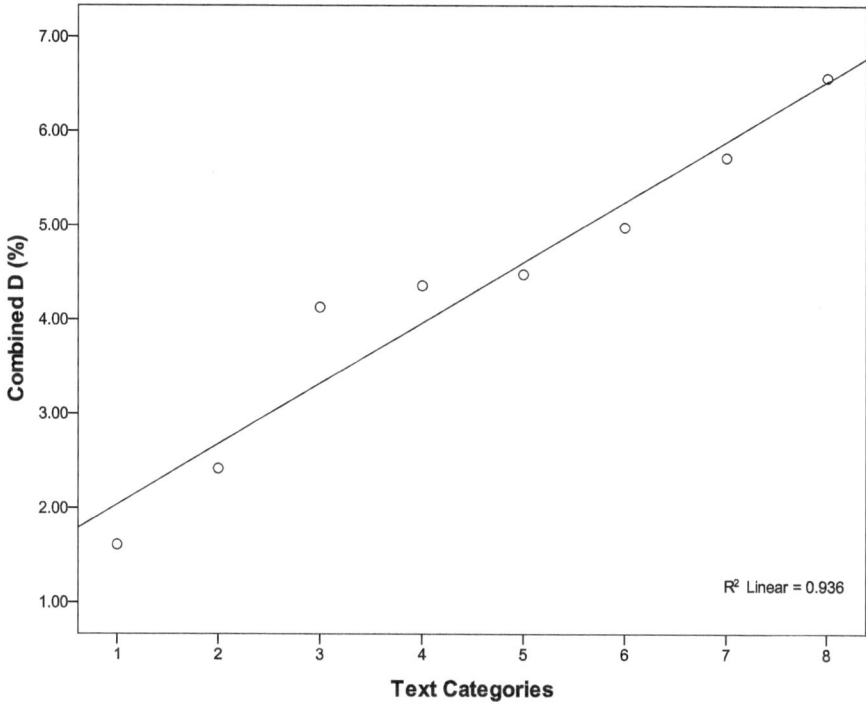

1=CONVRSN,2=OTHERSP,3=FICTION,4=UNPUB,5=NEWS,6=OTHERPUB,7=NONAC,8=ACPROSE

Fig. 4.4 Graph of combined *D* by text categories

Based on the observations above, the distribution of Latin, French and Greek appears to be a stylistic characteristic correlating with degrees of formality, which distinguishes not only speech from writing as two broad genres but also informal categories from the formal ones within the written genre. In other words, the interaction of social context and language use influences the proportion of the borrowed words concerned in the current study. Similar results were found in the test set.

4.4   Investigation of Subject Domains

Past studies have shown that Latin and Greek are suppliers of vocabulary for science and technology, and yet it is not clear what the exact composition is of such words in arts and humanities, technology and medical science, etc. The investigation to be reported in this section is thus intended to fill in such a gap. We observed a close correlation between the distribution of borrowed words and degrees of formality of text categories. An associated question remains whether a similar correlation can be found between the use of borrowed words and a set of subject domains.

Table 4.7 Tokens sampled in subject domains

Subject domain (domain code)	Token
Humanities and arts (HUM)	524,224
Medicine (MED)	504,857
Natural sciences (NAT)	536,499
Politics, law and education (POL)	511,935
Social sciences (SOC)	511,655
Technology and engineering (TEC)	535,380
Total	3,124,550

4.4.1 Creation of a Sub-corpus

The category of academic prose (ACPROSE) in the BNC was chosen as the basis of our experiment to investigate the use of borrowed words in relation to subject domains. ACPROSE comprises six subject domains, from each of which 500,000 word tokens were randomly sampled to form the sub-corpus. As Table 4.7 shows, the sub-corpus comprises a total of 3,124,550 word tokens.

Again, the sub-corpus was then divided into a training set containing 80 % of the total tokens and a test set with the remaining 20 %.

4.4.2 Descriptive Statistics

For each of the six domains, borrowed words were extracted as individual word tokens and then sorted for the extraction of their unique types. The type-token ratio (TTR) was also calculated. See Table 4.8.

Two observable patterns emerge from Table 4.8. First, in terms of TTR, domains belonging to arts have a higher TTR, all above 12 % (except for Greek), while domains belonging to sciences have a comparatively lower TTR, all below 10 % (except for Greek). This phenomenon appears to suggest that there is a higher degree of lexical flexibility or variation for foreign words in arts domains than in science domains. Second, in terms of occurrences, science domains tend to have a more intensive use of foreign words than their counterparts in the arts domain. Consider Fig. 4.5.

MED, NAT and TEC, as an example, have a much higher use of Latin than the other domains. It can be explained by the observable fact that the sciences domains seem to make a heavier use of Latinate words than the arts domains, thus yielding some initial indication of a different degree of preference for Latinate words between arts and sciences.

Table 4.8 Basic stats for Latin, Greek and French for different domains

Domain	Latin			Greek			French		
	Token	Type	TTR	Token	Type	TTR	Token	Type	TTR
HUM	14,750	2159	14.64	241	70	29.05	12,870	1674	13.01
MED	24,915	1846	7.41	1056	91	8.62	10,553	925	8.77
NAT	22,619	2018	8.92	1012	124	12.25	9910	1060	10.70
POL	10,803	1523	14.10	249	44	17.67	8744	1139	13.03
SOC	11,350	1431	12.61	574	54	9.41	6506	906	13.93
TEC	18,675	1116	5.98	356	42	11.80	7300	635	8.70
Total	103,112	4541	4.40	3,488	273	7.82	55,883	3145	5.63

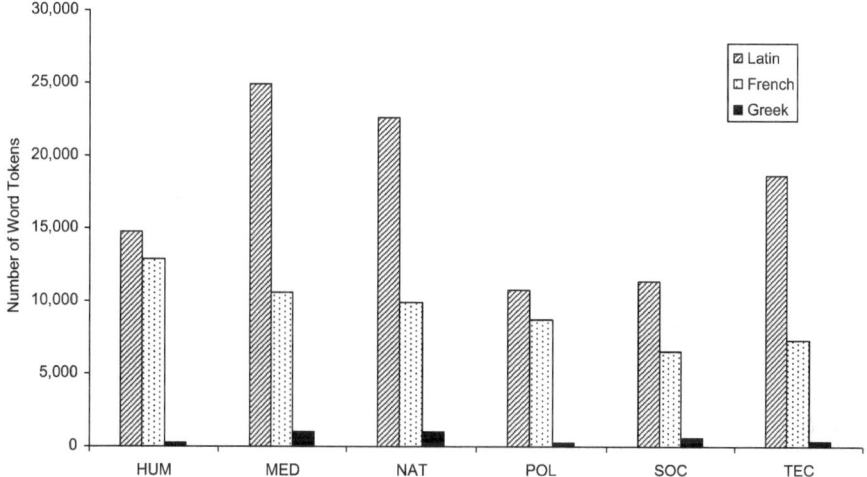

Fig. 4.5 Distribution across subject domains in word tokens

4.4.3   Borrowed Words and Domains

Distribution of borrowed words (D) was computed for the six component domains in the training set and summarised in Table 4.9.

As can be seen, as a whole, Latin, French and Greek account for 6.58% of the total word tokens from training set. Of the three languages, Latin has the most significant presence, forming 4.18% of the training set, followed by French (2.26%). Again, Greek is shown to have a marginal presence of 0.14%. Across the six subject domains, MED and NAT demonstrate a higher combined D with POL and SOC on the lower side of the scale, suggesting that in general the science domains make more use of borrowed words than the arts domains.

Individual distributions of Latin, French and Greek are charted in Fig. 4.6 over the six subject domains. Again, Latin and French demonstrate an opposed pattern

Table 4.9 Distribution of borrowed words (*D*) across subject domains

Rank	Text Code	Combined		Latin		French		Greek	
		#	D	#	D	#	D	#	D
1	SOC	18,430	4.59	11,350	2.83	6506	1.62	574	0.14
2	POL	19,796	4.86	10,803	2.65	8744	2.15	249	0.06
3	TEC	26,331	6.29	18,675	4.46	7300	1.74	356	0.09
4	HUM	27,861	6.79	14,750	3.60	12,870	3.14	241	0.06
5	NAT	33,541	7.82	22,619	5.27	9910	2.31	1012	0.24
6	MED	36,524	9.09	24,915	6.20	10,553	2.62	1056	0.26
Total		162,483	6.58	103,112	4.18	55,883	2.26	3488	0.14

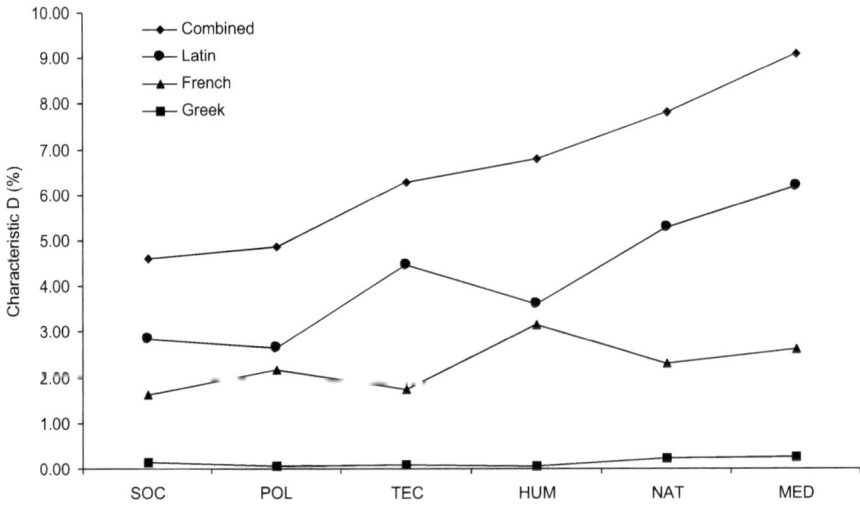

Fig. 4.6 Subject domains arranged according to combined *D* in ascending order

of distribution: a lower proportion of one would be accompanied by a higher proportion of the other, suggesting different preferences by different subject domains for a different language. On the whole, empirical data seem to suggest that Latin is preferred in science domains while French in arts domains.

Again, a linear regression analysis was done to examine the relation between subject domains and the distribution of borrowed words. See Fig. 4.7.

Figure 4.7 shows that the points neatly follow a linear pattern with a positive slope. Both the linear correlation coefficient ($r = 0.988$, with $p < 0.01$) and the coefficient of determination ($r^2 = 0.975$) indicate a strong positive correlation between combined *D* and subject domains, suggesting that different domains are likely to have a different preference for the use of borrowed words. Table 4.10 is a summary of the correlation between text formality and the three borrowing origins concerned in the study.

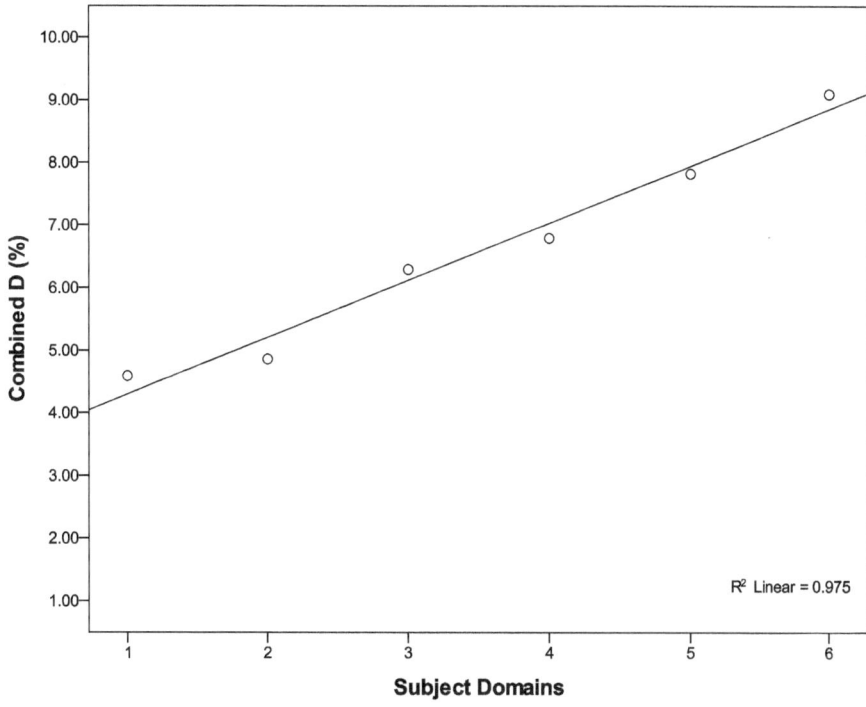

1=SOC, 2=POL, 3=TEC, 4=HUM, 5=NAT, 6=MED

Fig. 4.7 Graph of combined D by subject domains

Table 4.10 Correlation between D and subject domains

	r	r^2
French	0.650	0.423
Greek	0.666	0.444
Latin	0.908	0.825
Combined	0.988	0.975

4.4.4 Summary

We examined the use of Latin, French and Greek word tokens across a set of six subject domains, which fall into two broader categories of sciences versus arts. We have the following observations supported by empirical evidence:

- As a whole, subject domains of sciences tend to have a higher proportion of borrowed words than those of arts.
- When it comes to individual foreign sources, Latin and French again are polarised in terms of use in different domains. Latin is preferred in science domains while French in arts domains. In this regard, Greek demonstrates a pattern

similar to Latin despite its marginal occurrence compared with the other two languages.

Our empirical results here show that the use of borrowed words is also closely correlated to subject domains. The findings indicate that the distribution of borrowed words can be possibly used as a subject-specific differentia for the separation of texts in arts and sciences at least. Similar results were also found in the test set.

4.5   Conclusion

In this chapter, we described a corpus-based investigation of borrowed words according to linguistic settings that involve not only a spectrum of text categories ranging from informal speech to formal academic writing but a variety of subject domains in arts and sciences. The machine-readable CED was used as our lexical resource for a reference list of borrowed words from Latin, French and Greek. The BNC was used as the basis of the study for authentic texts. A sub-corpus was created with 3 million words for each of the eight text categories. A second sub-corpus of six subject domains was created from academic prose with a total of 500,000 word tokens for each domain, totalling 3 million word tokens. The distribution of borrowed words was calculated as the total number of borrowed word tokens over the total number of word tokens, first across the eight different text categories and then across the six subject domains in the study.

The findings show that there is an uneven use of borrowed words across the text categories. To be more exact, the distribution can be used to distinguish speech from writing, and moreover, between formal and informal writing. The distribution of borrowed words therefore suggests that this measure can be used as a stylistic characteristic that relates unambiguously to degrees of formality with good potentials for application in natural language processing systems to classify texts and to detect novel genres. The investigation also shows that even different subject domains have their own preferences for the use of borrowed words. Domains in the sciences have a higher proportion of borrowed words than those in arts. The findings indicate that the distribution of borrowed words can be possibly used as a subject-specific differentia for the separation of texts in arts and sciences at least.

The survey thus demonstrates on an empirical basis that the use of borrowed words not only distinguishes texts on a scale of different formalities but that different domains seem to have a different proportion and therefore preference for the use of borrowed words, a finding that will contribute to applications in automatic text classification and genre detection.

Chapter 5
Part-of-Speech Tags and ICE Text Classification

Part-of-speech (POS) tags have been employed in automatic genre classification in that they do not 'reflect the topic of the document, but rather the type of text used in the document' (Finn and Kushmerick 2003, p. 1) and that their distribution has been observed to vary across different genres (e.g., Nakamura 1993; Rayson et al. 2002). The current study introduces a new set of linguistically fine-grained POS tags generated by AUTASYS (Automatic Text Analysis System; Fang 1996 and 2007) for automatic genre classification. The experiment was designed to investigate the impact of the proposed feature set when compared and contrasted with word unigrams as a bag of words (BOW) and an impoverished POS tag set. Machine-learning tools were used to evaluate the classification performance in terms of F-score. The component from Great Britain for the International Corpus of English (ICE-GB; Greenbaum 1996) was employed as a resource of different text genres. Ten different genre classification tasks were identified based on the existing ICE-GB categories, which are grouped according to different granularities. As our results will show, the use of linguistically rich POS tags as discriminative features produces superior accuracy when compared with BOW for fine-grained genre classification. Our results will further demonstrate that the superior performance is due to the rich linguistic information since an impoverished tag set yielded worse classification results.

5.1 Research Background

A majority of past studies have included POS tags with other features to form a combined feature set. Karlgren and Cutting (1994) included six POS tags (i.e. adverb, preposition, second person pronoun, first person pronoun, noun and present tense verb) in classifying genres of the Brown Corpus. They carried out the classification

This study was originally presented at the 24th Pacific Asia Conference on Language, Information and Computation, Sendai, Japan, 4–7 November 2010.

tasks in terms of 2, 4 and 15 genre classes according to Brown categories. The combined feature set achieved an accuracy of 96, 73 and 52 % in the three classification tasks respectively. Dewdney et al. (2001) included POS tags of content words (i.e. noun, verb, adjective and adverb), where verbs were further defined in past, present and future tenses. Again, with a combined feature set, the performance of classifying seven genre classes reached 92 %. Eissen and Stein (2004) included ten POS tags (i.e., noun, verb, relative pronouns, relative preposition, adverb, article, pronoun, modals, adjective and alphanumeric words) in classifying eight genre classes. The performance of the combined feature set was 70 %.

Some other studies have not specified the POS tags, while they do report the performance using a combined feature set. For instance, Boese and Howe (2005) reported an accuracy of 79.6 % when classifying five genre classes, and an accuracy of 74.8 % for seven genre classes. Lim et al. (2005) reported a much lower performance of about 38 %.

Still, some studies have treated POS tags as independent feature set for automatic genre classification. For example, Finn and Kushmerick (2003) used 36 POS features in subjectivity classification (three genre classes) and review classification (two genre classes), and achieved 84.7 and 61.3 % accuracy respectively. More recently, Stein and Eissen (2008) used ten POS tags to classify eight genre classes and reported an accuracy of 74 %. Santini (2004) further computed POS tags into unigram, bigram and trigram. When classifying ten genre classes, POS trigram achieved the best performance with 82.6 % accuracy, compared with 77.6 % for bigram and 77.3 % for unigram. The study also investigated four spoken and six written genre classes, and POS trigram again performed the best.

It is fair to say that past studies have shown encouraging and suggestive results of using POS tags in genre classification, and yet there are some limitations. For example, it is difficult to evaluate whether POS tags are discriminatory features for a given classification task when they are included in a complex feature set. Limited studies have regarded POS tags as independent feature set. It is also noticeable that the number of genre classes is comparatively small.

5.2 Methodology

In this section we will first explain the experimental setup, then describe the corpus, and finally briefly introduce the machine-learning tools.

5.2.1 Experimental Setup

A goal of the experiment that we designed was to investigate the performance of a set of linguistically fine-grained POS tags for various levels of genre classification tasks. Currently, we are more interested in verifying the contribution of such a feature set in the classification task than ascertaining the comparative performance of different feature selection methods. The BOW approach was used to generate the baseline statistics, which has been commonly used in past studies (e.g. Scott and Matwin 1999; Diederich et al. 2003; Koster and Seutter 2003; Gupta and Ratinov 2008; Li et al. 2009). Besides, an impoverished POS tag set was also examined for indication of effect of linguistic granularity on classification performance. All the performance results were evaluated according to F-score, which is defined as in (3.3) in Chap. 3.

A series of genre classification tasks were identified based on the division of corpus in terms of different genre granularities, and also on the division of each granularity into speech vs. writing.

5.2.2   Corpus Resources

Given the purpose of investigating genre attribute performance, the ICE-GB (Greenbaum 1996) was employed. Based on the ICE-GB categories, four genre levels were identified according to granularity, namely, super, macro, micro and sub-micro. See David (2001) and Boese and Howe (2005) for a similar division of genre granularity. Table 5.1 is a summary of the four-level granularity of ICE-GB. The numbers within brackets indicate the number of genre classes at each level.

As can be seen in Table 5.1, the genre system of ICE-GB can be seen as a systemic hierarchy, with each level commanding a number of subdivisions. For example, the super genre Speech has 2 macro genres (Dialogue and Monologue), which

Table 5.1 Four levels of genre classes

Super (2)	Macro (4)	Micro (11)	Sub-micro (32)
Speech	Dialogue	Private	Direct conversation, distanced conversation
		Public	Class lessons, broadcast discussions, broadcast interviews, parliamentary debates, legal cross-examinations, business transaction
	Monologue	Unscripted	Spontaneous commentaries, unscripted speeches, demonstrations, legal presentations
		Mixed	Broadcast news
		Scripted	Broadcast talks, nonbroadcast talks
Writing	Nonprinted	Student writing	Untimed essays, timed essays
		Correspondence	Social letters, business letters
	Printed	Informational	Learned humanities, learned social sciences, learned natural sciences, learned technology, popular humanities, popular social sciences, popular nature sciences, popular technology, press news reports
		Instructional	Administrative writing, skills and hobbies
		Persuasive	Press editorials
		Creative	Fiction

in turn command 5 micro genres (such as Private and Public) to be divided into 15 sub-micro classes such as direct conversation and class lessons.

5.2.3   Machine-Learning Tools

Weka (Hall et al. 2009) was employed to estimate classification performance in terms of average weighted *F*-score. Naïve Bayes Classifier (NB) was used to evaluate the present or absent property of features, while Naïve Bayes Multinomial Classifier (NB-MN) was used to evaluate the frequency of features. Considering data size, ten-fold cross validation was used to calculate the results.

5.3   Feature Sets

5.3.1   Fine-Grained POS Tags (F-POS)

We propose the use of linguistically fine-grained part-of-speech tags (F-POS) as a feature set for automatic genre classification. The proposed F-POS tags are produced by a probabilistic tagger named AUTASYS (Fang 1996, 2007) according to a tag-feature hierarchy that comprises a head tag indicating general classes such as nouns and verbs augmented with a sub-categorisation feature such as common nouns and monotransitive verbs. Often the tag also includes an additional feature indicating the grammatical status, such as singular common nouns and present-tense monotransitive verbs. Consider [1] as an example.

[1]   *The workshop was held to collect current data on the related laboratory investigations.*

Once tagged by AUTASYS, [1] is represented as:

```
The <tag ART(def)> workshop <tag N(com,sing)> was
<tag AUX(pass,past)> held <tag V(montr,edp)> to <tag
PRTCL(to)> collect <tag V(montr,infin)> current <tag
ADJ(ge)> data <tag N(com,sing)> on <tag PREP(ge)>
the <tag ART(def)> related <tag ADJ(edp)> laboratory
<tag N(com,plu):1/2> investigations <tag
N(com,plu):2/2> . <tag PUNC(per)><#000000>
```

As illustrated above, the tag-feature hierarchy for different part-of-speech in [1] can be analysed as follows.

word	Head tag	Subcategory	Feature	Meaning
The	ART	def	n.a.	Article, definite
workshop	N	com	sing	Noun, common, singular
was	AUX	pass	past	Auxiliary, passive, past tense
held	V	montr	edp	Verb, monotransitive, -ed participle
to	PRTCL	to	n.a.	Particle to
collect	V	montr	n.a.	Verb, monotransitive, infinitive
current	ADJ	ge	n.a.	Adjective, -ed participle
data	N	com	sing	Noun, common, singular
on	PREP	ge	n.a.	Preposition, general
the	ART	def	n.a.	Article, definite
related	ADJ	edp	n.a.	Adjective, -ed participle
laboratory	N	com	sing	Noun, common, plural
investigations	N	com	sing	Noun, common, plural

As a result, the pre-processing of the grammatical annotation extracted 487 different types of POS tags for the whole corpus, with 449 for spoken genres and 319 for written genres.

5.3.2   BOW

A BOW through word unigrams were tested as the baseline experiment. In the current study, the BOW has been filtered with a stoplist of functional items, and the orthographical word forms are retained without lemmatization. A total of 35,758 word types were found for the whole corpus and subsequently used as BOW attributes, with 21,198 for spoken genres and 27,305 for written genres.

5.3.3   Impoverished Tags (I-POS)

The third feature set was generated from F-POS but contains only the head tags without the subcategorisation features and hence linguistically impoverished. Again take [1] for example.

Word	Head tag
The	ART
workshop	N
was	AUX

Word	Head tag
held	V
to	PRTCL
collect	V
current	ADJ
data	N
on	PREP
the	ART
related	ADJ
laboratory	N
investigations	N

I-POS was used in the experiment in order to ascertain the effect of grammatical granularity on classification performance. As a result, there were altogether 36 I-POS attributes for the total corpus, 36 for spoken genres and 27 for written genres.

5.4   Experimental Results

In this section we report the results of a series of genre classification tasks in our experimental study. As noted earlier on, all results were obtained from two Naïve Bayes Classifiers (i.e. NB and NB-MN) in Weka. The first subsection will be devoted to the classification results based on the presence of the selected features. The second part of this section will present the results obtained according to feature frequency, followed by the discussion section.

5.4.1   Results Obtained From NB Classifier

As mentioned earlier, NB Classifier was used to evaluate the three feature sets according to presence or absence of genre attributes. Table 5.2 summarises the performance of the three feature sets in genre classification in terms of average weighted *F*-score. The first column lists the four levels of genres. The second column shows ten genre classification tasks, where *S* stands for speech, *W* stands for writing and the number indicates the number of genre classes in a given classification task.

Several interesting patterns can be observed in Table 5.2. First of all, there tends to be a continual drop in accuracy with the increase in number of classes in general. Take F-POS for example. The *F*-score of F-POS in *SW* classification tasks starts from 0.998 in *SW-2* and then decreases to 0.842 in *SW-4*, 0.747 in *SW-11* and finally drops to 0.582 in *SW-32*. Secondly, genre classification tasks regarding spoken texts generally receive better results than those of written texts. This is perhaps due to those F-POS tags that are specific to speech only. One example is REACT for 're-

Table 5.2 Average weighted *F*-score (NB)

Genre granularity	Code	BOW	F-POS	I-POS
Super genre	*SW-2*	0.871	0.998	0.998
Macro genre	*S-2*	0.885	0.917	0.858
	W-2	0.886	0.742	0.704
	SW-4	0.855	0.842	0.798
Micro genre	*S-5*	0.802	0.749	0.566
	W-6	0.709	0.769	0.513
	SW-11	0.746	0.747	0.549
Sub-micro genre	*S-15*	0.561	0.606	0.341
	W-17	0.586	0.550	0.216
	SW-32	0.551	0.582	0.288

action signal' such as um, yeah and wow, which practically occur exclusively in transcribed speech. Thirdly, F-POS achieves better performance than BOW in six classification tasks, and yields a competing performance in two tasks (i.e., *SW-4* and *W-17*) where the difference is not statistically significant. Finally, F-POS performs better than I-POS in almost all of the ten classification tasks, indicating that fine-grained POS tags with rich linguistic information can better represent text genres than simple POS tags.

In addition to the proposed new feature set, the current study also extended the genre classes up to 32 categories. Next we take a closer look at the three classification tasks (i.e. *SW-32*, *S-15* and *W-17*) at the sub-micro level. Figures 5.1, 5.2 and 5.3 illustrate the learning curves of the three feature sets with the increased training data set (from 10 to 100 %) in the three tasks respectively.

Three interesting patterns emerge in the learning curves. Firstly, the accuracy of performance increases when more training texts are added. Take F-POS in *SW-32* for example. With 10 % of the training data, F-POS achieves an accuracy of about 0.20 in terms of *F*-score; with 50 % of the training texts, the *F*-score reaches to 0.40, and with all of the training data, the ultimate *F*-score reaches over 0.50. Secondly, F-POS performs better than BOW in both *SW-32* and *S-15*, while BOW outperforms F-POS in *W-17*. Finally, F-POS outperforms I-POS in all the three tasks, indicating that fine-grained POS tags with rich linguistic information can better represent the type of texts.

5.4.2 Results Obtained from NB-MN Classifier

Results from the NB-MN were summarised in Table 5.3. As can be seen, the results are generally in line with the previous findings obtained from NB Classifier. First of all, a continual drop in accuracy gain can be observed in most cases with the increase in number of classes. Secondly, genre classification tasks regarding spoken

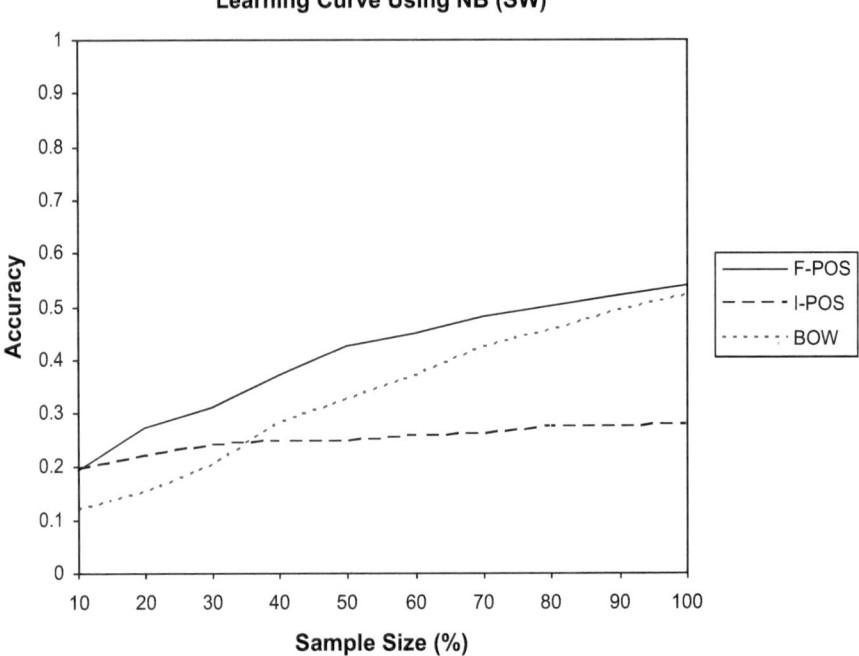

Fig. 5.1 Learning curve for *SW-32*

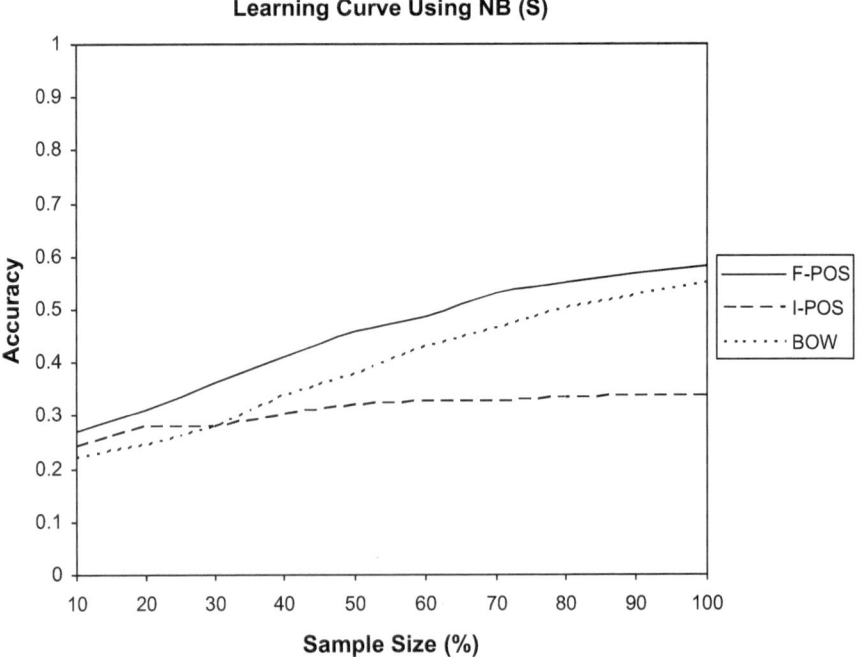

Fig. 5.2 Learning curve for *S-15*

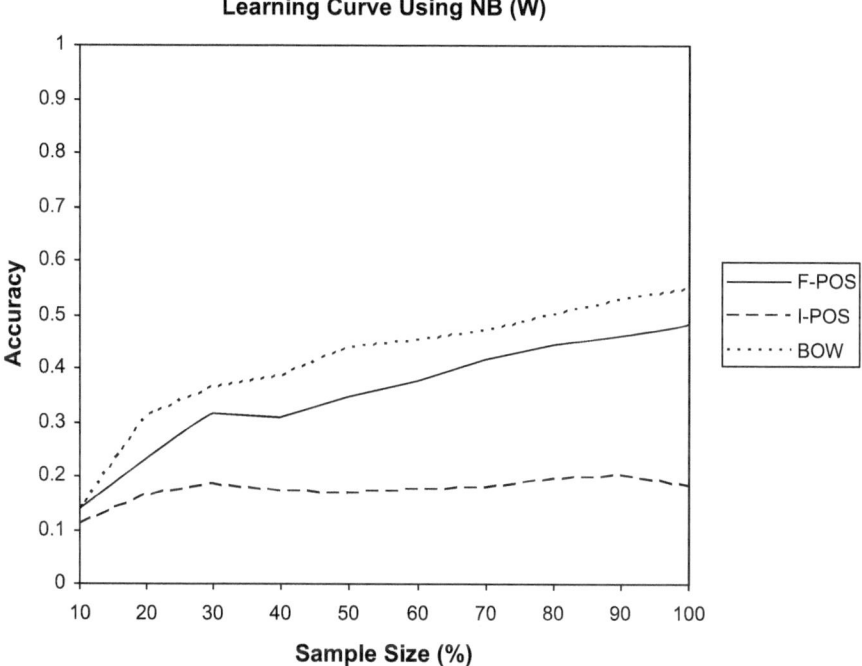

Fig. 5.3 Learning curve for *W-17*

Table 5.3 Average weighted *F*-score (NB-MN)

Genre granularity	Code	BOW	F-POS	I-POS
Super genre	*SW-2*	0.988	0.984	0.998
Macro genre	*S-2*	0.904	0.898	0.898
	W-2	0.892	0.778	0.728
	SW-4	0.895	0.850	0.833
Micro genre	*S-5*	0.773	0.816	0.775
	W-6	0.720	0.686	0.551
	SW-11	0.703	0.781	0.688
Sub-micro genre	*S-15*	0.499	0.785	0.647
	W-17	0.572	0.631	0.459
	SW-32	0.438	0.726	0.588

texts generally receive better results than those of written texts. Thirdly, F-POS outperforms BOW with deeper genre classes. It is also worth noticing that BOW achieves better results than frequency-based features when the number of classes is small. Finally, F-POS performs better than I-POS in nine out of ten classification tasks.

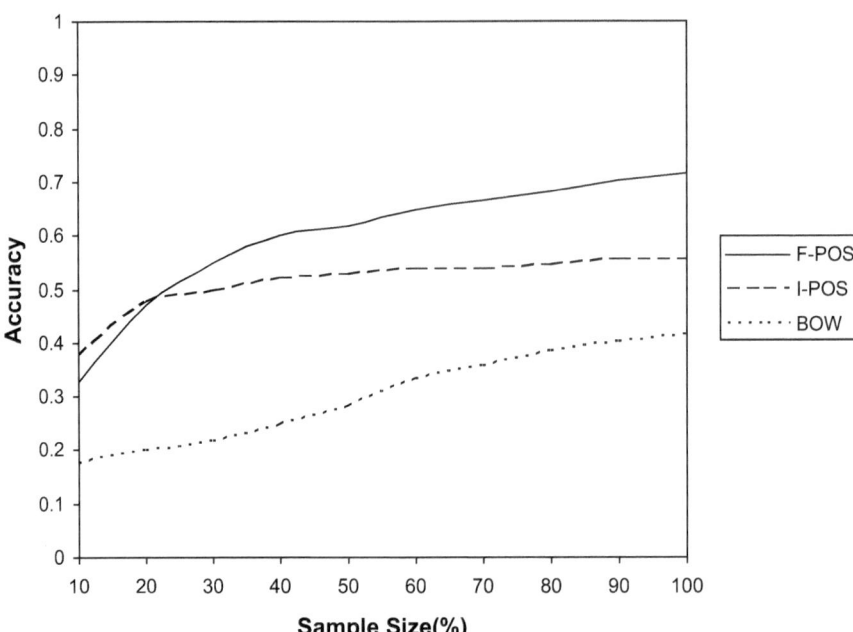

Fig. 5.4 Learning curve for *SW-32*

Next, with regard to the classification at the sub-micro level, the learning curves of the three feature sets with the increased training data set (from 10 to 100%) are illustrated in Figs. 5.4, 5.5 and 5.6. Again interesting patterns can be observed in the learning curves. Firstly, the accuracy of performance increases when more training texts are added. Secondly, F-POS demonstrates superior classification accuracy when compared with a bag of words and linguistically impoverished tags in all the three tasks.

5.4.3 Discussion

Our investigation suggests that F-POS tag set is shown to provide better generalization than the BOW and that it also has a tremendous advantage over BOW in feature size. The investigation also indicates that the contribution of the proposed F-POS tags to genre classification is achieved through detailed linguistic information provided by the descriptive features. This is evident through the fact that performance dropped with the use of head tags without the features indicating the subcategorisation and grammatical status.

Table 5.4 presents an overview of results from three previous studies with the use of POS tags as an independent feature set, as well as the performance from all

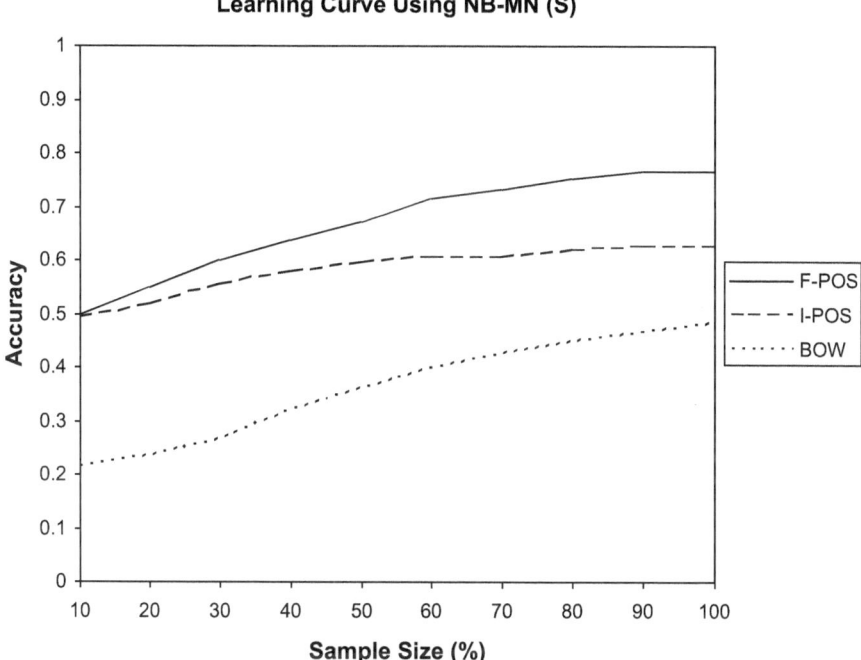

Fig. 5.5 Learning curve for *S-15*

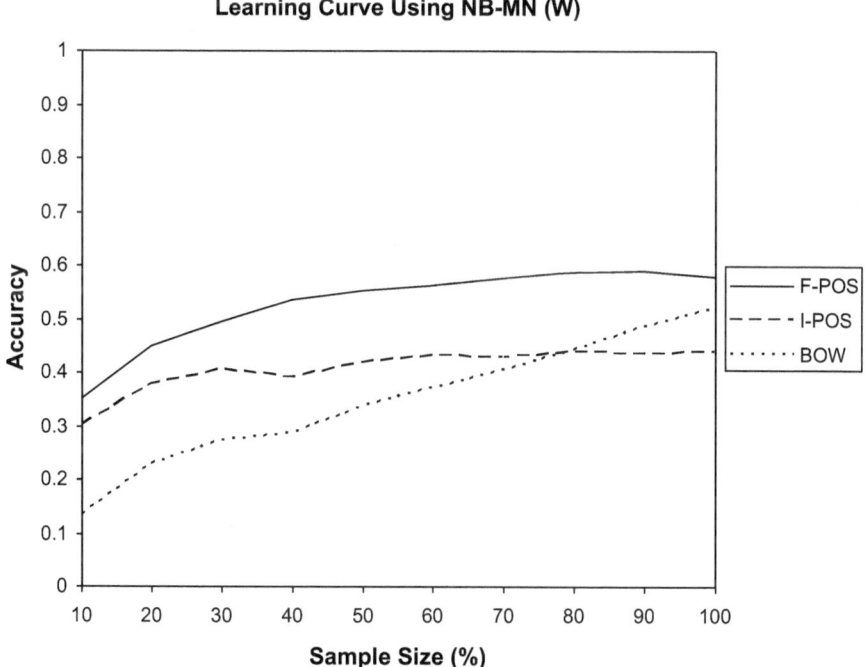

Fig. 5.6 Learning curve for *W-17*

Table 5.4 An overview of POS tag performance in accuracy (%)

No of genres	Past studies		Current study	
			NB	NB-MN
2	Finn and Kushmerick (2003)	61.3%	99.8%	98.4%
3	Finn and Kushmerick (2003)	84.7%	/	/
4	/	/	84.2%	85.0%
8	Stein and Eissen (2008)	74.0%	/	/
10	Santini (2004)	77.3%	/	/
11	/	/	74.7%	78.1%
32	/	/	58.2%	72.6%

the *SW* tasks in the current study. The numbers in the first column are the number of genres that have been involved in the classification tasks.

Although it is hard to compare the accuracy directly due to factors such as difference in genre class, corpus size or evaluation model, it is safe to say that the proposed F-POS tags achieve satisfactory accuracy and that they obtain more consistent performance when feature frequency is considered.

5.5 Conclusion

This section reported an experiment designed to investigate the performance of a linguistically fine-grained POS tag set in automatic genre classification when compared with word unigrams and a linguistically impoverished tag set. The ICE-GB was employed as a resource of text genres. Ten different genre classification tasks were identified, with a maximum of 500 sample texts. NB and NB-MN Classifiers were used to evaluate the performance of the proposed feature set in terms of *F*-score.

As a result of the experiment, the linguistically rich POS set demonstrated superior classification accuracy when compared with a bag of words and linguistically impoverished tags. The finding highlights the importance of grammatical properties represented in the form of POS tags for the separation of texts according to a predefined hierarchy of genres. In addition, our results also indicate that good classification performance is derived predominantly from the rich linguistic information conveyed through subcategorisation features. This indication is evidenced by the fact that when removed of detailed, subcategorisation features the head tags produced inferior performance.

Future work will include the use of a much larger collection of texts to verify the actual performance of the fine-grained POS entity tags. Tag bigrams and trigrams will also be investigated to verify if additional accuracy gain can be achieved.

Chapter 6
Verbs and Text Classification

6.1 Transitivity Type and Text Categories[1]

The investigation reported in this chapter was motivated by two considerations: to support theoretical research in verbs for better insights into the use and distribution of verbs across text categories and to facilitate attempts in the area of natural language processing (NLP) that draw on empirical data.

Researchers in NLP have increasingly felt the need to dynamically construct computational lexicons from text corpora, rather than relying on existent 'static' lexical databases (Pustejovsky and Boguraev 1994). The lack of accurate verb subcategorisation information causing half of the parse failures (Briscoe and Carroll 1993), attempts have been made to construct, from empirical data, lexicons that encode information about predicate subcategorisations that capture the valences of the verb and its structural collocations (cf. Brent 1991; Manning 1993; Ushioda et al. 1993; Briscoe and Carroll 1996). Work has also been carried out to construct formal grammars automatically from empirical data. Fang (1996a) describes an attempt to automatically generalise phrase structure (PS) rules from a syntactically pre-analysed corpus.

However, the feasibility of dynamic lexicon construction and the coverage of lexicons thus created still need to be tested. Moreover, the usefulness of phrase structure (PS) rules, especially those extracted from empirical data, has been seriously questioned by, for example, Sampson (1987), arguing that there is no clear cut distinction between grammatical and deviant sentences, an assertion that implies an immense deficiency of the use of PS rules in NLP systems. Though convincingly defended for the noun phrase (Briscoe 1990), the usefulness of PS rules still needs to be further explored with (1) a structured data set of a much larger size as both the objection and the rebuttal were conducted on a limited sample of about 20,000 words, (2) other syntactic categories and (3) a more extensive evaluation of the performance of NLP systems that employ these PS rules. Arising from these considerations, the

---

[1] An earlier version of this section was previously published as Fang, A. C. 1997. Verb forms and sub-categorisations. *Literary and Linguistic Computing* 12 (4): 209–217.

© Springer-Verlag Berlin Heidelberg 2015

A. C. Fang, J. Cao, *Text Genres and Registers: The Computation of Linguistic Features,*
DOI 10.1007/978-3-662-45100-7_6

authors conducted a series of investigations into English verbs based on empirical observations. We shall report results of a frequency study of lexical verbs in terms of their forms and transitivity subcategorisations based on the International Corpus of English (ICE) with a view to the eventual identification of useful characteristics regarding the use and distribution of verb transitivity types across different text categories. For a more detailed description of the ICE word class and syntactic analysis schemes, see Fang (1994, 1996c) and Greenbaum (1995).

6.1.1   *The Distribution of Lexical Verbs*

Palmer (1974, p. 15 ff) defines four subsets of the English verb: primary auxiliaries, modal auxiliaries, catenatives and the remaining full verbs. It is the full verbs, also called main or lexical verbs (Greenbaum 1996, p. 117), that concern us here. While catenatives are generally analysed as semi-auxiliaries in the ICE word class annotation scheme, lexical verbs in ICE-GB also include certain items that are ordinarily analysed as catenatives. For clarity, we list below those items that are analysed as semi-auxiliaries in ICE-GB:

appear to	*be sure to*	*happen to*
be about to	*begin to*	*have got to*
be apt to	*bease to*	*have to*
be bound to	*come to*	*mean to*
be certain to	*continue to*	*need to*
be due to	*dare to*	*seem to*
be going to	*fail to*	*start to*
be liable to	*get to*	*tend to*
be likely to	*had best*	*turn out to*
be meant to	*had better*	*used to*
be supposed to	*had rather*	

The following items are also analysed as semi-auxiliaries when followed by an *-ing* participle:

begin	*go on*	*start*
carry on	*keep*	*stop*
continue	*keep on*	

Modal auxiliaries in ICE include the following items:

can	*might*	*should*
could	*must*	*will*
may	*shall*	*would*

The above items, together with the primary auxiliaries *be*, *do* and *have*, form the auxiliary class of verbs in ICE-GB. Any other verb is analysed as lexical. For details, see Greenbaum (1995).

6.1.1.1   Observations

Disadvantages are obvious in the use of a mega-word corpus in the study of lexical forms. Frequency studies conducted in the past on both American and British English have already established that a fairly comprehensive list of word forms would require corpora of a size much larger than 1 million words, due to the log-normal distribution of English words in natural use. Frequently used lexical items converge quickly to form a sharp increase in the number of types as a factor of the increase of tokens, while less frequently used items create a long tail where the increase of types becomes much slower. Verbs are no exception; Figs. 6.1 and 6.2 demonstrate this phenomenon through the increase of verb types as a factor of the increase of corpus size in the spoken and written sections of ICE-GB.

The *Y*-axis represents the increase of verb types while the *X*-axis that of corpus size. Each graph has two reference lines, one indicating how much of the corpus is needed to develop 50% of the verb types and the other indicating what the increase is for verb types given 50% of the corpus. As can be observed, half of the spoken section produced over 80% of the verb types, forming a sharp slope in the graph. The rest of the verb types, however, took the other half of the spoken section to de-

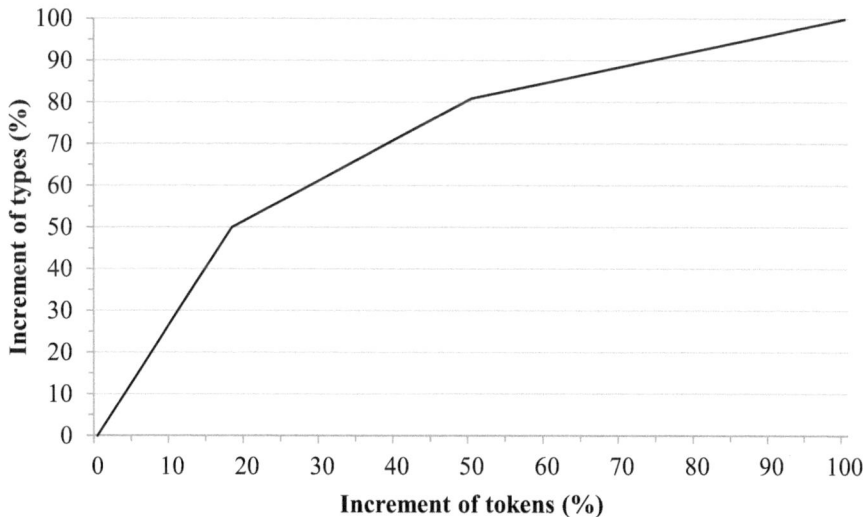

Fig. 6.1 The increment of verb types as a factor of the increment of tokens in speech

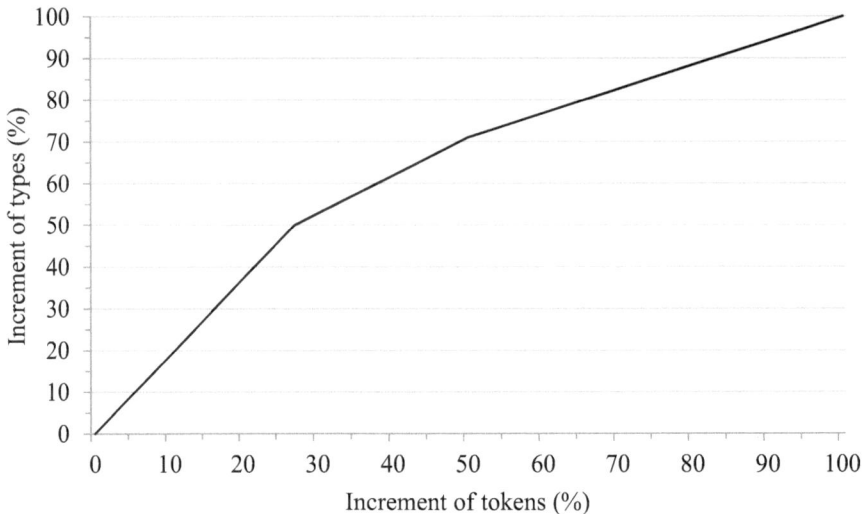

Fig. 6.2 The increment of verb types as a factor of the increment of tokens in writing

velop. Verbs in the written section revealed a similar curve (see Fig. 6.2), though the initial increase is not as sharp, with half of the written material generating slightly more than 70% of the verb types. This difference suggests that writing employs a larger variety of verbs than speech.

The ratio of hapax legomena (types or tokens that occur only once) is another indication of this feature in lexical distribution. The ratios of verbs that occur only once for speech and writing in ICE-GB are 0.42 and 0.43 respectively, as compared with 0.43 for nouns in ICE-GB and 0.45 in the Brown corpus of edited American English (cf. Kučera and Francis 1967) for general lexical items.

The discussion so far seems to suggest the impracticality of constructing a comprehensive list of verbs from moderately sized text corpora. However, if our question is 'what is the central core of English verb types and what coverage do they offer in the authentic use of the language', we then get a much more positive picture for verb distributions.

First of all, here are some basic statistics about verbs in ICE-GB:

From Table 6.1, another table may be generated:

Table 6.1 Some basic statistics about ICE-GB verbs

	Word tokens	Verb tokens	Verb types	Verb hapax
Speech	597,894	88,871	5233	2189
Writing	400,847	54,855	5911	2544
Total	998,741	143,726	7752	3003

Table 6.2 Hapax legomena in ICE-GB verbs

	Hapax/V. token (%)	Hapax/V. type (%)
Speech	2.5	41.8
Writing	4.5	43.0
Total	2.1	38.7

According to Table 6.2, over 40% of verb types in both speech and writing are hapax legomena. When the two sections are combined, some hapax legomena overlap and the ratio is now 38.7%, slightly reduced but still significant. However, verbs that occur once represent only a marginal portion of verb tokens: in speech verb hapax legomena represent only 2.5% of the total verb tokens. Writing yields a larger proportion of nonce verbs, 4.5%. When the corpus is considered as a whole, this ratio is reduced to only 2.1%. Moreover, we observe that naturally occurring texts make central use of a small group of verb types that account for the bulk of verb tokens. Indeed, to account for 90% of all the verb uses in ICE-GB, it was observed, only 20% of verb types are needed for speech, 32% for writing, and only 22% for the corpus as a whole. The tagged Lancaster-Oslo-Bergen Corpus of edited British English (LOB; cf. Johansson et al. 1986) was subsequently used to test the coverage of the 7752 verb forms from ICE-GB. As indicated by Table 6.3, ICE-GB verbs achieved a coverage of 95% and over for each of the 15 LOB text genres, the average being 96.4%.[2]

Verbs are productively inflected in order to reflect their intrinsic grammatical characteristics such as tense, phase and aspect (cf. Palmer 1974, p. 33 ff). Such inflections result in corresponding morphological changes of the verb; while irregular ones have no fewer than five, an English verb has at least four different

Table 6.3 The coverage of ICE-GB verb forms for LOB

Genre	Coverage (%)
A	97.1
B	97.9
C	95.1
D	96.4
E	96.3
F	96.2
G	96.5
H	98.0
J	97.1
K	96.3
L	96.5
M	95.3
N	95.1
P	97.0
R	95.1

---

[2] Considering that written English employs a greater variety of verbs than speech, ICE-GB could be expected to offer a higher coverage of LOB verbs if it was a homogeneous corpus of written samples.

forms: base, third person singular present tense (-s), past tense and past participle
(-ed) and present participle (-ing) (cf. Greenbaum 1996, p. 117). The number of
different verb forms can be thus further collapsed if, for instance, the verb forms
work, worked, working and works are regarded as the same verb type, a process of
morphological analysis generally known as lemmatisation. In the investigation, all
the verbs in ICE-GB were automatically lemmatised with AUTASYS 3.0 (cf. Fang
1996c) and manually checked. Results showed that lemmatisation can effectively
reduce the number of verb forms in English of natural use: the 5233 and 5911 verb
forms in speech and writing were respectively reduced to 2617 and 2912, and 3639
for the whole corpus, an overall reduction rate of more than 53%. The number of
verb hapax legomena for the whole corpus was reduced to 1133, a drop of 62.3%
from the original 3003. The coverage of these ICE verbs in LOB was subsequently
raised to more than 98%.

Table 6.4 lists the 100 most frequent lemmatised verbs in ICE-GB, which account for 76% of the total occurrences of verbs in speech and 58% of verb occurrences in writing. Rank in Table 6.5 refers to the overall ranking of a particular verb
in the corpus. S-rank refers to the verb's ranking in speech (with S-freq indicating
the absolute frequency) and W-rank in writing (with W-freq indicating the absolute
frequency). Think, for instance, has an overall ranking of 4. With a frequency of
2801 in speech, it is the second most frequent verb, while in writing it is the 14th
most frequent, occurring 816 times.

A Spearman's test for Table 6.4 found the rank correlation coefficient to be
0.5691, suggesting a tendency of greater difference between S-rank and W-rank
with the increase of rank, and therefore indicating a general disagreement in the
choice of verbs between speech and writing, an issue that warrants a separate investigation and shall not be discussed in the present study.

6.1.1.2 Summary

In the investigation, it was observed that the frequency distribution of verbs is similar to that of lexical items in general. However, due to the central use of a small
number of verbs, under-represented items (verb hapax legomena, for instance),
represent only a fraction of verb occurrences in actual use. Since this fraction can
be further reduced by lemmatisation, it may be concluded that a moderately sized
corpus can be used to generate a fairly comprehensive list of English verbs.

6.1.2   The Distribution of Verb Transitivity Types

This section describes an investigation into the use and distribution of different
verb transitivity types in the ICE corpus. It will first of all present an outline of the
verb subcategorisation in the ICE word class annotation scheme before present the
empirical observations.

Table 6.4 Hundred most frequent lemmatised verbs in ICE-GB

Rank	Verb	S-rank	S-freq	W-rank	W-freq
001	*be*	1	24,525	1	10,654
002	*have*	3	3,035	2	1,386
003	*say*	5	3,018	3	867
004	*think*	2	2,801	14	816
005	*get*	4	2,629	7	746
006	*do*	6	2,359	11	623
007	*go*	7	2,142	9	572
008	*know*	8	1,779	10	561
009	*make*	11	1,387	4	528
010	*see*	10	1,368	8	508
011	*come*	9	1,116	13	500
012	*take*	13	1,030	6	467
013	*want*	12	1,006	20	459
014	*use*	21	870	5	412
015	*look*	14	694	16	397
016	*give*	15	674	12	334
017	*find*	18	565	15	321
018	*mean*	16	557	35	292
019	*tell*	19	523	22	284
020	*work*	22	511	24	265
021	*try*	17	507	65	259
022	*put*	20	494	40	242
023	*call*	24	473	30	238
024	*show*	30	469	17	226
025	*like*	23	431	59	226
026	*become*	32	410	18	222
027	*feel*	29	343	21	218
028	*leave*	27	340	23	215
029	*happen*	26	339	74	192
030	*ask*	31	337	29	191
031	*talk*	25	314	128	190
032	*hear*	28	311	47	188
033	*write*	38	292	25	182
034	*bring*	35	283	33	182
035	*need*	39	276	32	179
036	*pay*	46	264	27	178
037	*play*	33	262	56	174
038	*believe*	37	261	52	173

Table 6.4 (continued)

Rank	Verb	S-rank	S-freq	W-rank	W-freq
039	*provide*	81	242	19	172
040	*keep*	45	234	34	169
041	*live*	44	232	39	162
042	*move*	41	228	44	161
043	*run*	40	226	48	157
044	*read*	34	218	119	157
045	*remember*	36	211	103	153
046	*produce*	72	210	26	152
047	*start*	42	208	69	150
048	*send*	48	206	55	148
049	*speak*	43	196	71	147
050	*allow*	73	193	28	145
051	*turn*	50	188	58	142
052	*meet*	51	186	62	138
053	*change*	49	176	73	138
054	*help*	63	169	41	138
055	*hold*	60	162	51	136
056	*hope*	68	160	42	135
057	*set*	57	159	60	133
058	*seem*	56	159	64	133
059	*agree*	52	154	85	132
060	*lead*	65	150	54	128
061	*describe*	69	142	49	127
062	*consider*	88	141	38	126
063	*decide*	55	139	80	125
064	*suggest*	66	139	57	125
065	*expect*	59	137	72	123
066	*carry*	70	135	53	118
067	*sit*	53	134	106	118
068	*cause*	87	131	43	118
069	*understand*	54	126	99	116
070	*follow*	89	124	46	115
071	*require*	119	124	37	115
072	*suppose*	47	124	236	113
073	*occur*	171	121	31	111
074	*include*	140	120	36	111
075	*develop*	71	119	67	111
076	*lose*	64	118	87	111

Table 6.4 (continued)

Rank	Verb	S-rank	S-freq	W-rank	W-freq
077	*involve*	76	115	75	108
078	*buy*	67	112	88	107
079	*stand*	62	112	97	106
080	*win*	58	110	152	106
081	*receive*	125	110	50	105
082	*increase*	146	107	45	103
083	*remain*	105	105	61	101
084	*learn*	75	104	95	101
085	*reach*	108	103	63	96
086	*apply*	99	102	70	96
087	*build*	97	98	79	95
088	*mention*	77	98	108	94
089	*offer*	112	98	68	94
090	*spend*	83	98	96	93
091	*add*	127	98	66	91
092	*fall*	100	95	83	91
093	*stay*	79	94	114	91
094	*achieve*	113	94	77	90
095	*sound*	61	93	221	89
096	*grow*	95	92	102	87
097	*explain*	96	91	101	87
098	*accept*	92	90	109	86
099	*pass*	104	89	93	86
100	*pick*	74	88	178	85

Table 6.5 Frequency distribution of verb subcategorisations in ICE-GB

Transitivity	Speech		Writing		Total	
	Freq	%	Freq	%	Freq	%
cop	22,833	25.8	10,495	19.2	33,328	23.3
cxtr	2644	2.9	1770	3.2	4414	3.1
dimontr	152	0.2	78	0.1	230	0.2
ditr	1129	1.3	663	1.2	1792	1.3
intr	21,355	24.2	11,668	21.4	33,023	23.1
montr	38,874	43.9	28,648	52.5	67,522	47.2
trans	1420	1.6	1209	2.2	2629	1.8
Total	88,407	100.0	54,531	100.0	142,938	100.0

Fig. 6.3 The ICE verb sub-categorisation schema

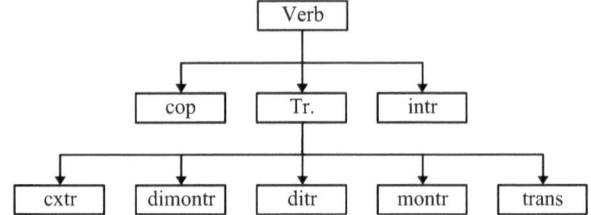

6.1.2.1 ICE-GB Verb Subcategorisations

ICE-GB has been annotated by the research team at the Survey of English Usage (SEU), University College London, with a tagset that is especially expressive in the representation of verb complementations. Verbs are first of all divided into three major types: copula (`cop`), intransitive (`intr`) and transitive, the last of which is further divided into complex transitive (`cxtr`), dimonotransitive (`dimontr`), ditransitive (`ditr`), monotransitive (`montr`) and transitive (`trans`). The verb subcategorisation schema is illustrated by Fig. 6.3.

The first four subdivisions of the transitive verb are illustrated by examples [1]–[4]:

a. Complex transitive, whose object is complemented by another phrase:

[1]   *If television was going to be bloody-minded, radio would <u>keep</u> me busy.*

b. Di-monotrantive, which takes an indirect object:

[2]   *The pen though, as Shakespeare will <u>tell</u> you, is more Mighty than the sword.*

c. Di-transitive, which takes both an indirect and a direct object:

[3]   *His parents were then recommended to stop comforting him as they were <u>giving</u> him positive reinforcement for undesirable behaviour.*

d. Monotransitive, which takes a direct object:

[4]   *The programme had a biggish audience (in radio terms) because it <u>fol-lowed</u> the Today programme, and because people listened to it in their cars on the way to work.*

The notation `trans` here is used in the ICE project to tag transitive verbs followed by a noun phrase that may be the subject of the following nonfinite clause. They are so tagged in order to avoid making a decision on their transitivity types.[3] This verb type is best demonstrated by the following sentences:

[5]   *Just before Christmas, the producer of Going Places, Irene Mallis, had asked me to make a documentary on 'warm-up men'.*

[6]   *They make others feel guilty and isolate them.*

[7]   *I can buy batteries for the tape - but I can see myself spending a fortune!*

[8]   *The person who booked me in had his eyebrows shaved & replaced by straight black painted lines and he had earrings, not only in his ears but through his nose and lip!*

In the above examples, asked, make, see and had are all complemented by nonfinite clauses with overt subjects, the main verbs of these nonfinite clauses being infinitive, present participial and past participial.

6.1.2.2   Observations

In the investigation, frequencies were collected and listed in Table 6.5 from ICE-GB for the seven transitivity types, with respect to speech and writing.[4] For the copula verbs, we can read from Table 6.6 that they occurred 22,833 times in speech, which amounts to 26 % (22,833/88,407) of all the verbs found in the spoken section, and that there are altogether 33,328 occurrences of copula verbs in the whole corpus which account for 23 % (33,328/142,938) of all the verb uses.

In speech, the three most frequent subcategorisations are monotransitive, copula and intransitive. In writing, they are monotransitive, intransitive and copula. The spoken section exhibits a substantially greater use of copula verbs than the written section, which in turn possesses a much higher percentage of monotransitive verbs. Complex transitive and trans verbs appear to have an even distribution across speech and writing. The other two transitivity types, dimontr and ditr, represent only a marginal use.

Table 6.6 lists the 15 most frequently used verbs for each of the seven subcategorisations, by descending frequency. As can be easily seen, speech and writing in

---

[3] This type of verb can be analysed differently according to various tests into, for instance, monotransitives, ditransitives and complex transitives (cf. Quirk et al. 1985; Mair 1990) . Accordingly, to avoid arbitrary decisions, the complementing non-finite clause is assigned a catch-all term 'transitive complement' in parsing.

[4] Note that there is a slight difference between the verb total reported here and that reported in the previous section. This is mainly because the investigation was conducted over a period during which new additions were made to the corpus. The slight difference is retained and reported in this article under the belief that it does not alter the overall picture of verb distributions.

Table 6.6 Fifteen most frequent verbs for the seven subcategorisations

Subcat	Genre	Verbs
cop	S	*be, become, get, look, feel, sound, seem, go, remain, form, stay, prove, make, appear, keep*
	W	*be, become, feel, seem, look, remain, get, sound, comprise, appear, prove, form, go, constitute, fall*
cxtr	S	*call, put, make, get, have, find, keep, take, leave, see, bring, describe, regard, send, know*
	W	*make, call, put, keep, find, see, place, know, regard, describe, leave, bring, consider, take, get*
dimontr	S	*tell, ask, assure, inform, show, remind, give, feed, offer, promise, quote, take, warn, write*
	W	*tell, ask, advise, assure, feed, grant, pay, remind, serve*
ditr	S	*give, tell, ask, show, get, send, offer, teach, convince, take, inform, cost, allow, lend, promise*
	W	*give, tell, send, offer, show, allow, ask, pay, teach, inform, assure, cause, grant, wish, deny*
intr	S	*be, go, come, think, know, look, get, work, talk, happen, say, do, see, live, speak*
	W	*be, go, come, say, look, work, occur, live, get, think, write, move, happen, lead, run*
montr	S	*have, think, say, do, get, know, see, want, take, make, mean, use, like, find, try*
	W	*have, use, take, say, make, do, see, know, get, provide, find, show, think, give, want*
trans	S	*have, get, want, see, make, allow, ask, let, expect, hear, enable, help, find, encourage, think*
	W	*allow, make, ask, enable, have, let, see, find, expect, encourage, help, force, cause, require, want*

ICE-GB tend to have a different preference for either the choice or the frequency of use of a particular verb.

Another purpose of the investigation was to classify verbs according to the number of subcategorisations they were observed to take in ICE-GB, in order to find out about verb distribution characteristics with one extra factor. The aim was to test the intuition that only a small subset of verbs are capable of taking a variety of subcategorisations, and that this subset corresponds to the centrally used set of verbs. If the intuitions are true, then the implication would be that it is feasible to generalise a comprehensive list of verb subcategorisations from a medium-sized corpus. Table 6.7 below presents the actual observations in ICE-GB with five columns:

Subcat no	Number of subcategorisations
Type no	Number of verb types with a certain number of subcategorisations
Token no	Number of verb tokens with a certain number of subcategorisations
Ratio/token	Ratio of token no over total number of verb tokens
Ratio/type	Ratio of type no over total number of verb types

Table 6.7 The distribution of verbs with a different number of subcategorisations

Subcat no	Type no	Token no	Ratio/token	Ratio/type
7	0	0	0.0	0.0
6	6	8491	0.06	0.0
5	17	11,388	0.08	0.0
4	72	24,139	0.17	0.02
3	234	59,432	0.41	0.06
2	956	27,167	0.19	0.26
1	2351	13,109	0.09	0.65
Total	3636	143,726	1.00	1.00

We may thus read that none of the verbs found in the corpus have all the seven subcategorisations. We may also read that in the whole corpus only 72 verbs were observed to have four subcategorisations, that they occurred a total of 24,139 times in ICE-GB, and that they jointly represent 17% of total verb tokens but only 2% of verb types.

The actual observations strongly confirmed our intuitions: only 9% of the verb types ($6 + 17 + 72 + 234 = 329$) in the whole corpus are capable of taking more than three different subcategorisations, and this small subset of verbs represent 72% of the total number of verb tokens. Conversely, 65% (2351) of the verb types have only one subcategorisation, either intransitive or monotransitive and 26% (956) of the verb types have two subcategorisations, intransitive and monotransitive. These two classes jointly constitute over 90% of the verb types, but account for only 28% of the verb tokens.

Table 6.8 lists the 50 most frequently used verbs in ICE-GB sorted first according to the number of subcategorisations (D) and then according to frequencies (Freq). In the same table, subfrequencies are provided for the verbs' distribution across the seven subcategorisations. The 50 verbs listed here represent only 1.4% of the total number of verb types but 16% of the total number of verb tokens.

6.1.2.3 Summary

In this section, observations were reported regarding the frequency distribution of ICE-GB verbs across the seven subcategorisations analysed according to the ICE word class annotation scheme. While it is evident that speech and writing tend to prefer a different set of verbs, the result of the investigation also confirmed that only a small subset of English verbs are capable of a variety of different subcategorisations and that this small subset correspond to the centrally used set of verbs.

6.1.3 Conclusion

In this section, we presented observations of the frequency distributions of verb forms, verb subcategorisations, and verb phrases, with an emphasis on whether a

Table 6.8 A list of 50 most frequent verbs sorted according to the number of subcategorisations

Word	Freq	D	cop	cxtr	dimt	ditr	intr	mont	tran
get	3373	6	296	260	0	29	681	1974	133
make	1932	6	15	463	0	7	32	1270	145
show	658	6	0	15	4	80	40	498	21
ask	506	6	0	4	42	87	88	162	123
keep	393	6	15	198	0	1	14	141	24
have	4404	5	0	151	0	1	50	4029	173
give	1161	5	0	4	2	547	29	579	0
find	954	5	0	191	0	2	33	663	65
tell	765	5	0	0	132	476	20	109	28
feel	598	5	272	4	0	0	35	267	20
leave	581	5	0	110	0	6	87	355	23
write	581	5	0	3	1	6	228	343	0
bring	458	5	0	90	0	8	4	348	8
pay	428	5	0	1	1	17	99	310	0
send	342	5	0	53	0	72	7	204	6
allow	336	5	0	7	0	20	30	63	216
set	287	5	0	46	0	2	35	197	7
offer	196	5	0	1	1	50	3	141	0
wish	161	5	0	1	0	8	8	140	4
advise	63	5	0	0	3	7	12	22	19
warn	40	5	0	0	1	9	1	21	8
persuade	33	5	0	1	0	7	1	6	18
say	3496	4	0	2	0	0	674	2792	28
think	3447	4	0	39	0	0	800	2572	36
know	2287	4	0	82	0	0	732	1461	12
see	1929	4	0	141	0	0	267	1363	158
want	1295	4	0	6	0	0	22	1134	133
use	1253	4	0	37	0	0	19	1181	16
put	680	4	0	381	0	0	19	278	2
like	605	4	0	8	0	0	58	511	28
hear	490	4	0	1	0	0	128	301	60
play	427	4	0	18	0	2	117	290	0
believe	400	4	0	4	0	0	71	305	20
provide	394	4	0	2	0	1	14	377	0
run	382	4	3	5	0	0	256	118	0
read	356	4	0	2	0	1	68	285	0
remember	348	4	0	2	0	0	67	265	14
turn	326	4	9	45	0	0	195	77	0
help	301	4	0	3	0	0	59	180	59
hold	292	4	0	33	0	0	29	224	6

Table 6.8 (continued)

Word	Freq	D	cop	cxtr	dimt	ditr	intr	mont	tran
lead	275	4	0	7	0	0	187	64	17
consider	271	4	0	44	0	0	1	201	25
expect	267	4	0	2	0	0	13	163	89
develop	242	4	1	1	0	0	68	172	0
lose	234	4	0	1	0	2	28	203	0
apply	204	4	0	1	0	0	135	67	1
build	197	4	0	6	0	1	31	159	0
accept	175	4	0	6	0	0	3	165	1
pass	175	4	0	5	0	2	63	105	0
form	170	4	43	1	0	0	18	108	0

moderately sized corpus, such as ICE-GB, can be used to generate a comprehensive picture about the English verb. It is evident that though verb forms share the characteristics of frequency distribution of lexical items in general, a one-million-word corpus can nevertheless generate a comprehensive and representative list of English verbs due to the strict productivity of inflected forms. In terms of verb subcategorisations, we observed that speech and writing are different in the choice of verbs and their frequency of use. More relevantly, it was confirmed that only a small subset of English verbs are capable of a variety of different subcategorisations and that they form the central set of verbs that are more frequently used than those with one or two subcategorisations. Due to this small subset, and hence the regularity in use, we find it reasonable to conclude that it is feasible to dynamically construct lexicons from medium-sized corpora for accurate information about verb subcategorisations.

6.2   Infinitive Verbs and Text Categories[5]

It is difficult to examine on a large scale the use of infinitives and their syntactic functions automatically. With unannotated collections of English texts stored on the computer (corpora), a huge amount of manual work is required to study the infinitives, as the researcher has to separate the infinitive marker to from the preposition to. If the texts have been analysed only at the word class level (tagged), however, the annotation is often inadequate to allow a reliable frequency count of infinitives. For instance, the Brown corpus of Present-Day American English (Francis and Kučera 1982) and the Lancaster-Oslo-Bergen Corpus (LOB, cf. Johansson and

---

[5] An earlier version of this section was previously published as Fang, A. C. 1995. The distribution of infinitives of contemporary British English: A study based on the British ICE Corpus. *Literary and Linguistic Computing* 10 (4): 247–257.

Hofland 1989), both tagged at word class level, do not note infinitive verbs. The underlined verbs in the following examples are not distinguished. All are tagged as verbs in the base form.

[9]   We _study_ English.
[10]   He will _give_ a lecture in Cambridge.
[11]   She sat closer to _hear_ me better.
[12]   The chairman demanded that he _attend_ the conference.
[13]   The sudden sound made her _shiver_.

These two corpora do separate the infinitive marker _to_ from the preposition _to_. But again this information is insufficient, as the infinitive marker itself does not guarantee a reliable count of infinitive verbs. Consider the following examples.

[14]   The Franks did make great efforts to _try_ and govern Brittany.

[15]   Imagination may _be_ misleading in more traditional displays but can _sow_ the seeds for discovering more if one wants to.

In [14], two infinitive verbs share one infinitive marker while in [15] the infinitive verb after _to_ is actually omitted. In both cases, counting the infinitive marker _to_ does not give an exact count for the actual number of infinitive verbs. Nor can we rely on counting the number of modals and auxiliaries for the number of infinitives.

  In spite of these difficulties, many corpus-based studies have been devoted to English infinitives. Mair (1987, 1990) investigated _to-_ and _for/to_-infinitival complement clauses in the manually analysed SEU corpus, and Biber (1988) investigated _to_-infinitival complementations in his study on variations across speech and writing. The written material used by Biber comprised the untagged BROWN and LOB corpora for writing, and the London-Lund Corpus of Spoken English for speech (Biber 1988, p. 211 ff). Earlier studies include van Ek (1966), Huddleston (1971), Levine (1977) and Andersson (1985). They are based on written material only and lump together British and American evidence (Mair 1987, p. 545).

  The British component in the ICE-GB allows for a detailed study of infinitives. It is a collection of 1 million words of contemporary British English produced in 1990–1993 and has been designed to cover both spoken and written English. With its 32 text categories, this corpus offers opportunities for the study of linguistic variations across speech and writing. See Table 2.3 in Chap. 2 for an overview of the categories that underlie the structure of the corpus. To assist various investigations into language use, ICE-GB has been tagged at word-class level with a tagset developed at the SEU (Greenbaum 1993; Greenbaum and Ni 1994; Fang and Nelson 1994) . The ICE tagset not only notes complementation types of verbs but also distinguishes other detailed features. The underlined verbs in [9]–[13], for instance, are all tagged as infinitive except [12], where attend is tagged as subjunctive. ICE-GB is currently being analysed at syntactic level. This annotation explicitly indicates not only phrase categories (e.g. noun phrase, verb phrase) but also their sentential functions (e.g. subject, verb, noun phrase postmodification). In [11], for example, *She* is analysed as the sentential subject realised by a noun phrase whose head is a singular personal pronoun, and *to hear me better* is analysed as an infinitive clause functioning as a sentential adverbial, with features indicating the clause type (dependent), the voice (active), the word order (unmarked) and the transitivity type of the verb (monotransitive). For a more detailed description of the ICE syntactic annotation scheme, see Fang (1994) .

This study based on the tagged British ICE corpus has two sections. The first section presents the distribution of infinitives in the 32 text categories and tries, where applicable, to speculate on differences in distribution. The following three types of infinitives are noted:

1.	aux infinitives	*I will come.*
2.	bare infinitives	*Did you notice anyone leave the house?*
3.	*to*-infinitives	*He asked me to leave immediately.*

Quirk et al. (1985) treat types 1 and 2 as bare infinitives. Here we informally use the term aux infinitive to indicate those that are used together with auxiliaries. Bare infinitive is used to refer to those that are used as complementations of certain verbs of coercive meaning and perception, and also those used in certain pseudo-cleft sentences through the use of the substitute verb do and their variances (cf. Quirk et al. 1985, pp. 15.15 and 16.52). *To*-infinitives cover those with the infinitive marker to but do not include those whose subjects are introduced by for. Statistics in this section were automatically collected from the tagged ICE-GB with ICECUP (ICE Corpus Utility Program) developed at SEU. In the second section, *for/to*-infinitives are counted separately and the distribution of their syntactic functions in the higher clause will be discussed with frequent reference to Mair (1987). Statistics were automatically collected from the parsed section of ICE-GB.

6.2.1   The Overall Distribution of Infinitives

The tagging of auxiliaries in the British ICE corpus requires some explanation. Four types are noted that directly involve the use of infinitives. These are *do, let,* modals and semi-auxiliaries. The *do* auxiliary consists of the dummy operator *do* and the introductory imperative marker *do*:

[16]	*You didn't say that, did you?*
[17]	*I do remember him.*
[18]	*Do tell me.*
[19]	*Don't be so noisy.*

while the *let* auxiliary is the introductory imperative marker *let*:

[20]   *Let me see now. What should I do next?*
[21]   *Let's play some jazz.*

The central modal auxiliaries are:

can	*might*	*should*
could	*must*	*will*
may	*shall*	*would*

Marginal modal auxiliaries (*dare, need, ought to* and *used to*) sometimes function as lexical verbs. But they are always tagged as auxiliaries when followed by a bare infinitive or *to*-infinitive. The class of semi-auxiliaries (*be about to, be apt to, be bound to*, etc.) also includes modal idioms (*had better, would rather, have got to, be to*, etc.) and catenatives (*appear to, come to, fail to, get to*, etc. cf. Quirk et al. 1985, pp. 3.45–49). Those followed by an infinitive—with or without *to*—are all tagged as semi-auxiliaries, all of which, including the infinitive marker to, are treated as compounds. For detailed discussions, see Greenbaum (1992) and relevant sections in Quirk et al. (1985).

Table 6.9 gives an overview of the distribution of infinitives across the categories in the corpus. The figures are absolute frequency counts. Refer to Table 2.3 for more information about the text categories (*Cat*).

As can be seen from Table 6.9, the spoken section outnumbers its written counterpart for all four types. This is not surprising at all, as there are more running words (tokens) in the spoken section than in writing in the British ICE corpus. Categories also differ radically in size. Direct conversations (S1A1), for instance, contain 90 texts, and this explains its very high numbers in Table 6.9. However, because of the different number of tokens and verbs in the categories, the absolute frequency counts do not present a true picture of the distribution of infinitives, especially when we want to know the percentage of verbs that are used infinitivally. Thus, in our following discussions, we shall use, instead of raw frequency counts, the ratio of the number of infinitives over the number of verbs in a category.

6.2.2 Aux Infinitives

The distribution of aux infinitives, which include those following semi-auxiliaries, is directly influenced by the distribution of auxiliaries. As there tend to be more modals in speech, we expect there to be more aux infinitives in the spoken categories than in written material, even as a percentage of the total number of verbs.

In the British ICE corpus, the mean ratio of verbs used as aux infinitives is 0.16, that for the spoken section 0.18 and for written material 0.13. These figures point to the general indication that there are more aux infinitives in spoken language (18 out

Table 6.9 Distributions of infinitives across text categories

Spoken					Written				
Cat	Aux	Bare	To	For	Cat	Aux	Bare	To	For
S1A1	5790	192	1563	45	W1A1	206	6	273	5
S1A2	636	25	163	2	W1A2	275	9	235	6
S1B1	1275	26	366	3	W1B1	929	30	510	16
S1B2	1112	17	480	14	W1B2	748	7	579	29
S1B3	576	25	263	11	W2A1	169	4	239	1
S1B4	560	4	243	17	W2A2	323	12	302	3
S1B5	567	7	224	12	W2A3	183	17	128	3
S1B6	779	19	200	4	W2A4	210	17	325	8
S2A1	490	19	370	15	W2B1	173	12	227	5
S2A2	1272	25	751	28	W2B2	364	12	320	7
S2A3	498	4	231	8	W2B3	383	23	253	1
S2A4	316	0	221	11	W2B4	312	11	306	7
S2B1	758	5	615	19	W2C1	692	15	651	20
S2B2	678	26	540	14	W2D1	577	1	302	7
S2B3	329	15	303	9	W2D2	331	22	266	13
					W2E1	447	9	345	7
					W2F1	952	31	561	22
Total	15636	409	6533	212	*Total*	7274	238	5822	160
Token: 597894		Verb: 87684			Token: 400847		Verb: 53990		

of every 100 verbs) than in written language (13). Table 6.10 presents such ratios for all the categories, arranged accordingly in descending order.

From Table 6.10, we learn that the two modes are 0.26 (business transactions) and 0.07 (learned and popular humanities). As can be easily discerned, spoken categories mainly occupy the upper half of the scale, with written ones clustered in the lower half, another indication of the uneven distribution of aux infinitives across speech and writing. Except S2A1 (spontaneous commentaries), four of the five spoken categories that fall below the corpus mean are speeches (S2A2, S2B3), talks (S2B2) and broadcast news (S2B1). These are closer to written English because they are all understandably carefully prepared; indeed, S2B1, S2B2 and S2B3 have simply been read aloud from scripts. One explanation for spontaneous commentaries, which have the least aux infinitive content in the spoken section, is probably the prevalence of verbless sentences and sentences depicting actions that either happen at the same time as the commentary or have just happened (Greenbaum, personal communication).

Four written categories are higher the corpus mean. These are press editorials (W2E1), social and business letters (W1B1, W1B2) and administrative writing (W2D1). Letters as a means of social communication undoubtedly share features of spoken English and thus have a relatively higher aux infinitive content. Editorials

Table 6.10 Distribution of aux infinitives across text categories

Ratio	Spoken	Written
0.26	Business transactions	
0.22	Distanced conversations	Administrative writing
0.21	Class lessons	
0.20	Direct conversations	Business letters
	Parliamentary debates	
0.19	Legal cross-examinations	Social letters
0.18	Broadcast discussions	Press: Editorials
0.17	Broadcast interviews	
	Demonstrations	
0.14	Unscripted speeches	Learned: Social sciences
	Broadcast news	Popular: Social sciences
	Broadcast news	Popular: Natural sciences
		Fiction
0.13	Broadcast talks	Press: News reports
0.12		Skills and hobbies
0.10	Spontaneous commentaries	Timed essays
0.09		Learned: Natural sciences
0.08		Untimed essays
		Learned: Technology
0.07		Learned: Humanities
		Popular: Humanities
Spoken mean: 0.18		
Written mean: 0.13		
Corpus mean: 0.16		

are argumentative discourse while administrative writings are mostly regulatory, and both require a considerable amount of modality. And since they serve different purposes, these two genres display different features in the use of modals and auxiliaries. Editorials generally aim at persuasion and prediction, e.g.:

[22]   *But the Government, including the Prime Minister, should be entirely willing to accept that its own proposed hard ecu, which addresses the problem of inflation while the Delors plan does not, might well prove so popular that economic and monetary union would come about within a very much shorter time than M Delors himself expects.*

[23]   *Yet it is hard to believe that this attempt is likely to be successful against the weight of bombardment directed against Iraqi facilities and the high level of target intelligence the allies seem to possess.*

Table 6.11 Ten most frequent auxiliaries in W2D1 and W2E1

Rank	Administrative writing		Press: editorials	
	Modal	Semi	Modal	Semi
1	*will*	*have to*	*will*	*have to*
2	*would*	*be likely to*	*may*	*be to*
3	*should*	*be to*	*can*	*be likely to*
4	*could*	*seem to*	*must*	
5	*can*	*appear to*	*should*	
6	*must*	*begin to*	*shall*	
7	*may*	*fail to*	*cannot*	
8	*might*	*be going to*	*would*	
9	*cannot*	*appear to*	*need to*	
10	*need to*	*be unlikely to*	*could*	

Administrative writings tend to aim at obligation and necessity:

[24]   *Other people will have to pay for their sight test the cost of which may vary from one optician to another, so it may pay you to shop around.*

[25]   *If at the end of this period the professor or reader is unable to resume his duties, his appointment shall continue but he shall not have a right to any remuneration except and in so far as the Governing Body of the Central Activity or School concerned shall otherwise determine.*

An exhaustive examination of the auxiliaries in the two categories reveals that in editorials both modals and semi-auxiliaries are very frequent, while in administrative writing, modals are predominant in terms of frequency. This implies that the distribution of aux infinitives points not only to such gross categorisations as spoken and written English but also other dimensions in discourse functions, such as argumentative writing. Table 6.11 lists the ten most frequent auxiliaries arranged in descending order according to frequency.

6.2.3   Bare Infinitives

Quirk et al. (1985) list the following uses of bare infinitives:

1. Object + bare infinitive complementation (Quirk et al. 1985, p. 16.52)

[26]   *We must make the public take notice of us.*
[27]   *The crowd saw Gray score two magnificent goals.*
[28]   *I have known John (to) give better speeches than that.*

2. Pseudo-cleft sentences through use of the substitute verb *do* (Quirk et al. 1985, pp. 18.29, 15.15)

[29]   *What he's done is (to) spoil the whole thing.*
[30]   *All I did was (to) turn off the gas.*
[31]   *Turn off the gas was all I did.*

3. With rather than (Quirk et al. 1985, p. 14.6)

[32]   *Rather than you do the job, I'd prefer to finish it myself.*

When the British ICE Corpus was being tagged, another type of bare infinitives was found necessary:

4. Elliptical use of aux infinitives

[33]   <#205:1:A> *Anyway if it's really bad weather we'll just you know stay in*
         <#206:1:A> *Or watch two videos*
         <#207:1:A> *Absolutely*
         <#208:1:B> *Stay in and watch two videos*
         <#209:1:B> *Yeah*
         <#210:1:A> *That's all you've got to do*

The underlined utterance by speaker B could be understood as imperative. But as the context shows, it is only an elliptical use of aux infinitives that follow <#205:1:A>. Thus, this use of verbs has been tagged as infinitives rather than imperatives. In this study, those elliptical aux infinitives are counted together with bare infinitives.

The distribution of bare infinitives, expressed as a ratio of total number of verbs, is presented in Table 6.12 (cf. Table 6.9 for absolute frequencies).

The ratios do not differ greatly across the categories, which are spread over the scale without a clear pattern of distribution. However, it is interesting to note the extremes in both sections. In the spoken section, legal presentations (S2A4) do not have any bare infinitives, while telephone conversations (S1A2) have the most. With written texts, administrative writing has only one occurrence while learned and popular natural sciences and skills/hobbies have the most. As can be well expected, most of the bare infinitives in the spoken section are due to the elliptical use of aux infinitives. In telephone conversations, for instance, elliptical use covers 64% of bare infinitives. With written sections, however, that use is rare, though occasionally found with letters and novels.

The most frequent verbs requiring bare-infinitive complementation are *make*, *see*, *help*, *let* and *watch*. All of the four types were found in the corpus. It is perhaps worth mentioning that Type 3, which occurred twice, was found only in the spoken section, not in writing. However, there is no clear indication of whether the underlined verbs in [34] and [35] are really bare infinitives instead of finite ones. The corpus failed to produce any example where a clear number difference can be seen between the subject and the verb.

Table 6.12 Distribution of bare infinitives across text categories

Ratio	Spoken	Written
0.009	Distanced conversations	
0.008		Learned: Natural sciences
		Popular: Natural sciences
		Skills and hobbies
0.007	Direct conversations	
	Broadcast interviews	
0.006	Business transactions	Social letters
	Non-broadcast talks	Learned: Technology
0.005	Broadcast talks	Learned: Social sciences
		Popular: Humanities
		Fiction
0.004	Class lessons	Popular: Social sciences
	Spontaneous commentaries	Popular: Technology
		Press: Editorials
0.003	Broadcast discussions	Timed essays
	Unscripted speeches	Press: News reports
0.002	Parliamentary debates	Untimed essays
	Legal cross-examinations	Business letters
		Learned: Humanities
0.001	Demonstrations	
	Broadcast news	
0.000	Legal presentations	Administrative writing

[34]   *How about the the the union in our office who knows really rather than
      hold an election ... has been organised*

[35]   *They do everything but uhm uhm rather than actually buy stuff from them
      direct it's just as well to make out that you might be buying from them but
      just to get a get a an idea of the manufacturer and whoever does the job*

Generally speaking, there are not enough examples to warrant any sound conclusion
about bare infinitives.

6.2.4   To-Infinitives

To-infinitives have four major syntactic functions. First, they can be used as clausal
subjects:

[36]   *To disregard the past is very often the surest means of becoming its slave.*
[37]   *It is dangerous to disregard the past.*

Second, they can be used as complements of transitive verbs:

[38]   *He wanted to leave.*
[39]   *The police ordered them to leave.*

Additionally, they are used as complements of adjectives or adjective postmodifiers:

[40]   *He was not anxious to acquaint himself with this stranger.*
[41]   *We'll be glad to see you next Friday.*

Finally, they can function as adverbials of purpose and result:

[42]   *She put on glasses in order to see more clearly.*
[43]   *We woke up only to find ourselves in a dark cabin.*

To-infinitives as clausal subjects, whether or not extraposed, are a stylistic feature attributed more to written than spoken English. In his analysis of infinitival complement clauses, Mair observed that

> About 60 % of all extraposed infinitival subject clauses attested in the corpus [SEU] are from the written sample—a slight imbalance which does not warrant far-reaching conclusions. For non-extraposed infinitival subject clauses, however, the disparity between the spoken and the written language is highly significant. Forty-one of a total of fifty-two collected instances are from written texts, and most of the few remaining spoken examples are from formal genres such as scripted orations. (Mair 1990, p. 40)

If we consider expressing the percentage as a ratio of total number of verbs in the material examined, the 'slight imbalance' becomes much greater, as shown by an examination of 11,550 spoken sentences and 16,664 written ones in the ICE corpus. The ratio of *to*-infinitives used as subjects is 0.1304 in written material in contrast with only 0.0072 in spoken material.

Infinitival clauses as verb complementation undoubtedly depend on verbs that are transitive, especially monotransitives as they are unquestionably the most frequent pattern of infinitival complementation in modern English (Mair 1990, p. 101). Remarkably, in the ICE corpus more than half (53 %) of the verbs are used as monotransitives in writing while less than half (43 %) in speech, including scripted material. We may therefore hypothesise that a greater proportion of infinitive clause are used as verb complements in writing than in speech.

No frequency indications were found in the literature about *to*-infinitival complementation of adjectives or adverbials of purpose and result. However, through the sentences examined in the ICE corpus, the distribution of these two types also demonstrates great variations between speech and writing. The ratio of adjective postmodifiers in writing is 0.0216 as compared with 0.0116 in speech. A similar difference was found when counting infinitival clauses as adverbials, both of purpose and result. For writing, the ratio is 0.466, in sharp contrast with 0.0294 in speech.

Table 6.13 Distribution of *to*-infinitives across text categories

Ratio	Spoken	Written
0.16		Business letters
0.14		Press: Editorials
0.13	Nonbroadcast talks	Learned: Social sciences
0.12		Learned: Technology
		Popular: Social sciences
		Popular: Technology
		Press: News reports
		Administrative writing
0.11	Broadcast news	Untimed essays
0.10	Broadcast talks	Social letters
		Learned: Humanities
0.09	Parliamentary debates	Timed essays
	Unscripted speeches	Popular: Humanities
	Legal presentations	Popular: Natural sciences
		Skills and hobbies
0.08	Broadcast discussions	Fiction
	Broadcast interviews	
	Legal cross-examinations	
	Spontaneous commentaries	
	Demonstrations	
0.07	Business transactions	
0.06	Direct conversations	Learned: Natural sciences
	Distanced conversations	
	Class lessons	
Spoken mean:0.07		
Written mean:0.11		
Corpus mean:0.09		

Thus, combining results from previous studies in infinitival clauses and the findings in the examination of both spoken and written sentences in the ICE corpus, we can say that there are more *to*-infinitives in writing than in speech.

Table 6.13 lists figures of distribution of *to*-infinitives in the British ICE corpus.

From the ratios we learn that roughly seven out of a hundred verbs in the spoken section are used as *to*-infinitives while in the written section this percentage is much higher, 11 %. Considering the corpus as a whole, an average of nine verbs out of every hundred are used infinitivally with the marker *to*. This indicates that, unlike aux infinitives, there are more *to*-infinitives in writing, which strongly confirms our expectation at the beginning of the section.

Most of the spoken categories fall under the corpus mean (0.09) while most written texts are higher on the scale, a reverse picture of Table 6.10. In the spoken section, strongly interactive speech—S1A1 (conversations), S1A2 (phone calls) and S1B1 (classroom lessons)—has the least *to*-infinitive content, with another form of interactive speech, S1B6 (business transactions), coming next. Three texts are higher than the corpus mean. Again, these are the scripted news, talks and speeches, categories that have been shown to be more closely related to written English in terms of aux infinitive content (cf. Table 6.10). In between are broadcast talks, parliamentary debates, legal cross examinations, commentaries and unscripted public speeches. Thus, with the arrangements of spoken categories on the scale, as *to*-infinitive content increases, categories move up on the scale from casual interactions to occasion-conscious utterances, and finally to formal, scripted speech.

Only two out of the 17 written categories are below the corpus mean: W2A3 (learned natural sciences) and W2F1 (novels/stories). It goes without saying that the latter, especially novels, is very close to spoken English in many respects because of the considerable amount of direct and reported speech. It is surprising that the category of learned natural sciences has the fewest *to*-infinitives among the written categories (cf. Table 6.9), a matter that requires further investigation. With informational writings centred round 0.10, categories move up to press editorials, and finally to business letters (W1B2), which unexpectedly occupies the top of the scale.

An examination of business letters showed that they typically require *to*-infinitives. Here are some examples of their use at the beginning of the letters:

[44]   *I am writing to invite you to a formal dinner to be held at the Grosvenor Hotel, London, on Saturday the 14th September, 1991.*

[45]   *This is essentially a very important letter to let you know that I have moved to Johnson with effect from Monday 29 April.*

[46]   *This is to confirm that you are booked on a First Aid Requalification course on 11 and 12 February.*

[47]   *I am pleased to inform you that the notes are available for purchase at a cost of word.*

The end of the business letter also tends to entail their uses:

[48]   *We hope to hear from you in the near future.*

[49]   *Do not hesitate to contact me if you need any more information.*

[50]   *Once again, thank you for taking the time and trouble to write to Dillons and for being one of our regular customers.*

The body of the letters is most revealing:

[51]   *If you have any questions then I would be happy to hear from you, but*
       would you please allow me until Tuesday 7 May to give me a little time to
       sort things out at this end.

[52]   *It has not and now I feel it is necessary to take formal legal action to pro-*
       tect my own property and to stop the nuisance.

[53]   *If you were not able to work on this basis, then it might be possible to*
       split the Box Office (we would perhaps be able to operate a 60/40 split in
       your favour).

The contents of these letters show that, like editorials and regulatory writing, business letters are a form of writing that involves a large amount of modality, either through the use of auxiliaries or *to*-infinitives. We recall that in Sect. 6.2.2, business letters are shown to be the second highest in aux infinitive content in writing (cf. Table 6.10). High in both auxiliary and *to*-infinitive contents, this category suggests itself to be an interesting area of studies in English modality.

Nevertheless, since the corpus mean of *to*-infinitives does pick out the scripted texts from the rest and this value distinguishes novels/stories from other writings, except learned natural sciences, we can say that the distribution of *to*-infinitives is not uniform across spoken and written categories. Rather, like that of aux infinitives, this distribution reveals variations that cut across speech and writing.

6.2.5   For/to-Infinitives

Clearly, like bare infinitives, the occurrences of *for/to*-infinitives here do not produce enough evidence to become statistically reliable, though the means do show slight differences between spoken and written categories. What is more interesting here will be to classify the syntactic functions of these *for/to*-infinitival clauses in the higher clause and see if there are any differences across the two modes (Table 6.14).

Mair investigated five types of *for*-clauses in the SEU corpus (Mair 1987), which include

1. Subject
2. Object
3. Subject complement
4. NP-postmodification
5. Adverbial

Two subsets of Type 4, NP-postmodification, were noted, the first being the appositional clause:

[54]   *Earlier, the university authorities refused a request by the University*
       Conservative Association for Mr. Wall to speak in a university hall.

Table 6.14 Distribution of *for/to*-infinitives across text categories

Ratio	Spoken	Written
0.0078		Business letters
0.0062	Parliamentary debates	
0.0045		Skills and hobbies
0.0044	Legal presentation	
0.0041	Legal cross-examinations	
0.0038	Non-broadcast talks	Press: News reports
0.0034	Broadcast news	
0.0033	Spontaneous commentaries	Social letters
	Unscripted speeches	Fiction
0.0032	Broadcast interviews	
0.0029		Learned: Technology
0.0028		Press: Editorials
0.0027	Demonstrations	Popular: Technology
		Administrative writing
0.0026	Broadcast talks	Popular: Social sciences
0.0022	Broadcast discussions	Timed essays
0.0020		Untimed essays
0.0019		Popular: Humanities
0.0016	Direct conversations	
0.0014	Business transactions	Learned: Natural sciences
0.0012		Learned: Social sciences
0.0007	Distanced conversations	
0.0005	Class lessons	
0.0004		Learned: Humanities
		Popular: Natural sciences
Spoken mean: 0.0024		
Written mean: 0.0030		
Corpus mean: 0.0026		

The other subset is the relative clause:

[55]   *Think of something nice for us to do soon...*

In the same study, adverbials of purpose and adverbials of result were separately discussed. What was not studied in his investigation, however, is adjectival complementation by *for/to*-infinitival clauses. Table 6.15 presents the distribution of those functions (including adjectival complementation) in the British ICE corpus.

Table 6.15 Distribution of functions of *for/to*-infinitival clauses

Function		Spoken		Written	
		Raw	Relative	Raw	Relative
Subject clause	Extraposed	73	122.09	42	104.77
	Non-extraposed	1	1.67	0	0.00
Subject complement		13	21.74	7	17.46
Object clause		24	40.14	30	74.87
NP postmodification	Appositional	12	20.07	11	27.44
Adverbial clause	Relative	22	37.42	16	39.91
	Purpose	30	50.17	24	59.87
	Result	5	8.36	16	39.91
Adjectival complement		2	3.34	0	0.00

Since the spoken section outnumbers writings in terms of running words, care should be taken to interpret the figures presented in Table 6.8. For a better comparison, both raw and relative (per million words) frequencies are given in the table. However, we can still see some unusual features. There is only one non-extraposed subject clause, for instance, in the corpus and this one example was found in speech, not in writing.

[56]   *And I think for Nell to know that a happy sex life is going on in the same house when you're fourteen is the worst age than if she was seven or eight or if she was eighteen.*

Mair had found just four such examples in the SEU corpus, which comprised only 800,000 words at the time. No adjectival complement was found in the written section, but two in spoken English, both with the adjective *happy*. The following sections discuss those distributions that show a clear difference between speech and writing.

6.2.5.1   Object Clauses

Object clauses are found to be more frequent in writing (30) than in speech (24), as in Mair's study. This is another reflection of the fact that more verbs are used transitively in writing than in speech. Examples attested in the corpus reveal that *for/to*-infinitival clauses as transitive complements are limited to a very small set of verbs. They are, in order of frequency, *arrange, wait, make* and *ask*. The verb *wait* is the most frequent in spoken texts, while in writing the most frequent verbs are *arrange, wait* and *make*.

[57]   *Otherwise there would've been two groups sitting there waiting for me to*
         lecture on Tuesday.

[58]   *At the moment I'm waiting for ten o'clock to come so I can go and phone*
         Antonio.

[59]   *I shall be grateful if you could arrange for me to be represented at the*
         Inquiry on 26 February 1991.

[60]   *This will make it easy for the receiver to move towards the ball and head*
         it through its top half, directing it down to the feet of the thrower.

6.2.5.2 Adverbial Clauses of Result

There are altogether 21 occurrences of adverbial clauses of result, 5 in spoken and
16 in written texts. It is interesting to note that in his study, Mair (1987) found such
clauses to be more frequent in speech (9) than in writing (5). Such clauses typically
co-occur with too (as in [64] and [65]). Two examples ([61] and [62]) were found
co-occurring with *enough*, both in speech, and only one with *only* ([63]).

[61]   *But they make sure they sort of they seem to make sure that the processes*
         take long enough for you to miss your train.

[62]   *But not here beside me, not close enough for me to be 'serious' to, to ca-*
         ress, to....

[63]   *It's rather like sending your opening batsmen to the crease only for them*
         to find the moment the first balls are bowled that their bats had been bro-
         ken before the game by the team captain.

[64]   *It takes far too long for us to get rid of the poll tax.*

[65]   *He had never met Edward Schumacher, but the politician's face had ap-*
         peared on too many news programmes in recent months for him to go un-
         recognized.

6.2.5.3 Appositional Clauses

The *for/to*-infinitival clauses postmodifying noun phrases are said to be appositional if the head noun is not at the same time a constituent in the infinitival phrase
(Mair 1987). Mair observed that 'the majority of *for*-infinitival clauses postmodifying noun phrases is of the appositional type' (Mair 1987). However, this remark

does not apply to what is found in the British ICE Corpus. Of the two types of noun phrase postmodification considered, relative clauses, which occurred 37 times, outnumber the appositional use which accounted for 23 instances of use. Here are some examples of appositional clauses:

[66]   *And if there was supposed to be some system for the maintenance man to check the swimming pool out you certainly didn't yourself check to see if he was doing his job did you.*

[67]   *There was also a trend for the caesarian subjects' illnesses to be shorter than the illnesses among the control group but this achieved significance only at the ten per cent level.*

[68]   *The existential model, which is one type of phenomenological model focuses on the need for each person to develop his/her own meaning for life, and to take responsibility for guiding personal growth.*

[69]   *Some Conservative MPs on either side privately argued that Mr Heseltine had gone too far this time to be able to draw back without fatal loss of face, and had, moreover, insulted his colleagues with a call for the Cabinet to enforce a collective line to save the party from defeat.*

Some Unclear Cases Quite a few examples show structural indeterminacy for various reasons. The first type is the fuzzy connection between postmodification and adverbial. In [70] below, the problem is the relation between information and the *for/to*-infinitival clause.

[70]   *We have the information from those tombs which are not finished from ostraka that's sketches on limestone flakes produced by Egyptian artists for them to work on the larger surface uh from and putting it together we can accept this reconstruction by the Metropolitan museum New York of a tomb being cut.*

Two possible interpretations include (1) We have the information with which they can work … and (2) We have the right information in order for them to work….
    Another type is demonstrated by [71].

[71]   *All it needs is one pregnant female rat left alive for the plan to have failed.*

The perfect aspect in the infinitival clause strongly indicates that it is an adverbial of result, but it is also possible to interpret it as an adverbial of purpose.

Example [72] involves nested *for/to*-infinitival clauses, which can be interpreted two ways, or even three ways.

[72]   *Is it in order for a member who did not vote for the debate to be continued then to stand up to continue the debate after that vote is taken?*

6.2.5.4   Gerundial Clauses Following NP Introduced by for

This is only a minor but interesting point to note. A few utterances were also found, where gerundial clauses follow the NP introduced by *for*. In Examples [73]–[75], all of the gerundial clauses can be replaced by a *to*-infinitive clause without any discernible change of meaning.

[73]   *<#96:1:A> Paul we heard there about the Soviet Union's regrets that longer hadn't been given for the peace process to work Was there any realistic prospect ever for it working*
         <#98:1:G> No I don't think so and I think this idea that Mr Gorbachev wants the Americans to negotiate at this stage is completely unrealistic.

[74]   *Right that's that's the dangerous point for the thing cracking off.*

[75]   *But for us going to Vienna it would have been all right.*

It is worth pointing out that the three examples all came from the spoken texts. Sentences similar in structure were also found in written material. But contexts proved all the gerundial clauses to be postmodifying the NP following the preposition *for*. In view of the fact that such citations are found only in spoken material, it is likely that they are deviant use of the *for*-NP-*to* construction, though this needs further proof.

As a brief summary, we realise in this section that there is not enough evidence to make any sound comments about the distribution of *for/to*-infinitives. The few examples that are found in the corpus to illustrate their different functions do not lend themselves to indications of their distribution across spoken and written categories. However, while some of the observations further confirm previous studies, this analysis of *for/to*-infinitives has presented some differences from what has been reported, and it has also revealed some phenomena that have not been previously noted. What is needed is a much larger corpus.

6.2.6   Summary and Conclusion

In this study, the British ICE corpus was used to investigate the distribution of four types of infinitives. Their contents as ratios of total number of verbs in every text category were examined. The mean ratios of aux and *to*-infinitives for the corpus as a whole successfully discriminated spoken genres from written English, especially in separating scripted categories, which are included in speech, from the genuine spoken material. The distribution of these two types of infinitives is thus shown to be uneven in their distributions across the spoken and written categories in the corpus. Aux infinitives tend to occur in spoken English, while *to*-infinitives are more frequent in writing. Where both types are frequent, it is likely that the text category in question is strong argumentative and persuasive writing, as exemplified by administrative writing and business letters. The other two smaller types, bare and *for/to*-infinitives, did not present significant differences across speech and writing, for lack of enough examples. When investigating linguistic features that are closely connected with certain lexical items, much more material than 1 million words is needed to present a reliable picture of their use.

Thus, it may be concluded that the distribution of infinitives in contemporary British is not neutral of styles or genres. It directly points to variations that are subject to the need of communication in both speech and writing.

Chapter 7
Adjectives and Text Categories

7.1 Adjective and Formality[1]

This section reports an investigation into the use of adjectives to classify texts. In particular, the investigation focuses on the density of adjectives, defined as the proportion of adjectives amongst word tokens, as a characteristic of text formality that can be applied to effective text classification. The investigation attempts to address the question how strongly adjective density correlates with text formality, a research question that past studies have not explicitly addressed. Such a correlation will be measured in both the training and test sets, and compared with the standard of human ranking. We shall report empirical results that suggest a strong and significant correlation between degrees of text formality and adjective density that can be used to mimic human ranking of the categories. It will be shown on empirical basis that adjective density successfully separates speech from writing and, within writing, academic prose from nonacademic prose. Our study significantly extends past studies by further simplifying the set of characteristic features for text classification.

7.1.1 Research Background

Text classification according to degrees of formality has been a long-standing issue that is both linguistically complex and computationally challenging. Word classes, as one of the linguistic features, have been employed for automatic text classification. For example, various word classes are combined into a joint index to measure text formality. As mentioned in Sect. 4.2.1, Heylighen and Dewaele (1999, 2002) propose such a formula of formality based on word classes, which is repeated here as Eq. (7.1).

---

[1] An earlier version of this study was presented at the 23rd Pacific Asia Conference on Language, Information and Computation, 3–5 December 2009, Hong Kong.

© Springer-Verlag Berlin Heidelberg 2015
A. C. Fang, J. Cao, *Text Genres and Registers: The Computation of Linguistic Features,*
DOI 10.1007/978-3-662-45100-7_7

$$F = \frac{\left[\sum freq(\text{n., adj., prep., art.}) - \sum freq(\text{pron., v., adv., interj.})\right] + 100}{2}$$

(7.1)

Results show that such a formality score is quite effective in separating speech from writing and that imaginative writing can be separated from informational writing.

In other studies, sets of a certain grammatical class are also employed to distinguish text categories. Dempsey et al. (2007) investigate whether phrasal verbs can distinguish writing from speech, and formal from informal registers. The frequency counts of 397 most frequently used phrasal verbs were calculated and used to measure the formality of texts in three corpora. The results show that in most cases phrasal verbs can significantly distinguish writing from speech, and formal from informal registers. It is worth noticing that although a wide range of text categories are represented in the chosen corpora, the study only proposes a broad dichotomy classification, writing vs. speech and formal vs. informal registers. Rittman (2008) employs a set of trait adjectives, speaker-oriented adverbs, and trait adverbs to examine three chosen genres (i.e. academic, fiction and news) in the British National Corpus (BNC). The results show that it is possible to use the particular sets of adjectives and adverbs to classify genres. In particular, speaker-oriented adverbs are found to be more effective than trait adjectives and adverbs.

This study focuses on the use of adjectives in text classification. The investigation attempts to address the question how strongly the use of adjectives correlates with text formality, a research question that past studies have not explicitly addressed.

7.1.2 Methodology

The investigation required a large corpus of texts that represents a range of text categories to be ranked manually according to degrees of formalities. The corpus needs to be grammatically tagged to enable the retrieval of adjectives, whose density, defined as the proportion in word tokens, will be computed and used to rank the same range of text categories. The two rankings will be subsequently analysed for possible correlation. In the event of significant correlation between human ranking and automatic ranking according to adjective design, unseen data in the test set will be used to verify such correlation.

The randomly sampled subset of the BNC was used as the corpus resource for the investigation. See Table 5.1 in Chap. 5 for the size and different types of text categories. Here, a training set was created that accounted for 80 % of the total word tokens. The remaining 20 % was kept as the test set for unseen data.

At the same time, seven human subjects (six PhD students and one professor in linguistics) were invited to evaluate the formality of the eight text categories independently. They were asked to rank the text categories in the order of formality by specifying 1, 2, 3, etc. with 1 being the most informal and 8 the most formal. The intra-class correlation (ICC) coefficient was computed to test the inter-rater

Table 7.1 Manual ranking of
the eight text categories

Text category	R_m
Conversation (CON)	1
Other spoken (OSP)	2
Unpublished writing (UPUB)	3
Fiction (FIC)	4
Nonacademic prose (NAC)	5
Newspapers (NEWS)	6
Other published writing (OPUB)	7
Academic prose (AC)	8

reliability. The value of the ICC coefficient is 0.857 with $p < 0.001$, which is considered as outstanding inter-rater reliability (Landis and Koch 1977). The means of the human judgments were then computed, according to which the eight different text categories were ranked. See Table 7.1 for the results, where R_m stands for manual ranking.

As can be observed from Table 7.1, spoken texts, including *conversation* (CON) and *other spoken* (OSP), are considered more informal than written texts. In addition, among written categories, academic prose (AC) is regarded as the most formal, and expectedly separated from nonacademic prose (NAC), which is ranked in the fourth place.

7.1.3   Adjective Use across Text Categories

7.1.3.1   Adjective Density and Automatic Ranking

Adjective density (D_{adj}) is defined as the proportion of adjectives in all the word tokens for each category and normalised by 100:

$$D_{adj} = \frac{\text{Frequency of adjectives}}{\text{Frequency of word tokens}} \times 100 \tag{7.2}$$

Table 7.2 presents adjective density of the eight text categories in the training set in ascending order.

As noted in Table 7.2, AC has the highest density of adjectives, 9.63 %, whereas CON has the lowest density of 3.49 %. From the viewpoint of speech and writing, we notice that the written texts are grouped together towards the bottom of the scale and that the spoken texts are clustered together at the top of the scale. Moreover, within writing, AC has the highest adjective density, separated from NAC, a similar result to the manual ranking. Also similar to manual ranking, FIC has the lowest density among the written texts, bordering the spoken texts on the scale. In other words, spoken categories have a generally lower adjective density while written texts show an overall higher proportion of adjectives. The initial results, therefore,

Table 7.2 Adjective density of the training set

R	Text category	Total tokens	ADJ tokens	D_{adj}
1	Conversation (CON)	2,368,324	82,599	3.49
2	Other spoken (OSP)	2,382,061	111,126	4.67
3	Fiction (FIC)	2,382,786	139,894	5.87
4	Newspapers (NEWS)	2,360,843	159,046	6.74
5	Unpublished writing (UPUB)	2,395,601	162,826	6.80
6	Other published writing (OPUB)	2,354,825	197,100	8.37
7	Nonacademic prose (NAC)	2,451,482	213,128	8.69
8	Academic prose (AC)	2,468,802	237,709	9.63

seem to suggest that informal categories, such as the spoken ones, tend to have a lower adjective density, while formal categories are more likely to have a higher adjective density.

7.1.3.2 Evaluating Manual and Automatic Rankings

This automatic ranking according to adjective density (R_{adj}) was then compared with the manual ranking (R_m). The absolute difference of each paired rankings (D) was calculated and Table 7.3 presents the results.

Table 7.3 Manual ranking vs. automatic ranking in the training set

Text category	R_m	R_{adj}	D
Conversation (CON)	1	1	0
Other spoken (OSP)	2	2	0
Fiction (FIC)	4	3	1
Newspapers (NEWS)	6	4	2
Unpublished writing (UPUB)	3	5	2
Other published writing (OPUB)	7	6	1
Nonacademic prose (NAC)	5	7	2
Academic prose (AC)	8	8	0

Based on D, the Spearman rank correlation coefficient r_s was calculated between the automatic ranking of adjective density and human ranking according to the formula:

$$r_s = 1 - \frac{6 \sum D_i^2}{n(n^2 - 1)}.$$
(7.3)

As a result, the value of the Spearman rank correlation coefficient is 0.833, which is significant at the level of 0.02. In other words, there is strong evidence of agreement between the automatic ranking of adjective density and the manual ranking. This result also suggests a strong correlation between adjective density and text formality.

7.1.3.3   Linear Regression Analysis

To further examine the relation between adjective density and formality of text categories, linear regression was computed and analysed. The regression equation was first graphed to determine if there is a possible linear relationship (see Fig. 7.1).

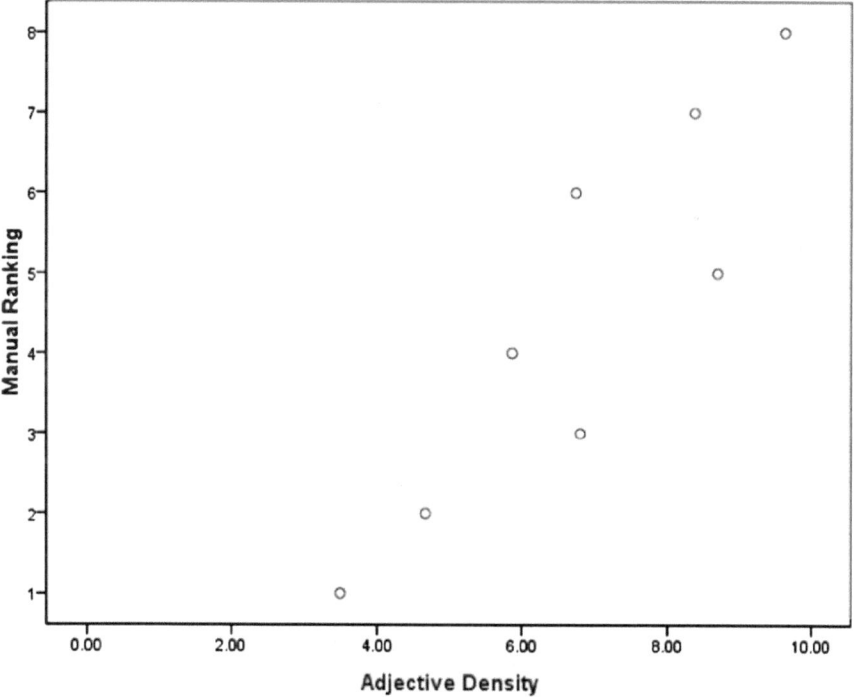

1=CON, 2=OSP, 3=UPUB, 4=FIC, 5=NAC, 6=NEWS, 7=OPUB, 8=AC

Fig. 7.1 Graph of adjective density by manual ranking

As shown in Fig. 7.1, the points follow a linear pattern with a positive slope. Next, the linear correlation coefficient (r) was computed.

The value of r is 0.897 and again suggests a strong positive linear relationship between adjective density and degree of text formality. Accordingly, the coefficient of determination (r^2) is 0.805, indicating that about the variation in the density data can account for 80.5% of the degree of text formality. More importantly, since the value of r^2 is 0.805, the regression equation from the training data set can be seen as a potentially useful model for the prediction of unseen data sets.

7.1.3.4   Adapting to Unseen Data Sets

A model can then be constructed based on the results from the training set for possible adaptation to unseen data sets. The linear regression equation allows us to obtain two parameters: intercept (α) and gradient (β), given adjective density (X) and automatic ranking (Y) from the training set:

$$Y = \alpha + \beta X. \tag{7.4}$$

The equation is, therefore, seen as a model characterising the correlation between adjective density and ranking along a continuum of text formality. Such a model can be used to predict the ranking and therefore the text category given an unseen text for which only adjective density is known. Effectively, an automatic classifier can be constructed that operates on adjective density alone. However, it is necessary to make sure that such a model will show a good level of consistency when tested with unseen data from the test set, that is, the high level of correlation can be replicated and observed on the test set. The following sections will first describe the construction of a model based on the regression equation, and then the expected ranking of text categories in the test set will be calculated, and finally the expected ranking will be evaluated by both manual and automatic rankings.

Based on the data from the training set, the regression equation is determined and graphed in Fig. 7.2.

According to Table 7.4, the acquired parameters are: $\alpha = -2.652$ and $\beta = 1.054$. In this way, given adjective density of the unseen data set (X), Eq. (7.4) can be converted into a model to predict the expected automatic ranking (Y) of the unseen data set. The expected automatic ranking of adjective density (ExR_{adj}) was presented in Table 7.5.

As shown in Table 7.5, there is again a clear dividing line between spoken texts and written texts, where two subdivisions of spoken texts (i.e. *conversation* and *other spoken*) are grouped together towards the top of the scale. Among writing, *fiction* is the most informal while *academic prose* is the most formal one appearing at the bottom of the scale. It is also noticeable that *unpublished writing* vs. *newspapers* seem to have the same expected ranking, and that the same situation also involves *nonacademic prose* vs. *academic prose*. The possible explanation is that the values of the expected rankings are in round numbers, when the actual values

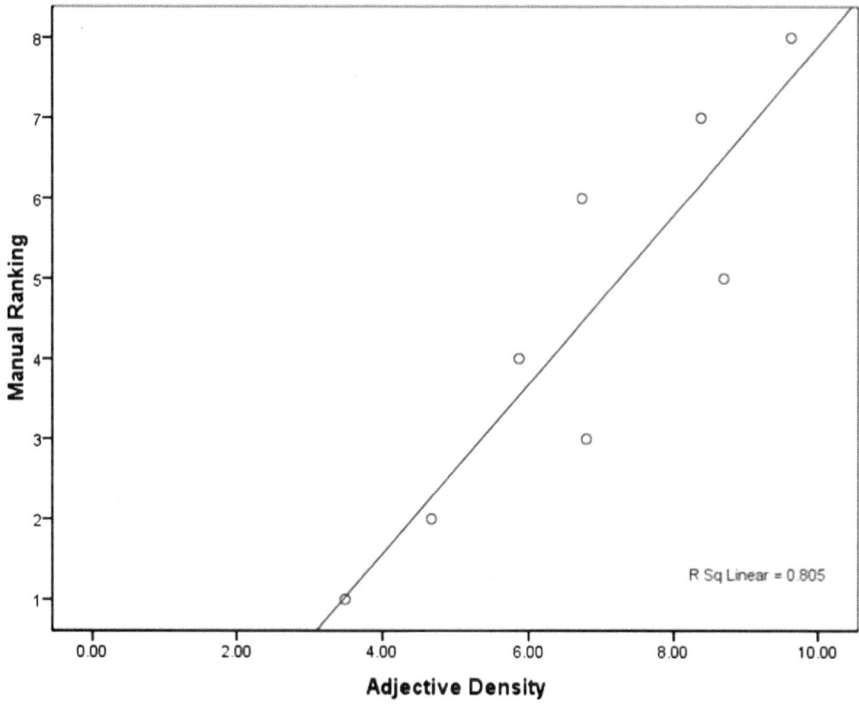

1=CON, 2=OSP, 3=UPUB, 4=FIC, 5=NAC, 6=NEWS, 7=OPUB, 8=AC

Fig. 7.2 Graph of $Y = -2.652 + 1.054X$

Table 7.4 Results from linear regression test

	R	r^2	α	B
ADJ	0.897	0.805	-2.652	1.054*

*$p < 0.01$

Table 7.5 Expected automatic ranking of the test set

Text category	ExR_{adj}
Conversation (CON)	1
Other spoken (OSP)	2
Fiction (FIC)	3
Unpublished writing (UPUB)	5
Newspapers (NEWS)	5
Other published writing (OPUB)	6
Nonacademic prose (NAC)	6
Academic prose (AC)	7

Table 7.6 Adjective density of the test set

R	Text category	Total tokens	ADJ tokens	D_{adj}
1	Conversation (CON)	649,613	25,506	3.93
2	Other spoken (OSP)	636,982	29,327	4.60
3	Fiction (FIC)	643,410	37,508	5.83
4	Unpublished writing (UPUB)	606,149	41,441	6.84
5	Newspapers (NEWS)	657,458	46,807	7.12
6	Other published writing (OPUB)	658,762	52,466	7.96
7	Nonacademic prose (NAC)	632,003	53,816	8.52
8	Academic prose (AC)	655,748	60,468	9.22

are 4.6 (*unpublished writing*), 4.9 (*newspapers*), 6.6 (*nonacademic prose*) and 7.4 (*academic prose*), respectively. Therefore, although obtaining the same expected ranking number, those two-paired subcategories are placed in order.

Next, the expected automatic ranking (ExR_{adj}) was evaluated through comparison with both manual and automatic rankings. The Spearman rank correlation coefficient (r_s) was calculated based on the difference of paired rankings (D) in three settings:

1. The first setting measured the correlation coefficient r_s between ExR_{adj} and manual ranking (R_m); the value of r_s is 0.869, which is above the significant level of 0.02, indicating a strong evidence of agreement between these two rankings.
2. In the second setting, r_s was measured between ExR_{adj} and R_{adj}, the automatic ranking of the training set. The value of r_s in this setting is 0.976, which is significant at level of 0.01.
3. In the third setting, r_s was measured between ExR_{adj} and the automatic ranking based on the adjective density in the test set (cf., Table 7.6). The data show that the rankings are identical and therefore the value of r_s is 1.

The results in all of the three settings show that the expected automatic ranking correlates significantly well with both manual and automatic rankings. In other words, the adaptation of the model to test data sets demonstrates a satisfactory performance. This finding suggests that the regression model can be adapted to unseen data sets with reliable performance, which again proves the intrinsic value of adjectives in texts.

7.1.4 Adjective Density and Automatic Text Classification

As previously shown, experiments on both training and test sets indicate that adjective density is significantly correlated to degrees of formality of different text categories and hence the prospect of using this measure to automatically classify texts. To verify how adjective density as a characteristic could contribute to text classification, an experiment was further carried out by using the naïve Bayes clas-

Table 7.7 Precision, recall and *F*-score in eight BNC text categories

Text category	Precision	Recall	*F*-score
Conversation	0.000	0.000	0.000
Other spoken	0.492	0.970	0.653
Academic prose	0.167	0.053	0.080
Fiction	0.000	0.000	0.000
Newspapers	0.000	0.000	0.000
Nonacademic prose	0.246	0.538	0.337
Other published writing	0.000	0.000	0.000
Unpublished writing	0.250	0.214	0.231
Weighted average	0.223	0.373	0.267

sifier available in Weka (Hall et al. 2009). Weka was used to perform an 80–20 split of all the instances (1180 in total). Naive Bayes was selected to train a model based on adjective density as the sole feature from the training set (80 % of all the instances), which was subsequently applied to the test set (20 % of all the instances). Table 7.7 summarises the results for the eight text categories in terms of precision, recall and *F*-score.

The classification results are summarised in the following matrix:

```
a b c d  e f  g  h    < -- classified as
1 0 0 0  8 4  5  1  | a = ACPROSE
0 0 0 0  0 0 25  0  | b = CONVRSN
0 0 0 0  0 1 12  2  | c = FICTION
0 0 0 0 13 0  4 12  | d = NEWS
2 0 0 0 14 1  3  6  | e = NONAC
1 0 0 0  8 0  1  4  | f = OTHERPUB
0 0 0 0  0 0 64  2  | g = OTHERSP
2 0 0 0 14 1 16  9  | h = UNPUB
```

It can be noticed that all the files of *conversation* have been classified into *other spoken*. There are two possible explanations. Firstly, there is significant difference in instance number between the two categories: *conversation* has only 102 instances while *other spoken* has 378 instances. Secondly, *other spoken* also includes dialogues, which blurs the distinction of *conversation*. For the same reason, a majority of *fiction* has been classified as *other spoken*. In addition, *unpublished writing* and *other published writing* were observed as the less clearly defined categories. The training of the model and the subsequent prediction by the model were, thus, biased as a result of the unbalanced classes (Eibe and Bouckaert 2006).

The less clearly defined categories were excluded and a second try on the classifier was made. The results are presented in Table 7.8.

Almost every category shows a better performance. *Conversation* shows the best results, with an *F*-score of 88 % based on a recall of 91.7 % and a precision rate of 84.6 %. It is encouraging to see that the average precision, recall and *F*-score

Table 7.8 Performance of using ADJ density for text categorisation

Text category	Precision	Recall	*F*-score
Conversation	0.846	0.917	0.880
Academic prose	0.556	0.333	0.417
Fiction	0.524	0.733	0.611
Newspapers	0.667	0.467	0.549
Nonacademic prose	0.448	0.591	0.510
Weighted average	0.626	0.613	0.606

have been all over 60 %, which indicates that with distinctively defined categories, adjective density can be used as a powerful characteristic for automatic text classification. Indeed, the same experiments were carried out on the other three open classes, namely, nouns, verbs and adverbs. Results show that adjectives remain a powerful indicative of text categories with a weighted average *F*-score of 0.606, close to nouns (weighted average *F*-score $= 0.756$) and followed by adverbs (0.511) and verbs (0.448).

7.1.5 Conclusion

In this section, we described our investigation into the relation between adjective density and text formality for the purpose of automatic text classification. According to empirical results collected from the training set, adjective density exhibits a significant positive correlation with text formality. The Spearman rank correlation coefficient shows a significant degree of agreement between such an automatic ranking and manual ranking. In other words, formal text categories tend to have a higher adjective density than informal text categories. A linear regression analysis also confirms such a positive linear relationship, and more importantly, it helps to construct a linear regression model to describe the relation between adjective density and category prediction. When adapted to assess unseen data in the test set, the model produced a satisfactory performance by obtaining a high value of correlation with automatic ranking as well as manual ranking. The results suggest that adjective density can be reliably used to predict text categories. A predictive model was created using a naïve Bayes classifier on adjective density, which achieved a weighted average *F*-measure of 0.606 across a set of five text categories, compared with 0.756 for nouns, 0.511 for adverbs and 0.448 for verbs. The experimental results establish adjective density as a powerful characteristic of text categories compared with the other open classes.

In conclusion, our investigation has shown on empirical basis that adjective density is significantly correlated to degrees of formality of different text categories. To be more specific, adjective density can effectively distinguish speech from writing, and within writing, academic prose from nonacademic prose. Our study has advanced past research in the sense that we have extracted a single linguistic feature that can be used to distinguish text categories according to degrees of formality. By employing adjectives alone, our study indicates that it would be technically more feasible when applied in automatic text classification and genre detection. A significant finding of the research reported here is the established of adjectives as an effective characteristic of text categories amongst the open classes, an important feature that has been generally ignored in past studies. In hindsight of our current investigation, each text category is treated as a homogeneous group without considering the effect that file size has on adjective density. In a future study, we plan to investigate the relation between file size and adjective density with a view to develop an enhanced model parameterised not only with adjective density but also with the file size.

7.2 Adjective Phrase (AJP) and Subject Domains[2]

Past work on terminological studies has typically concentrated on corpora of a specific-subject domain such as medicine or biochemistry (Ananiadou et al. 2000; Nenadic et al. 2005; Aubin and Hamon 2006; Ville-Ometz et al. 2007). However, there has been little in-depth investigation into the syntactic characteristics of terms for the purposes of a systematic description of the internal structure as well as the clausal functions of terms and relations between terms. Nor has there been any systematic study to investigate the use of terms across a set of different text categories or subject domains in order to ascertain the relation between term occurrence and extralinguistic settings.

The work discussed here results from a project that investigates the syntactic characteristics of terms and attempts to study terms based on a new corpus source that has been specially prepared to assist a syntactically oriented description of terms. We will first describe the new corpus resource that embodies two different kinds of annotations, i.e. that of syntax and that of terms and thus addresses the issue of harmonising syntax and terminology. We will then present some of the initial findings regarding adjectives in general as well as adjectives in terminological expressions across the chosen text categories and domains.

7.2.1 Corpus Resource

To achieve our objectives, the British component of the International Corpus of English (ICE-GB; Greenbaum 1996) was chosen as a basis for the following reasons: first, it is encoded for a variety of text categories and subject domains. Secondly, all the texts in ICE-GB are richly annotated grammatically and syntactically

---

[2] An earlier version of this section was previously presented at The Second International Conference on Global Interoperability for Language Resources, Hong Kong, January 2010.

(Fang 1996b, c, 2000, 2006a, 2007) . Two contrastive text types, i.e. academic writing and popular writing, were chosen. The two text types cover four different subject domains comprising ten texts each.

HUM   Humanities and arts
SOC   Social sciences
NAT   Natural sciences
TEC   Technology, computing and engineering

Table 7.9 presents the composition of the subcorpus created from ICE-GB.

7.2.1.1   Syntactic Annotation of the ICE-GB

When the 80 texts from ICE-GB were selected to create the subcorpus, a treebank was effectively created that comprises 8306 syntactic trees. Consider [1]:

[1] *The fibres of group B are found in the autonomic nervous system.*

The same example is syntactically parsed and represented in ICE-GB according to a formalism exemplified in Fig. 7.3.

At the grammatical level, words are coded with part-of-speech (POS) tags that include a head tag with a set of attributes indicating the subcategorisations of the head tag. For instance, the verb found enclosed within a pair of curly brackets is tagged as V(montr, edp), namely, a monotransitive verb in past participial form. Syntactically, each node comprises two labels: one representing its syntactic category and the other the syntactic function. Take the node SU NP () as an example, which indicates that it is a noun phrase (NP) functioning as the subject (SU) of the clause. See Fang (2007) for more details.

7.2.1.2   Term Annotation

Term annotation was carried out manually during a period of 4 months, and has gone through the four stages: training of the annotators, analysis of interannotator

Table 7.9 The structure of the subcorpus

Text types	Domains	Samples	Tokens
Academic writing	AHUM	10	24,363
	ASOC	10	24,280
	ANAT	10	24,165
	ATEC	10	23,386
Popular writing	PHUM	10	27,168
	PSOC	10	23,110
	PNAT	10	23,150
	PTEC	10	23,584
Total		*80*	*193,206*

Fig. 7.3 An example of syntactic analysis of [1]

```
PU CL(main,montr,pass,pres)
 SU NP()
  DT DTP()
   DTCE ART(def) {The}
  NPHD N(com,plu) {fibres}
  NPPO PP()
   P PREP(ge) {of}
   PC NP()
    NPHD N(com,sing) {group B}
 VB VP(montr,pres,pass)
  OP AUX(pass,pres) {are}
  MVB V(montr,edp) {found}
 A PP()
  P PREP(ge) {in}
  PC NP()
   DT DTP()
    DTCE ART(def) {the}
   NPPR AJP(attru)
    AJHD ADJ(ge) {autonomic}
   NPPR AJP(attru)
    AJHD ADJ(ge) {nervous}
   NPHD N(com,sing) {system}
      PUNC PUNC(per) {.}
```

agreement, actual annotation and finally the manual examination of terminological annotations. Three annotators were trained to mark-up terms. The working guidelines for annotation were made as follows:

- Among the NPs, proper names of places, countries, organisations or institutes are excluded from this study, and therefore, will not be annotated.
- Variant terms will be annotated.
- With nested terms, we only mark up the longest part as a multiword term.
- Terms are marked with <t> at the beginning and with <t> at the end in the tree diagram, and the resulting NP is described by an additional attribute 'term'. See Fig. 7.4.

To measure the interannotator agreement, two texts were taken from the preselected subcorpus from ICE-GB, with a total number of about 4000 words. The interannotator agreement was then evaluated using Kappa coefficient (Cohen 1960) defined in the following formula:

$$k = \frac{A_0 - A_e}{1 - A_e},$$
(7.5)

where A_0 is the observed agreement; A_e is the expected agreement.

Since Cohen's Kappa is originally used to find agreement between two annotators, the common practice for multiple-annotator agreement is to 'measure agreement separately for each pair of [annotators], and report the average' (Artstein and Poesio 2008, p. 562). Thus, in our case, the κ value is first computed for each pair with the total numbers of terms and nonterms for each annotator as well as the num-

Fig. 7.4 Examples of term annotations of [1]

```
PU CL(main,montr,pass,pres)
 SU NP(term)
  DT DTP()
   DTCE ART(def) {The}
   NPHD N(com,plu) {<t> fibres </t>}
   NPPO PP()
    P PREP(ge) {of}
    PC NP()
     NPHD N(com,sing) {group B}
 ...
 A PP()
  P PREP(ge) {in}
  PC NP(term)
   DT DTP()
    DTCE ART(def) {the}
   NPPR AJP(attru)
    AJHD ADJ(ge) {<t> autonomic}
   NPPR AJP(attru)
    AJHD ADJ(ge) {nervous}
    NPHD N(com,sing) {system </t>}
```

ber of disagreements, and then the average of the three κ values is computed as the overall Kappa coefficient.

Table 7.10 illustrates how the value of Kappa coefficient is graduated, a best known convention proposed by Landis and Koch (1977).

See Table 7.11 for the results of the interannotator agreement.

As shown in Table 7.11, the pairwised κ values are above 0.90 with $p < 0.001$, and the average Kappa coefficient reaches 0.934, indicating a high-level interannotator agreement.

Table 7.10 Interpretation of Kappa

Kappa	Agreement
<0	Less than chance agreement
0.01–0.20	Slight agreement
0.21–0.40	Fair agreement
0.41–0.60	Moderate agreement
0.61–0.80	Substantial agreement
0.81–0.99	Almost perfect agreement
1	Perfect agreement

Table 7.11 A summary of the interannotator agreement

Paired annotators	K*
A–B	0.917
A–C	0.920
B–C	0.965
Average	0.934

* $p < 0.001$

After the interannotator agreement test, the three annotators carried out the actual annotation and met to discuss the uncertain situations when necessary. Finally, the annotated corpus was manually validated by one annotator with the help of online resources and specialised dictionaries.

7.2.2   Investigation of Adjective Use

In Fang et al. (2009) , the syntactic functions of NPs constructions were investigated and observed to be conditioned by text types defined in terms of both subject domains and degrees of formality. In this section, we shall describe empirical observations of the distribution of adjectives according to the same setting. A major objective is to ascertain whether, like that of NPs, the distribution of AJPs is also conditioned by text types parameterised according to register and domain.

7.2.2.1   The Distribution of AJPs According to Category and Domain

Two groups of AJPs were investigated: AJPs in general and AJPs in terminological expressions (term-AJPs). Instead of the use of raw frequencies, AJP density was calculated according to Eq. (7.6):

$$\text{Density} = \frac{\text{frequency of AJPs}}{\text{frequency of word tokens}}. \tag{7.6}$$

Table 7.12 presents the basic statistics of AJPs among the total number of words and their associated density. The domains are arranged according to density in descending order.

Then all AJPs within the boundary of a term-NP were extracted as term-AJPs, with frequencies summarised and densities calculated according to Eq. (7.6). See Table 7.13, which is arranged according to density in descending order. As a gen-

Table 7.12 Basic stats of AJPs across domains

Domain	Tokens	AJPs	Density
ANAT	24,165	2238	0.0926
ASOC	24,280	1974	0.0813
PNAT	23,150	1690	0.0730
AHUM	24,363	1768	0.0726
ATEC	23,386	1675	0.0716
PTEC	23,584	1636	0.0694
PSOC	23,110	1410	0.0610
PHUM	27,168	1627	0.0599

Table 7.13 Basic stats of term-AJPs across domains

Domain	Tokens	Term-AJPs	Density
ANAT	24,165	1279	0.0529
ASOC	24,280	1098	0.0452
AHUM	24,363	1080	0.0443
ATEC	23,386	883	0.0378
PNAT	23,150	806	0.0348
PTEC	23,584	717	0.0304
PHUM	27,168	754	0.0278
PSOC	23,110	610	0.0264

eral observation, the density of term-AJPs amongst the total number of words corresponds to a predefined popular-vs.-academic division. To be more exact, popular texts have a lower density of term-AJPs than those in an academic setting. Such differences between the two groups of texts were evaluated to be significant by the independent T-test with $t = 5.591$ with $p < 0.05$. Our observations suggest that the use of term-AJPs can serve as a good text category differentiator and thus suggest the motivation for our next experiment to use adjectives to classify texts.

7.2.2.2   Use of Adjectives as Linguistic Feature to Classify Texts

The distribution of adjectives (ADJs) and adjectives in term expressions (term-ADJs) was computed respectively in terms of individual text for each domain. Naïve Bayes classifier, available in Weka (Hall et al. 2009), was used and results obtained using tenfold cross validation. Table 7.14 presents the precision, recall and F-score for the classification of the eight categories of texts using all the ADJs. The best performance was achieved for academic natural sciences (ANAT) with an F-score of 0.7273, twice as high as that for PTEC. As can be noted, academic texts (with the exception of PNAT) generally show a better performance than popular texts.

Table 7.14 F-score of ADJs across domains

Domain	Precision	Recall	F-score
ANAT	0.6667	0.80	0.7273
PNAT	0.8571	0.60	0.7059
AHUM	0.7500	0.60	0.6667
ATEC	0.5556	0.50	0.5263
PSOC	0.6667	0.40	0.5000
PHUM	0.3846	0.50	0.4348
ASOC	0.3333	0.40	0.3638
PTEC	0.3333	0.40	0.3638
Mean	*0.5684*	*0.53*	*0.5361*

Table 7.15 *F*-score by term-ADJs domains

Domain	Precision	Recall	*F*-score
PTEC	0.7500	0.90	0.8182
ATEC	0.7273	0.80	0.7619
PSOC	0.8571	0.60	0.7059
ASOC	0.7000	0.70	0.7000
ANAT	0.5000	0.60	0.5455
AHUM	0.4615	0.60	0.5217
PNAT	0.5714	0.40	0.4706
PHUM	0.3750	0.30	0.3343
Mean	*0.6178*	*0.61*	*0.6073*

Table 7.15 summarises the use of term-ADJs for the classification of the same texts. The mean *F*-score is 0.6073, 0.07 higher than the use of general adjectives, suggesting improved performance through the use of term-adjectives. With a general improvement in the *F*-score, we also notice that the drop in the performance in terms of two individual domains (i.e. NAT and HUM) in both academic and popular registers. Two possible explanations are revealed when we take a further look at the lists of term-ADJs that are used as the input to the naïve Bayes classifier. First, there are quite a few texts that have less than ten term-ADJs in the problematic categories concerning NAT and HUM, which cannot be observed in the other domains. Secondly, a more distinct distribution difference of term-ADJs among the individual texts can be noticed in the four problematic domains. Take ANAT as example. The shortest list consists of 25 term-ADJs while the longest one 133 term-ADJs, a difference of 108. Hindsight may show that the size of individual text in each domain could be also an important factor and that a further test in texts of similar size could help to clarify the situation.

7.2.3   Conclusion

In this section, we first described the new corpus resource that embodies two different kinds of annotations, i.e. that of syntax and that of terms and explained how the two different annotations were harmonised within the same representation formalism. The second focus of discussion concerned the relationship between terminological use and text types and between such uses and subject domains. Within this scope, we focused on adjectives, including those used within the boundary of term-NPs. Our results show that the occurrence of adjectives seems to be conditioned by registerial settings (popular and academic) and that AJPs in terminological expressions seem to be more effective than AJPs in general. A further experiment of using adjectives and term-adjectives as linguistic features to classify texts demonstrates that the use of term-adjectives tends to have a better performance than the use of adjectives in general.

Chapter 8
Adverbial Clauses across Text Categories and Registers

The methodology adopted in the current study was to investigate the distribution of different types of adverbial clauses across speech and writing based on a representative corpus of contemporary English. The scope of investigation would cover not only finite adverbial clauses but also the nonfinite ones, including infinitival, present participial and past participial constructions. The aim was to show the differences in the use of adverbial clauses, in frequential terms, across speech and writing. A second step would be to ascertain the variation of these clauses within the spoken and the written genres respectively.

The International Corpus of English (ICE; Greenbaum 1996) was used in the current study as source of empirical evidence. The British component of the corpus (ICE-GB) consists of 300 texts of transcribed speech and 200 texts of written samples, of 2000 word tokens each, generally dated from the period 1990 to 1994. The component texts were selected according to registerial specifications. ICE-GB provides an ideal setting for an empirical investigation of the variation in the use of adverbial clauses across speech and writing. First of all, the corpus is divided into spoken and written sections and thus allows for some general indications of distribution. Secondly, each major mode within the corpus contains genres that display a continuum between the spontaneous and the prepared, the informal and the formal, the timed and untimed, etc. thus allowing for the validation of hypotheses whether the use of adverbial clauses can be discussed in terms of degrees of preparedness, alongside the spoken–written division.

The experiments examined the frequency distribution of finite adverbial clauses as well as the nonfinite ones (infinitival, present participial and past participial) in ICE-GB. There are three procedures. Firstly, the experiment aimed to establish the

An earlier version of this chapter was previously published as Fang, A. C. 2006. A corpus-based empirical account of adverbial clauses across speech and writing in contemporary British English. In *Lecture Notes in Artificial Intelligence 4139: Advances in Natural Language Processing*. Berlin Heidelberg: Springer-Verlag. 32–43.

A. C. Fang, J. Cao, *Text Genres and Registers: The Computation of Linguistic Features*,
DOI 10.1007/978-3-662-45100-7_8

overall distribution of adverbial clauses across the spoken and the written sections. Secondly, samples of spontaneous and prepared speech were examined to ascertain whether preparedness could be seen as a continuum of changes for the use of adverbial clauses. Finally, samples of timed and untimed university essays were used to validate the hypothesis that adverbial clauses also demonstrate a predictable variation as a function of degrees of preparedness in written English.

8.1 Adverbial Clauses across Speech and Writing

As a first step, the complete corpus was used to obtain empirical indications of the different uses of adverbial clauses across speech and writing. Frequencies of occurrence were respectively collected from the spoken and the written sections of ICE-GB. The statistics include the total number of sentences and clauses in these two sections. Statistics were also collected for the total number of sentences involving the use of adverbial clauses and the exact number of adverbial clauses in these two sections. Two proportions were calculated: (1) the total number of sentences with at least one adverbial clause over the total number of sentences and (2) the total number of adverbial clauses over the total number of sentences. The former indicates the proportion of sentences in ICE-GB that make use of adverbial clauses. The latter shows the proportion of adverbial clauses in the corpus since there often are multiple adverbial clauses in one sentence or utterance and it is useful to have such an indication. These two proportions thus indicate how often adverbial clauses are used and how complex the sentence structure is (assuming that structural complexity can be measured in terms of clause subordination). Table 8.1 summarises the results.

In Table 8.1, we find that there are 59,470 sentences or utterances in the spoken section, 24,084 in the written section, with a total of 83,554. Each section has two columns: # and %, the former indicating the absolute frequency of occurrence and the latter the corresponding percentage. As Table 8.1 indicates, a much higher proportion of sentences in writing make use of adverbial clauses. To be exact, adverbial clauses are more than twice likely to occur in writing than in speech. In writing, 26.88 % of the sentences make use of adverbial clauses in contrast to only 11.98 % of the sentences with an adverbial clause in speech. The same difference can be observed in terms of the number of adverbial clauses: there are over 29 adverbial clauses per 100 sentences in writing compared with just over 13 adverbial clauses per 100 sentences in speech. The spoken section has a total of 569,637 tokens,

Table 8.1 Adverbial clauses in speech and writing

	Spoken (59,470)		Written (24,084)		Total (83,554)	
	#	%	#	%	#	%
Sentence	7124	11.98	6474	26.88	13,598	13.27
Clause	7809	13.13	7052	29.28	14,861	17.79
Word	569,637	1.37	390,586	1.81	960,223	1.55

Table 8.2 Types of adverbial clauses in speech and writing

		Spoken (59,470)		Written (24,084)		Total (83,554)	
		#	%	#	%	#	%
A_{sub}	Sentence	5172	8.69	3954	16.42	9126	10.92
	Clause	5787	9.73	4430	18.39	10,217	12.23
A_{infin}	Sentence	1122	1.89	1254	5.21	2376	2.84
	Clause	1177	1.98	1308	5.43	2485	2.97
A_{ing}	Sentence	691	1.16	1023	4.25	1714	2.05
	Clause	704	1.18	1066	4.43	1770	2.12
A_{edp}	Sentence	139	0.23	243	1.01	382	0.46
	Clause	141	0.24	248	1.03	389	0.47
Total	Sentence	7124	11.98	6474	26.88	13,598	16.27
	Clause	7809	13.13	7052	29.28	14,861	17.79

yielding an average of 13.7 adverbial clauses per 1000 tokens. The written section, which has 390,586 tokens, has an average of 18.1 adverbial clauses per 1000 tokens. We thus have the initial indication that on a general scale there are more adverbial clauses in writing than in speech.

The distribution of different types of adverbial clauses was investigated to verify that the observed difference was not the result of a skewed use of any one particular type. The second experiment examined the distribution of finite adverbial clauses with an overt subordinator and the nonfinite ones, which include infinitival, present participial and past participial adverbial clauses. The results are summarised in Table 8.2. As can be clearly seen, this second experiment also indicates that written samples of the ICE corpus make much more extensive use of the adverbial clause, be it finite, infinitival, or participial. The finite ones occur twice as many times in writing than in speech. For the other three types of adverbial clauses, the proportion for the written genre is even higher than for the spoken genre. Consider the infinitival clauses, for example. In writing, they are nearly three times more likely to be used than in spoken discourse (5.43% vs. 1.98%), largely echoing previous observations that writing is characterised by a higher content of infinitives compared with spoken English. See, for example, Mair (1990) and Fang (1995). This proportion is even greater with the other two types of nonfinite adverbial clauses.

We may incidentally note that past participial clauses are the least frequent type of adverbial clauses, with only 141 found in speech and 248 in writing in the whole corpus.

8.1.1   Adverbial Clauses across Spontaneous and Prepared Speech

Empirical indications thus suggest that adverbial clauses are a marked characteristic of the written genre, in line with nonfinite clauses that also characterise writing. However, to conclude that this difference in terms of use is due to different levels

Table 8.3 Types of adverbial clauses in spontaneous and scripted speech

		Spontaneous (29,490)		Scripted (5793)		Total (35,283)	
		#	%	#	%	#	%
A_{sub}	Sentence	1574	5.34	742	12.81	2316	6.56
	Clause	1757	5.96	784	13.53	2541	7.20
A_{infin}	Sentence	271	0.92	253	4.37	524	1.49
	Clause	279	0.95	260	4.49	539	1.53
A_{ing}	Sentence	190	0.64	161	2.78	351	0.99
	Clause	193	0.65	163	2.81	356	1.01
A_{edp}	Sentence	21	0.07	35	0.60	56	0.16
	Clause	21	0.07	36	0.62	57	0.16
Total	Sentence	2056	6.97	1191	20.56	3247	9.20
	Clause	2250	7.63	1243	21.46	3493	9.89

of elaboration, we need further empirical evidence. We need to prove that such variations can be observed not only across speech and writing, but also within the spoken and the written sections as a function of varying degrees of elaboration. To this end, a sub-corpus of 180,000 words was created from ICE-GB, representing spontaneous private conversations. A second sub-corpus was also created, this time with ICE-GB texts representing talks prepared and scripted for public broadcast. These two genres thus form a continuum between what was unprepared and what was carefully prepared, therefore a measure of different degrees of elaboration.

The results are summarised in Table 8.3, where we can read that, as an example, the subcorpus of spontaneous conversations contains a total number of 1574 sentences that make use of finite adverbial clauses, accounting for 5.34 % of the total number of sentences in the sub-corpus. On the other end of the continuum, as another example, we duly observe a higher proportion of finite adverbial clauses, that is, 12.81 % in terms of sentences and 13.53 % in terms of clauses. It is important to note that this general trend can be observed for all of the different types of adverbial clauses.

It is thus reasonable to suggest that within speech the proportion of adverbial clauses increases as a function of degrees of elaboration, formality and preparedness.

8.1.2 Adverbial Clauses across Timed and Untimed Essays

Having established that in speech the proportion of adverbial clauses is largely a function of elaboration or formality or preparedness, we want to do the same for the written samples. We want to argue, on empirical basis, that adverbial clauses not only mark a spoken–written division, that they also mark a continuum between what is spontaneous and what is scripted in speech, and that they also mark a degree of preparedness in writing.

Table 8.4 Types of adverbial clauses in timed and untimed essays

		Timed (1057)		Untimed (1046)		Total (2103)	
		#	%	#	%	#	%
A_{sub}	Sentence	156	14.76	203	19.41	359	17.07
	Clause	171	16.18	235	22.47	406	19.31
A_{infin}	Sentence	62	5.87	61	5.83	123	5.85
	Clause	65	6.15	64	6.12	129	6.13
A_{ing}	Sentence	59	5.58	51	4.88	110	5.23
	Clause	59	5.58	55	5.26	114	5.42
A_{edp}	Sentence	10	0.94	16	1.53	26	1.23
	Clause	10	0.94	16	1.53	26	1.23
Total	Sentence	287	27.15	331	31.64	618	29.29
	Clause	305	28.86	370	35.37	675	32.09

Conveniently, the ICE-GB corpus contains a category coded W1A, which includes 20 texts evenly divided into two sets. Both sets were unpublished essays written by university students. The only difference is that the first set was written within a predesignated period of time while the second set comprises samples written without the time constraint. If the higher use of adverbial clauses were indeed the result of a higher degree of elaboration or preparedness, then we would observe more uses in the untimed set than in the timed set. This consideration led to a third experiment, whose results are summarised in Table 8.4.

Again, we duly observed a consistent increase in the proportion of adverbial clauses from one end of the continuum, timed essays, to the other end of the continuum, untimed essays. For instance, we observe that there are 16.18 finite adverbial clauses per 100 sentences for the timed essays. The untimed essays make more uses of finite adverbial clauses, 22.47 per 100 sentences. The same trend can be observed for all of the different types of adverbial clauses, except the infinitival ones. In timed essays, 62 sentences were observed to contain a total of 65 adverbial clauses. In the untimed essays, 61 sentences were found to use a total of 64 infinitival adverbial clauses. While the differences are only marginal and can be dismissed as occasional, this group of texts will be examined in a future study for a possible relation between text types and uses of infinitival clauses.

8.2   Frequency Distribution of Adverbial Subordinators

The experiments have collected all of the adverbial subordinators from ICE-GB and grouped them according to speech and writing. They were subsequently sorted according to their frequency of use in descending order in order to show which ones were typically used by the two modes of discourse. Consider Appendixes F and G, which show adverbial subordinators in speech and writing arranged according to frequency in descending order. Both lists have the following headed columns:

Rank	Indicates the ranking of the subordinators in the list according to frequency, ten thus indicating a subordinator that is the tenth most frequent in the list
Freq	Indicates the frequency of use of a particular subordinator, 1408 thus indicating a subordinator that was used 1408 times in the corpus
%	Shows its corresponding proportion in the total occurrences of subordinators, 25.39 thus indicating that the subordinator accounts for 25.39 % of the total occurrences of subordinators
Acc freq	Indicates an accumulative frequency from the beginning of the list till the current position in the list, 2372 thus indicating that all of the subordinators till this position in the list so far account for a joint frequency of 2372
Acc %	Indicates an accumulative proportion of the total occurrences of subordinators till the current position in the list, 42.77 thus indicating that all of the subordinators till this position in the list so far account for a joint proportion of 42.77 % of the total occurrences of subordinators

Both lists have columns headed by *rank*, *subord*, *freq*, *%*, *acc freq* and *acc %*. They reveal that both speech and writing have a common set of most frequently used subordinators: *if*, for example, is the most frequent subordinator for both speech and writing, accounting for 25.39 and 24.26 % respectively for the two genres and suggesting a more or less even distribution across speech and writing. If we look at the top four for both groups, we find a common set comprising *if*, *when*, *because* and *as*, suggesting that conditional, temporal and causal clauses are the most commonly used adverbial clauses and thus constitute the norm of use for such clauses.

A closer look reveals that there are also differences between speech and writing in terms of the use of most frequent subordinators. As an example, the top four in speech account for 71.84 % of the total uses of subordinators while in writing they account for only 62.04 %. This difference in proportion suggests that writing has a more varied use of subordinators than speech. A second difference can be found in the fact that in speech the top four subordinators respectively account for over 10 % of the total uses. The fourth most frequent subordinator *as*, for example, occurred 723 times, accounting for over 13 % of the total uses. The fifth most frequent, *cos*, has a drastically lower proportion of only 2.79 %. The top four then constitute the mode of use for adverbial subordinators in the spoken genre. The written genre, however, has a different distribution. Only the top three respectively account for over 10 % of the total uses, namely, *if*, *as* and *when*. The fourth most frequent subordinator, *because*, accounts for only 6.13 % of the total uses in writing. It is thus reasonable to suggest that speech and writing have a different mode of uses for adverbial subordinators: in speech, the mode comprises *if*, *because*, *when* and *as* while in writing, the modes comprises only three items—*if*, *as*, and *when*. The differentiating one in this regard between speech and writing seems to be the causal subordinator *because*. This in its own right may lead to an interesting research question for a future study regarding the subordinator *as*, which can be used both temporally and causally. Speech and writing may have different preferences concerning these two semantic possibilities.

8.3 Discussions and Conclusion

We have thus observed that, in the first place, adverbial clauses mark a division between spoken and written English in the sense that the spoken samples have a lower
proportion of adverbial clauses than the written samples. This is true not only for
finite adverbial clauses but also for nonfinite ones, including infinitival, present participial and past participial constructions. Secondly, the experiments also produced
empirical evidence that the frequency distribution of adverbial clauses follows a
predictable and regular growth curve from spontaneous conversations to scripted
public speeches. The same trend can be observed from within the written sample,
where the proportion of adverbial clauses in general increase from timed essays to
untimed essays. As Fig. 8.1 clearly demonstrates, the proportion of adverbial clauses per 100 sentences in ICE-GB consistently increases along a continuum between
spontaneous conversations and untimed university essays. What is remarkably surprising is the fact that the occurrence of adverbial clauses in spontaneous conversations accounts for only about 7.5 % of the utterances. What is equally surprising is
that the occurrence of adverbial clauses in untimed university essays accounts for
over 35 % of the sentences, over 4.6 times as much as that in speech.

The graph also shows the average proportions of adverbial clauses in the two
modes are nicely situated between the two sections within the same continuum.

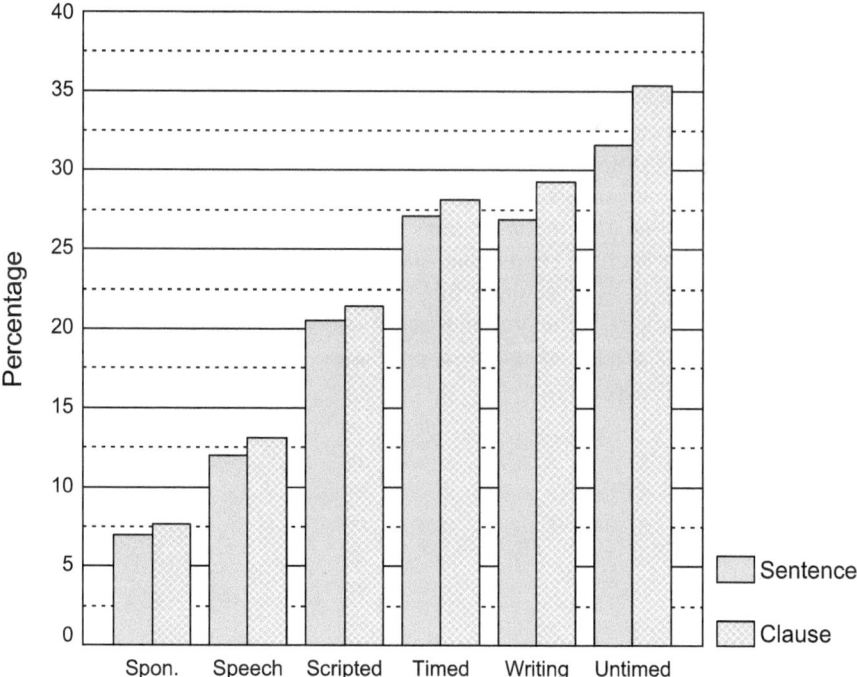

Fig. 8.1 The increase of adverbial clauses as a function of degrees of preparedness

First of all, the average proportion of adverbial clauses in speech is shown in the figure to be between spontaneous conversations and scripted public speeches, suggesting a consistent increase in speech along the 'preparedness' register. In the written section of the continuum, the average proportion of adverbial clauses in writing rests between timed and untimed essays, again suggesting a consistent increase, continuing the trend from the spoken section, along the 'preparedness' register. This is therefore clear and concrete evidence that there are more adverbial clauses in writing than in speech, at least as far as contemporary British English is concerned and there is no obvious reason why other varieties of English should be seen otherwise.

While it is evident from Fig. 8.1 that speech and writing demonstrate a vast difference in terms of the use of adverbial clauses, it is clear at the same time that adverbial clauses are not as much a factor of speech vs. writing division as a degree of preparedness in discourse. To be exact, it is acceptable to suggest on the basis of empirical evidence that degrees of information elaboration dictate the proportion of adverbial clauses: the more elaborate the sample (defined in terms of preparedness), the more adverbial clauses.

To conclude, this section described an experiment to investigate the distribution of adverbial clauses across speech and writing. The experiment used ICE-GB, a corpus of contemporary British English that contains both transcribed speech and written samples. The detailed syntactic annotation of the corpus and manual validation of the analysis ensured that adverbial clauses could be accurately retrieved. The results demonstrate that the proportion of adverbial clauses is much lower in speech than in writing. It is also shown that adverbial clauses do not simply mark a division between the spoken and written genres. Empirical evidence also shows that the proportion of adverbial clauses is a function of varying degrees of preparedness, which can be independently demonstrated from within the spoken and written genres. It is thus reasonable to postulate that the spoken–written division is perhaps better perceived as a continuum of preparedness, from spontaneous private conversations at one extreme to untimed carefully prepared writing at the other, along which the proportion of adverbial clauses consistently change in a predictable fashion. Finally, it is observed that while speech and writing have a common norm of uses for conditional, temporal and causal subordinators, the two genres have different modes of use for adverbial subordinators, suggesting interesting research questions for the future.

Chapter 9
Coordination across Modes, Genres and Registers

As any representative corpus of English will readily show, the coordinator *and* is one of the most frequently used lexical items. It ranks the third most frequently used word type in the Brown, the Lancaster-Oslo-Bergen Corpus of British English (LOB) and the British component of the International Corpus of English (ICE-GB) corpora of American and British English (Table 9.1; refer to Chap. 2 for detailed descriptions.). In addition to its consistently high rank across varieties of English, the same coordinator also demonstrates a consistently high ranking across different modes of production such as speech and writing. According the ICE-GB, which comprises both spoken and written texts, *and* is the second most frequently used word in the spoken genre and the third in the written genre, right after the definite article *the* in speech and additionally the preposition *of* in writing (Table 9.2). Similarly, empirical data also suggest that this coordinator enjoys a high ranking across different text categories such as news report, business correspondence and academic writing. If we count the other canonical coordinators and include *but* and *or*, the three coordinators would jointly rank the second most frequently used in contemporary English after the definite article.

The ubiquitous use of coordinators across varieties, genres and registers in English owes to their deep root in syntax, where, grammatically speaking, coordination is a pervasive construction that can be found at all possible junctures in the English sentence, conjoining words, phrases and clauses. Here are some illustrative exam-

[1]   *Our urban property essentially the London estate together with various trading **and** investment activities both in the United Kingdom and overseas are held in a form through a UK holding company.* <#s2a-045-040>

[2]   *I think <,> the main perception that I had of <,,> what was described as integrated work was that the contributions from <,> able-bodied people **and** disabled people were often <,> uhm <,> unbalanced <,> <#s1a-001-012>*

[3]   *You either study pure dance <,> **or** you study dance therapy <,> uhm **and** there seems to be no connection between the two <,> <#s1a-001-104>*

© Springer-Verlag Berlin Heidelberg 2015   143
A. C. Fang, J. Cao, *Text Genres and Registers: The Computation of Linguistic Features*,
DOI 10.1007/978-3-662-45100-7_9

Table 9.1 The top ten most frequent word types in Brown, LOB and ICE-GB

Rank	Brown		LOB		ICE-GB	
	Freq	Type	Freq	Type	Freq	Type
1	70,002	*the*	67,516	*the*	57,565	*the*
2	36,472	*of*	35,355	*of*	26,945	*of*
3	28,935	*and*	27,537	*and*	26,679	*and*
4	26,239	*to*	26,492	*to*	21,417	*a*
5	23,547	*a*	22,485	*a*	21,243	*to*
6	21,422	*in*	20,895	*in*	18,696	*in*
7	10,789	*that*	11,295	*that*	17,343	*I*
8	10,102	*is*	10,975	*is*	16,222	*that*
9	9815	*was*	10,576	*was*	15,940	*it*
10	9797	*he*	10,396	*it*	12,914	*you*

Table 9.2 A list of the top ten most frequent word types in ICE-GB across speech and writing

Rank	ICE-GB		Speech		Writing	
	Freq	Type	Freq	Type	Freq	Type
1	57,565	*the*	30,325	*the*	27,240	*the*
2	26,945	*of*	16,074	*and*	13,216	*of*
3	26,679	*and*	14,180	*I*	10,605	*and*
4	21,417	*a*	13,729	*of*	9,876	*to*
5	21,243	*to*	12,399	*a*	9,018	*a*
6	18,696	*in*	12,207	*that*	8,345	*in*
7	17,343	*I*	12,155	*it*	5,300	*is*
8	16,222	*that*	11,367	*to*	4,086	*for*
9	15,940	*it*	10,351	*in*	4,015	*that*
10	12,914	*you*	10,283	*you*	3,785	*it*

ples extracted from the ICE-GB corpus, with their textual reference IDs enclosed within pointed brackets.

In [1], coordination is used within the noun phrase (NP) at the word level between *trading* and *investment* while [2] is an example where the conjunction *and* conjoins two full NPs, that is, *able-bodied people* and *disabled people*. Clause-level coordination can take place with both main clauses, as is exemplified in [3], and subordinate clauses as exemplified in [4] below.

[4]   *Uhm <,> so I think there's a difficulty an initial difficulty uhm but I think that very very quickly goes **and** people <,> uh begin to dance with each other <#s1a-001-066>*

As the examples above illustrate, the basic English sentence structure of subject–predicate–complement can be altered to different extents through the use of coordination and subordination. According to Halliday (2004, p. 375), such

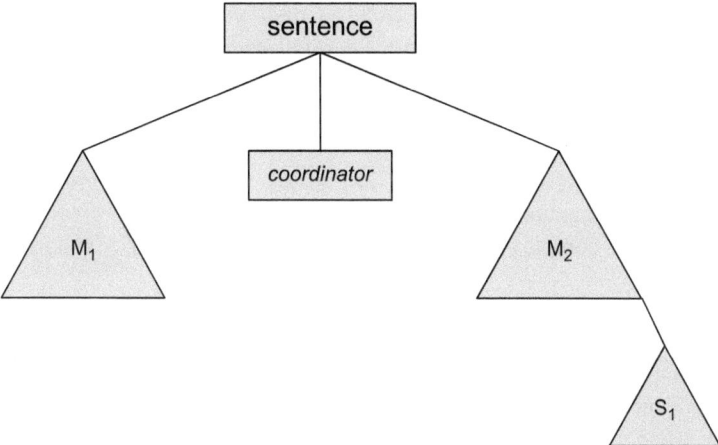

Fig. 9.1 Interplay Type I: subordination within coordination

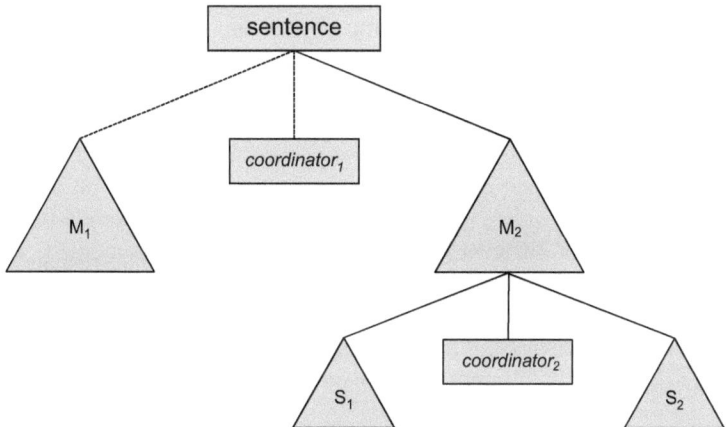

Fig. 9.2 Interplay Type II: coordination within subordination

a mixture of coordination and subordination is the driving force for the formation of clause complexes. Their interplay therefore contributes to the complexities of the clausal structure to the effect that there may be subordination within coordination and that there may be coordination within subordination. The two relations are charted in Figs. 9.1 and 9.2, adapted from Greenbaum (1996, p. 315).

In Fig. 9.1, the interplay is between the subordinate clause, S_1, and the two coordinated main clauses, M_1 and M_2. A second type of interplay represented in Fig. 9.2 is between the main clause, M_2, and the two coordinated subordinate clauses, S_1 and S_2. This schema has the potential to recursively embed each other, resulting in even more complex structures if required by specific discourse types. [5] is such an example,

[5]   *Once language has been acquired, auditory feedback is used <u>to monitor</u>*
        <u>the levels of volume and pitch</u> and <u>to regulate the timing and rhythm of</u>
        <u>speech</u> <u>to keep them constant with the environmental conditions</u> and <u>to</u>
        <u>ensure comprehension.</u> <#w1a-016-002>

which commands the schematic view in Fig. 9.3, showing the high level of structural complexity that nonetheless does not affect the clarity of expression. One can argue that such a complex structure here actually enhances clarity and transparency of meaning.

Coordination, along with subordination, therefore is a major factor that contributes to the complexity of the sentence structure. In the recent past, structural complexity has been measured in terms of the T-unit, which is an abbreviation of the minimal terminable unit of language proposed initially in Hunt (1965). Syntactically speaking, the T-unit comprises a main clause and any subordinate clauses the main clause governs. According to Hunt, the length of such a unit is a good indication of the cognitive development of a child. The length of the T-unit has been used to evaluate the writing quality. Crowhurst (1983) contains a review of various studies that support the view that, when measured in terms of the T-unit and clause length, syntactic complexity is positively related to the quality of written composition. However, the same study, based on its observations, concludes differently that neither the T-unit nor the clause length is a good predictor of writing quality. Beers and Nagy (2011) investigate differences among four different genres of text, namely, narrative, descriptive, comparative and contrastive and persuasive according to the T-unit, or clauses per T-unit and words per clause to be exact. The texts were written by two groups of students in different grades on two occasions 2 years apart. The study did not find any significant difference between the two groups of students, which suggests that syntactic complexity measured in T-unit did not increase as the grade level increased. An interesting finding of the study, however, is that persuasive essays were significantly different from the other three genres in terms of clauses per

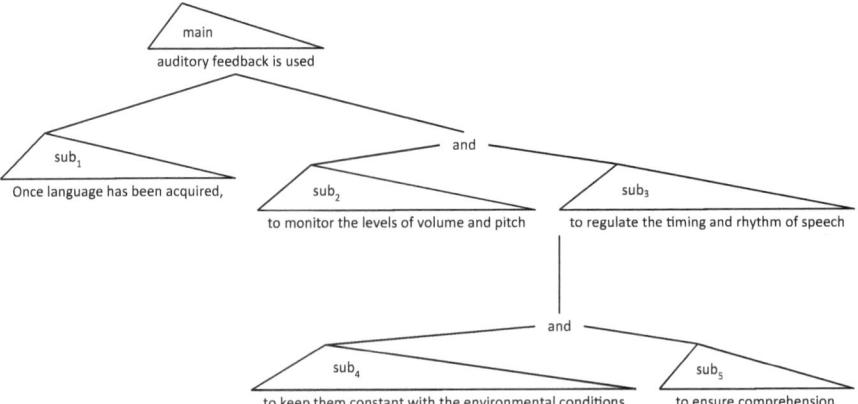

Fig. 9.3 A schematic view of coordination and subordination in [5]

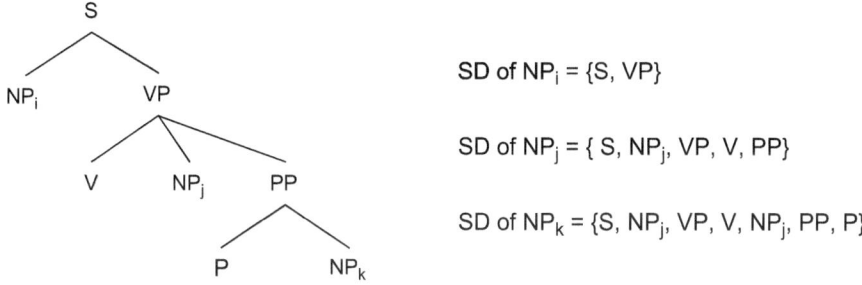

Fig. 9.4 Syntactic complexity and structural domain in Hawkins (1994, p. 29)

T-unit, which is a measure of subordination. A second interesting finding is that clauses per T-unit and words per clauses are negatively correlated; descriptive essays of an academic register were found to have more words per clause but fewer clauses per T-unit compared with persuasive essays. Beers and Nagy (2011) seem to suggest that syntactic complexity is more a matter of difference between different genres and registers. Subordination is found to be characteristic of persuasive essays while clause length is characteristic of descriptive essays. However, the study did not examine the role of coordination since the T-unit is limited in that it only considers Interplay Type II, where a single main clause interacts with multiple and/or coordinated subordinate clauses, and leaves out Interplay Type I, where coordinated main clauses interact with subordinate clause.

Hawkins (1994) is more explicit in associating structural complexity with coordination and subordination, where it is argued that the syntactic complexity of a node X in constituent C is to be defined in terms of the number of structural relations that structurally integrate X in C (p. 50). The integration that is mentioned here forms a structural domain (SD) that consists of 'a grammatically and/or psycholinguistically significant subset of structurally related nodes' in a tree where nodes A and B are 'considered to be structurally related if one dominates the other, if they are sisters, or if one is a sister of some other node that dominates the other' (Hawkins 1994, p. 25).

Figure 9.4 is an illustration of Hawkins's syntactic complexity, which is measured in SD, where we see that the three NPs have different SDs involving different number of syntactic constituents. A node is said to have a higher syntactic complexity if it involves more syntactic relations. Extending beyond the sentence, we say a sentence is more complex if it governs more constituents than another sentence. The notion can be well extended to compare different texts for their syntactic complexity. An interesting point is that this notion gives more emphasis to the number of nonterminal nodes, which is intuitively a better complexity measure than the T-unit, which uses the number of terminal nodes or word tokens in the clause. A particularly interesting aspect of this notion of syntactic complexity is that by emphasizing the dominant and the sister nodes it gives emphatic consideration to coordination as well as subordination while the T-unit ignores coordination of the main clauses. In this sense, Hawkins's notion of syntactic complexity is more attractive than Miller and Chomsky's (1963) notion of syntactic complexity as the ratio between nonterminal and terminal nodes, which does not consider hierarchical relationships between nonterminal nodes.

Stylistically speaking, such uses of subordination and coordination, which result in varying degrees of structural complexity, are linguistic devices that characterise specific genres and text types. Subordination, for instance, used to be described as a feature that is typical of casual and spontaneous language production such as speech, which is supported in Halliday (1978), Thompson (1984) and Biber (1988). Empirical results in Chap. 8, however, have suggested that this construction, when taken as exemplified by the adverbial clause, is actually found to be more commonly used in the written genre than in speech. Through the use of the ICE-GB corpus, which comprises sets of texts ranging from spoken to written discourse along with indications of preparedness such as spontaneous and prepared speech as well as timed and untimed essays, the study shows, in Fig. 9.5, that the subordination is used in proportion with elaboration, that is, the higher the preparedness of the text, the more subordination is to be found. Similar findings were reported in Hasselgard (2010).

While the findings above remain to be verified further and independently, they have nonetheless given rise to the question of how the coordination is actually used in speech and writing. Naturally, given its significant role, coordination has been substantially discussed in the past. A notable study is Crystal and Davy (1969), which is an investigative account of prosodic and grammatical features related to English style. Analysing two newspaper reports on the same subject, evidently one more casual and the other more formal, the authors observe that there is a variety of coordinating devices in the latter that is almost entirely absent from the former, suggesting that coordination might be taken as a stylistic feature of formal discourse. This preference of coordination is explained as a way of 'packing a large amount of information into a fairly simple grammatical structure' (Davy 1969, p. 183), suggesting further that coordination is a co-occurring feature with simpler grammatical structures, echoing Halliday's observation that written English is characterised by simple clausal structures but complex nominal groups while speech has the feature of simpler noun groups and the feature of complex clausal constructions. We are thus presented with a nice layout about the polarised aspects about speech and language: the former with more subordination but more simple nouns and the latter with more coordination but more complex nominal groups. However, this theory was contradicted later on. For one, Ochs (1979) holds an opposite view: 'A distinction between planned and unplanned discourse is that unplanned discourse uses syntactic structures similar to those of childhood with more coordination than subordination'. Later, through a study on the utterances by 14 faculty and graduate students, Chafe (1982) observed a high frequency of coordinating conjunctions in spoken discourse and interpreted it as evidence of fragmentation that is typical of speech.

Additionally, it remains to be investigated whether subordination and coordination represent two opposing polarities of stylistic features that demonstrate significant difference preferences across speech and writing as well as across different

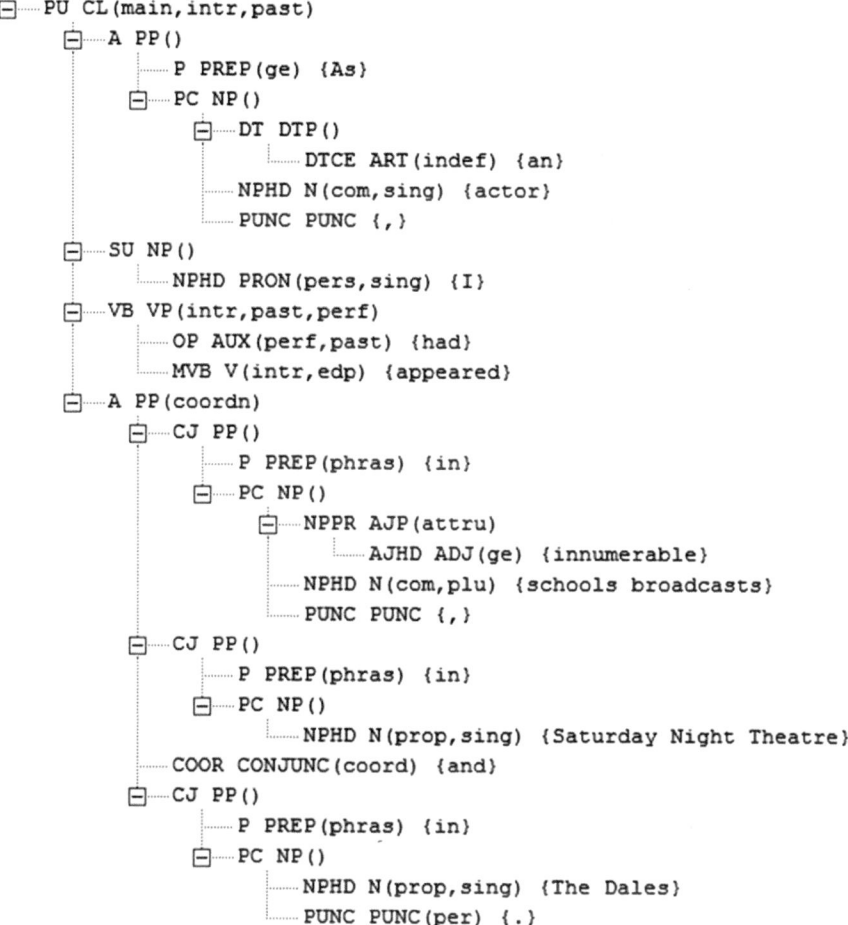

Fig. 9.5 An ICE-GB tree structure for [6]

registers. Newkirk (2003) clearly hints at such a contrasting pattern of use: 'Since young children tend to connect short main clauses with "and", they tend to use relatively few words/T-unit. But as they mature, they begin to use a range of appositives, prepositional phrases, and dependent clauses that increase the number of words/T-unit'. That coordination and subordination might have a mutually exclusive, polarised distribution is also partly hinted at in Biber (1988), where Factor 6 seems to suggest that phrasal coordination, which is described by Chafe (1982; Chafe and Danielewics 1987) as a device for idea unit expansion and informational integration, has a salient negative weight while three subordination features involving the various uses of *that* have a high positive weight (Chafe and Danielewics 1987, p. 113). His overall interpretation seems to confirm Halliday's hypothesis that speech is marked with a higher structural complexity and a lower lexical density compared with writing, as a result of 'informational elaboration that is produced under strict real-time constraints, resulting in a fragmented presentation of information accomplished by tacking on additional dependent clauses, rather than an integrated presentation that packs information into fewer constructions containing more high-content words and phrases' (Chafe and Danielewics 1987, p. 113).

In the light of the different, and often opposing, views regarding coordination and its relation with subordination, new studies are necessary, especially those that are empirically based on corpus evidence. The present chapter represents such an attempt and intends to first of all focus on the issue whether coordination can be observed to characterise spontaneous, unplanned spoken production if subordination is a feature of elaborate, planned written discourse. Answers to this question would help to unveil parataxis and hypotaxis as potential demarcations of informal and formal discourse in terms of register as exemplified by speech and writing. Second, this chapter will attempt to take a closer look at coordination at three different syntactic levels, i.e. words, phrases and clauses and see whether speech and writing demonstrate any special preference for any of these. Answers to the second question will undoubtedly provide for better insight into the use of coordination, not as a monolithic issue but more in a stratified view of finer details. Such a study of coordination is important since coordination represents a conscious or subconscious linguistic choice that reflects the psychological process underlying linguistic productions. More specifically, it can be taken to offer a significant linguistic feature that serves to characterise different registers and genres.

The rest of the chapter is organised as follows: the corpus material will be described first, which comprises text categories that can be taken to represent different registers. The chapter will then discuss observations on the distribution of coordinators across speech and writing before a discussion on whether or not speech and writing demonstrate any preference for different types of coordination. The chapter will finally conclude based on the observations and raise suggestions for future research.

9.1   Methodology and Corpus Data

A primary methodology of the current study is to use a representative corpus of contemporary English. It is important that the corpus comprises a range of text categories identifiable with degrees of text formality. Statistics regarding the use of coordination across the text categories will thus be directly compared and associated with their inherent registerial degrees in order to verify any possible correlation between the two. Last but not least, the same corpus needs to be syntactically annotated to such an extent that coordinated constructions can be retrieved unambiguously and according to different types such as the word, the phrase and the clause. This effectively means that every sentence in the chosen corpus will need to have been globally parsed according to a linguistically motivated annotation scheme and, to ensure the reliability of data about the use and distribution of coordination, the parsing will need to have been manually validated. Nowadays, while corpora of different kind abound, there are few that satisfy the conditions set above and the British component of the International Corpus of English (ICE-GB; Greenbaum 1996) quickly became the only option.

ICE-GB, with a total of one million word tokens, contains 500 samples of around 2000 word tokens each. Its overall text composition is shown in Table 2.3, where the numbers indicate the number of samples assigned to each component text category. As an example, the text category *S1A1 Direct Conversations* contains 90 samples. As can be seen from Table 2.3 in Chap. 2, ICE-GB is divided into spoken and written sections. The spoken section comprises dialogues and monologues while the written section is divided into nonprinted and printed material, suggesting a varying degree of preparedness and hence a varying degree of formality. The varying degree of preparedness is further emphasised through the subsections within the corpus. Dialogues, for instance, are divided into private and public dialogues. Monologues, as other examples, are divided into unscripted, scripted and mixed. The same principle is observed for the written section. For student writings, we see two sets of ten samples each, one for timed essays and the other for untimed ones, setting out a possible registerial division between the two. The *Correspondence* section is also divided into sets of 15 samples each, one for social letters and the other for business letters, which, again, can be conceived in terms of formality differences. In all, the spoken section has 300 samples and the written section has 200.

Most appropriately, the whole corpus has been syntactically parsed according to a framework that represents possibly one of the most detailed parsing schemes. Each syntactic constituent is not only labelled for its category such as NP or prepositional phrase but explicitly indicated for its function such as subject, direct object or adverbial. Coordinated constructions are similarly annotated with all the participating conjoins and the coordinator clearly marked up, thus allowing for unambiguous retrieval of such constructions. Consider [6] below.

[5]   *As an actor, I had appeared in innumerable schools broadcasts, in Saturday Night Theatre and in the Dales. <#w2b-001-004>*

In the example above, the main clause governs a coordination of three adverbial functions, each realised through a prepositional phrase. This analysis is shown graphically in the corresponding ICE tree structure in Fig. 9.5, with the node A PP (coordn) indicating an coordination (coordn) of prepositional phrases (PP) as the sentential adverbial (A). Within the same coordinated construction, we see three conjoins (CJ), each performed by the prepositional phrase, along with a coordinator (COOR).

Such an explicit analysis allows for the extraction of the component conjoins as well as the whole coordinated construction. In this specific example, for instance, we can extract the coordinated PP as a sentential adverbial as well as the three component PPs as conjoins of the same coordination. Obviously, this is not easily achievable without the detailed syntactic analysis embodied in ICE-GB. With its

Table 9.3 Some basic statistics about the ICE corpus

	Spoken section	Written section	Total
Token	595,223	441,429	1,036,652
Type	21,107	28,415	36,780
Type-token ratio	3.55%	6.44%	3.55%

representative text categories and the vast repertoire of syntactic structures found in its 80,000-strong sentences, the ICE-GB is well suited for the research objective and is expected to produce some new evidence regarding the use of coordination in contemporary British English, both spoken and written.

Two data sets were subsequently created for the study. The primary data consists of the corpus as a whole divided into spoken and written sections. An intended use of the primary data set is to test whether or not speech and writing demonstrate a different preference for coordination. Table 9.3 below summarises the basic statistics of the corpus.

As can be seen from Table 9.3, the corpus comprises just over 1 million word tokens, the spoken section accounting for roughly 60% with 595,223 tokens and the written section for about 40% with its 441,429 tokens. The corpus as a whole has a type-token ratio of 3.55%, equating to 3.55 types per 100 word tokens. A difference between the two component sections is that the written section demonstrates a higher lexical content of 6.44% than the spoken section, which has a type-token ratio of 3.55%.

A secondary data set was constructed from some of the component text categories of the corpus. The overall division is still between speech and writing but each with two additional subsections. The spoken section is divided into *unprepared speech* comprising the private conversations of 100 samples (S1A1 and S1A2 in Table 1) and *prepared speech* comprising mixed and prepared monologues of 50 samples (S2B1, S2B2 and S2B3). The written section also comprises two subsections, one for timed student essays of ten samples (W1A1) and the other for untimed student essays of ten samples (W1A2). A major rationale for the construction of such a secondary data is to highlight the formal–informal contrasts between the sections. The primary division between speech and writing is based on the understanding that spoken production is generally more informal than written production. Then we also see registerial differences within the sections. The spontaneous section, for instance, is understandably more informal than the prepared monologues. Untimed essays are more likely to be better organised and deliberated and hence have a higher register than the timed essays. An underlying feature that factors the subsections is production time, reflecting the view that a more informal style is expected when the language is produced under time constraint while complexing at lexical and syntactic levels is expected as a result of better preparation and information packing without the time constraint. A major intended use is to see if the four component sections demonstrate a neat correlation between the use of coordination and the perceived registerial level of the texts. Table 9.4 is a summary of the secondary data used in the study.

Table 9.4 Some basic statistics about the secondary data

Categories		Token	Type	STTR (%)
Speech	Unprepared	190,614	9937	11.57
	Prepared	101,927	11,030	19.49
	Subtotal	292,541	16,383	14.62
Writing	Timed	22,327	3274	14.66
	Untimed	22,385	4471	19.97
	Subtotal	44,712	6697	17.48
Total		*337,253*	*18,918*	*16.42*

Table 9.4 gives the statistics about the component sections of the secondary data regarding the tokens and the types. The overall size of this data is 337,253 tokens. It should be noted that the four subsections are of unequal sizes and therefore the *Standardised TTR* refers to the mean type-token ratios calculated on the basis of standardised text size of 22,300 tokens for all of the four subsections. We thus see that the spoken section has a lower TTR of 14.62 % than the written section's 16.42 %. Looking across the component sections, we see that unprepared speech has a lower lexical content than prepared speech. Within the written section, the untimed essays are lexically more varied than the timed essays. It is particularly interesting to note that prepared speech has a higher lexical content (19.49 %) than timed essays (14.66 %). As a matter of fact, prepared speech is closely similar to untimed essays with a negligible difference of only 0.48 %. Indeed, this observation is not surprising at all since prepared speech comprises largely broadcast news and broadcast talks, which have been carefully scripted and edited. This observation partly supports the presupposition that degrees of preparedness have an impact on lexical complexities. As far as subordination is concerned, Fang (2006) demonstrates strong evidence that this factor also has an important impact on syntactic complexities. What we shall aim to find out about is whether coordination is also correlated to the same factor or whether, unlike subordination, coordination is a feature of informal language production, in which case subordination and coordination will be seen as polarised as mutually exclusive features representing formal and informal discourse.

9.2   The Distribution of Coordinators

A first step of the investigation is to examine the distribution of coordinating conjunctions across speech and writing. The ICE-GB corpus, which is divided into spoken and written sections and also grammatically tagged for parts of speech, can readily produce a list of lexical items that are contextually analysed as conjunctions augmented by their frequencies of occurrences. It is interesting to see whether speech and writing demonstrate any significant difference in their use of coordinating conjuncts. Tables 9.5 and 9.6 present a summary of the empirical observations.

Table 9.5 Distribution of coordinators in speech

Rank	Freq	%	Cum %	Coordinator
1	10,613	74.86	74.86	*and*
2	1970	13.89	88.76	*or*
3	1436	10.12	98.89	*but*
4	67	0.47	99.36	*rather than*
5	38	0.26	99.63	*as well as*
6	15	0.10	99.73	*nor*
7	15	0.10	99.84	*for*
8	9	0.06	99.90	*let alone*
9	4	0.02	99.93	*than*
10	3	0.02	99.95	*yet*
11	2	0.01	99.97	*plus*
12	2	0.01	99.98	*as opposed to*
13	1	0.00	99.99	*or rather*
14	1	0.00	100.00	*and/or*
Total	14,176	100.00	100.00	
%	2.36%			

Table 9.6 Distribution of coordinators in writing

R	Freq	%	Cum %	Coordinator
1	10,263	73.49	73.49	*and*
2	1,873	13.41	86.90	*or*
3	1,257	9.00	95.90	*but*
4	221	1.58	97.48	*&*
5	99	0.70	98.19	*rather than*
6	79	0.56	98.76	*as well as*
7	43	0.30	99.06	*+*
8	40	0.28	99.35	*for*
9	36	0.25	99.61	*nor*
10	22	0.15	99.77	*and/or*
11	12	0.08	99.85	*yet*
12	8	0.05	99.91	*/*
13	7	0.05	99.96	*let alone*
14	3	0.02	99.98	*than*
15	1	0.00	99.99	*not to mention*
16	1	0.00	100.00	*not*
Total	13,965	100.00	100.00	
%	3.49%			

Table 9.7 Distribution of coordinators across text categories

Mode	Genre	Frequency	Word token	Proportion
Speech	Spontaneous speech	3741	190,614	1.96
	Prepared speech	3001	101,927	2.94
	Speech total	6741	292,541	2.30
Writing	Timed essays	650	22,385	2.90
	Untimed essays	759	22,327	3.39
	Writing total	1409	44,712	3.15
Total		16,301	674,506	2.41

From Tables 9.5 and 9.6, we first see that the spoken section has a total of 14,176 coordinators, which represent 2.36 % of the total number of the tokens in this section, indicating an occurrence of 2.36 coordinators per 100 tokens. The written section has 13,965 coordinators with a normalised occurrence of 3.49 per 100 tokens. Through this preliminary observation, writing appears to show a substantially higher preference for coordinating conjunctions than speech. Lexically speaking, we see that *and*, *or* and *but* remain the three canonical conjunctors for both speech and writing. However, they have a higher coverage of 98.89 % in speech than the 95.9 % in writing. This suggests a predominant preference for or use of the three in speech on the one hand and a wider lexical variation or choice in writing on the other, which is expected since, from Tables 9.5 and 9.6, we see that the written section exhibits the use of some special signs in place of lexical words such as the ampersand &, the plus sign + and the slash /, which are totally missing from the spoken language. The coordinating use of *plus* was observed twice in the spoken section, which is never used in writing.

That there is a substantially higher use of coordinators in writing than in speech yields a first indication that there might be a correlation between text registers and coordinator occurrence, that is, the higher the register, the more frequent is the occurrence of coordinators. To verify this possible correlation, the distribution of coordinators was investigated against the sub-corpus of secondary data, which comprises a range of text categories of different registers. Table 9.7 summarises the observations.

We observe again that speech has a lower use of coordinators than writing: the two spoken sections have a total number of 6741 coordinators, producing a combined percentage of 2.30 %, lower than 3.15 % found for the two written genres in writing. More interestingly, we see that prepared speech has a higher use of coordinators than spontaneous speech and that untimed essays show a greater preference for coordinators than timed essays. This observation suggests that increased degrees of preparedness might be a defining factor for increases in coordinator use. Figure 9.6 is a graphical representation of Table 9.7, which clearly visualises the increase of coordinator use along an increase in register levels, with the vertical axis representing the proportion of coordinators in all tokens and the horizontal axis representing register levels. Here, it is worth noting that prepared monologues demonstrate a slightly higher use than timed essays, which suggests the relatively

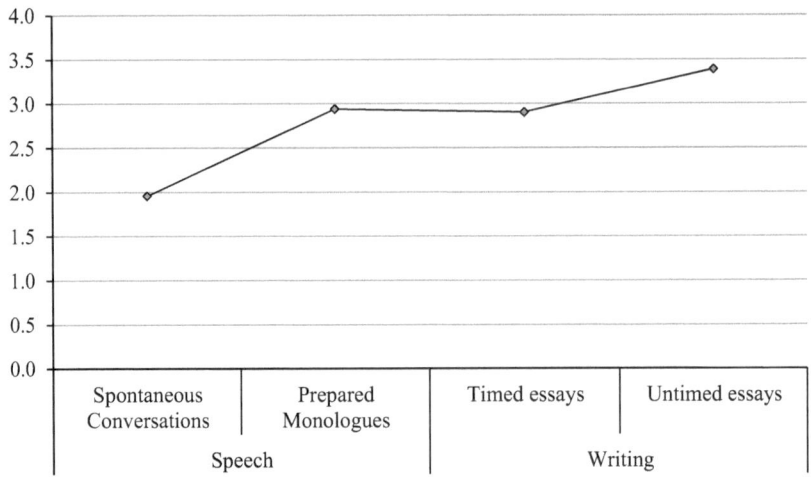

Fig. 9.6   The distribution of coordinators across speech and writing

high register associated with the kind of production found in broadcast talks that
have been written for spoken delivery and also the relatively lower register found in
written texts produced under a time constraint. This very phenomenon adds weight
to our earlier hypothesis that degrees of preparedness might be the decisive factor
for the occurrence of coordinators. We are thus taking a first glimpse into an important understanding that text formality is probably not defined in terms of modes of
production such as speech and writing but in terms of degrees of preparedness as
measured in terms of time.

In summary, coordinators are found to be more frequently used in writing than in
speech. Considering that subordination is also a feature of writing, we may conclude
here, albeit tentatively, that coordination and subordination are not polarised,
mutually exclusive features of English but important linguistic devices to perform
syntactic complexing, if we accept that writing as a whole is generally characterised
by a higher syntactic complexity than speech. Second, it is observed that the occurrence of coordinators cannot be defined in terms of modes of production such as
speech and writing. Rather, on the basis of the secondary data set, which comprises
a range of texts of different preparedness, the increased use of coordinators is found
to occur with an increased degree of preparedness, hence suggesting that the use
of coordinators is a linguistic feature that correlates with degrees of preparedness.

9.3   Syntactic Categories of Coordination Conjoins

This part of the investigation aims to identify the types of syntactic categories that
coordination associates with in the corpus. Syntactically speaking, coordination can
potentially occur at the word level, the phrase level and the clause level. Table 9.8
lists the syntactic constituents at which coordinations were found.

Table 9.8 Three levels of syntactic categories

Level	ICE symbol	Explanation
Word	ADJ	Adjective
	ADV	Adverb
	AUX	Auxiliary
	CONJUNC	Conjunction
	CONNEC	Connector
	N	Noun
	NADJ	Nominal adjective
	NUM	Numeral
	PREP	Preposition
	PROFM	Pro-nominal form
	PRON	Pronoun
	V	Verb
Phrase	AJP	Adjective phrase
	AVP	Adverb phrase
	DISP	Disparate coordination
	DTP	Determiner phrase
	NP	Noun phrase
	PP	Prepositional phrase
	PREDEL	Predicate group
	VP	Verb phrase
Clause	CL	Clause

Table 9.9, which has two major columns for speech and writing, provides more detailed statistics describing such occurrences. The columns labelled as Freq gives the frequency of occurrences, % the proportion of the frequency amongst all occurrences, %% the cumulative frequency and Category the syntactic category in ICE notation symbols. *Rank* indicates the ranking according to Freq in descending order. We thus read that the top ranking clause coordination occurred a total of 10,904 times in speech, accounting for 32.82% of total occurrences. For both speech and writing, the clause and the NP are the most frequent, jointly accounting for 60.81% for speech and 55.29% for writing.

An important observation according to Table 9.9 is that coordination in speech and writing is mostly differentiated through a respective preference for clauses and NPs. We see that coordinated clauses account for 32.82% of the total use of coordination in speech while this construction is much lower in writing, accounting for only 23.76% of coordinations. On the other hand, writing is significantly different from speech through its use of coordinated NPs as the most frequent coordination type, which accounts for 31.53% of the total use of coordination. Combining both NPs and Ns, according to Table 9.4, such coordinations account for 45.03%, that is, nearly half of the total occurrences of coordinations. Speech is considerably lower in this regard; NP and N jointly produce a moderate 34.95%. This observation therefore lends a strong weight to the suggestion that speech is marked through

Table 9.9 Coordination of syntactic categories across speech and writing

R	Speech				Writing			
	Freq	%	%%	Category	Freq	%	%%	Category
1	10,904	32.82	32.82	CL	10158	31.53	31.53	NP
2	9297	27.99	60.81	NP	7652	23.76	55.29	CL
3	4223	12.71	73.52	PREDEL	4350	13.50	68.79	N
4	2312	6.96	80.48	N	4345	13.49	82.28	PREDEL
5	1405	4.23	84.71	PP	1895	5.88	88.17	AJP
6	1399	4.21	88.92	AJP	1257	3.90	92.07	PP
7	1287	3.87	92.80	NUM	611	1.90	93.96	ADJ
8	375	1.13	93.93	ADJ	378	1.17	95.14	NUM
9	366	1.10	95.03	AVP	368	1.14	96.28	V
10	311	0.94	95.96	PROFM	311	0.97	97.25	VP
11	294	0.89	96.85	V	268	0.83	98.08	AVP
12	280	0.84	97.69	VP	124	0.38	98.46	PRON
13	179	0.54	98.23	CONJUNC	122	0.38	98.84	PREP
14	147	0.44	98.67	PRON	118	0.37	99.21	CONJUNC
15	132	0.40	99.07	ADV	93	0.29	99.50	ADV
16	109	0.33	99.40	NONCL	84	0.26	99.76	PROFM
17	98	0.30	99.69	PREP	34	0.11	99.86	NONCL
18	47	0.14	99.83	AUX	15	0.05	99.91	NADJ
19	27	0.08	99.92	NADJ	12	0.04	99.95	AUX
20	12	0.04	99.95	DTP	10	0.03	99.98	DTP
21	9	0.03	99.98	DISP	5	0.02	99.99	DISP
22	5	0.02	99.99	CONNEC	2	0.01	100.00	CONNEC
23	2	0.01	100.00	AUXEL				
Total	33,220				32,212			

a preference for clause coordinations while writing through a preference for NP coordinations. It is not surprising that NP coordinations are preferred in writing since it has long been established that the written discourse has a fundamental feature of complex NPs. However, it is surprising to see that speech is characterised through its preference for coordinated clauses, since past studies have invariably argued for a preference for subordination. Nonetheless, it is too early here to draw the conclusion, since clausal coordination may occur as subordinate constituent in the clausal structure. This will be the focus of investigation to be reported in the following section. For the moment, let us take some time and look at the sub-corpus of secondary data to see if the observations here can be replicated (Table 9.10).

Here, our control data showing varying degrees of registers reveal the same pattern of distribution: spontaneous speech has a higher preferred use of coordinated clauses (43.97%) than that of NPs (28.09%). Prepared speech, on the other hand, sees coordinated NPs as the most preferred construction, accounting for 45.79%

Table 9.10 Coordination of syntactic categories across registers

R	Speech								Writing							
	Spontaneous speech				Prepared speech				Timed essays				Untimed essays			
	Freq	%	Cum %	Cat	Freq	%	Cum %	Cat	Freq	%	Cum %	Cat	Freq	%	Cum %	Cat
1	4180	43.97	43.97	CL	2507	35.64	35.64	NP	604	37.84	37.84	CL	615	36.50	36.50	NP
2	2229	23.45	67.42	NP	1576	22.40	58.04	CL	368	23.06	60.90	NP	302	17.92	54.42	N
3	1271	13.37	80.79	PREDEL	739	10.50	68.54	PREDEL	254	15.91	76.82	PREDEL	235	13.95	68.37	CL
4	441	4.64	85.43	N	714	10.15	78.69	N	127	7.96	84.77	N	197	11.69	80.06	PREDEL
5	305	3.21	88.64	AJP	441	6.27	84.96	AJP	89	5.58	90.35	AJP	127	7.54	87.60	AJP
6	269	2.83	91.47	NUM	374	5.32	90.28	PP	38	2.38	92.73	PP	55	3.26	90.86	ADJ
7	195	2.05	93.52	PP	220	3.13	93.40	NUM	22	1.38	94.11	ADJ	39	2.31	93.18	PP
8	132	1.39	94.91	PROFM	116	1.65	95.05	ADJ	17	1.07	95.18	AVP	26	1.54	94.72	VP
9	86	0.90	95.81	AVP	76	1.08	96.13	VP	16	1.00	96.18	V	26	1.54	96.26	V
10	85	0.89	96.71	V	75	1.07	97.20	AVP	11	0.69	96.87	NUM	18	1.07	97.33	NUM
11	50	0.53	97.23	NONCL	65	0.92	98.12	V	10	0.63	97.49	NONCL	14	0.83	98.16	AVP
12	49	0.52	97.75	CONJUNC	36	0.51	98.64	CONJUNC	10	0.63	98.12	CONJUNC	9	0.53	98.69	ADV
13	46	0.48	98.23	PRON	17	0.24	98.88	PRON	7	0.44	98.56	PRON	6	0.36	99.05	PREP
14	44	0.46	98.70	VP	16	0.23	99.10	PREP	7	0.44	99.00	PROFM	4	0.24	99.29	DTP
15	43	0.45	99.15	ADV	16	0.23	99.33	NADJ	7	0.44	99.44	ADV	4	0.24	99.53	CONJUNC
16	42	0.44	99.59	ADJ	16	0.23	99.56	ADV	6	0.38	99.81	VP	3	0.18	99.70	PRON
17	19	0.20	99.79	PREP	14	0.20	99.76	PROFM	2	0.13	99.94	PREP	2	0.12	99.82	PROFM
18	9	0.09	99.88	AUX	9	0.13	99.89	AUX	1	0.06	100.00	AUX	2	0.12	99.94	AUX
19	5	0.05	99.94	DISP	7	0.10	99.99	NONCL					1	0.06	100.00	CONNEC
20	3	0.03	99.97	DTP	1	0.01	100.00	AUXEL								
21	2	0.02	99.99	NADJ												
22	1	0.01	100.00	AUXEL												
	9506				7035				1596				1685			

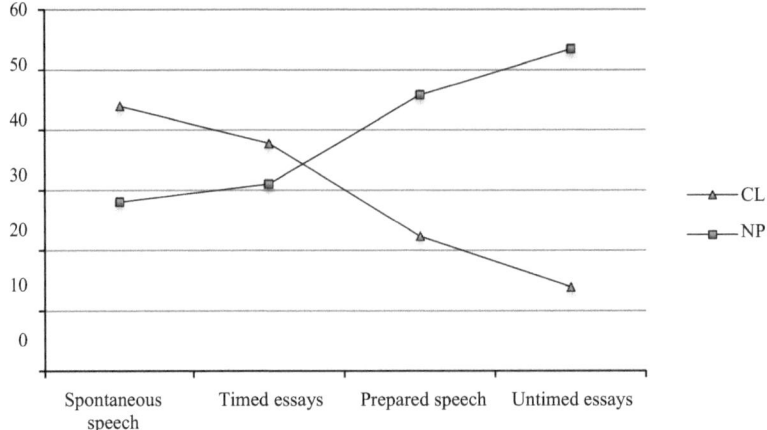

Fig. 9.7 The opposing distributions of CL and NP coordinations across texts of different registers

of the total, compared with 22.40 % for coordinated clauses. Timed essays shows a
small dip in the use of coordinated clauses, 37.84 %, compared with 31.92 % for coordinated NPs, a much smaller margin of difference than spontaneous speech, and
lower than prepared speech just like what has been previously shown with speech
and writing. Untimed essays demonstrate a predominant preference for coordinated
NPs with a proportion of 54.42 % accounting for more than half of the total use
of coordinated constructions. Clause coordination, in comparison, has fallen to
13.93 % compared with 43.97 % in spontaneous speech. See Fig. 9.7 for a graph
visualising the opposing pattern of distribution.

It is therefore reasonable to conclude, based on empirical evidence, that, in the
first place, coordination is correlated with text register. Texts of a higher register
tend to show a higher use of coordinations. Second, speech and writing have a different preference for the type of syntactic categories that typically occur within a
coordinated construction; while frequent in both speech and writing, coordinated
constructions tend to prefer NPs in writing and clauses in speech, which largely
corresponds with findings from previous studies that writing is characterised by
complex NPs and speech by complex clausal structures. More specifically, we see
that clausal complexing in speech is facilitated by coordination in speech and subordination in writing.

9.4 Syntactic Functions of Coordination

Obviously, an interesting endeavour would be to examine the syntactic functions
of the coordinated constructions identified in the ICE corpus, which was a rather
straightforward business given the detailed syntactic annotation that had already
been performed on the corpus. The results are summarised in Table 9.11, according to which it is evident that utterance- or sentence-level coordination (PU), or

Table 9.11 The distribution of syntactic function of coordinations across speech and writing

R	Speech				Writing			
	Freq	%	%%	Function	Freq	%	%%	Function
1.	3143	24.01	24.01	PU	2495	18.42	18.42	PU
2.	1755	13.40	37.41	PC	2136	15.77	34.18	PC
3.	1700	12.98	50.39	PREDGP	1986	14.66	48.84	PREDGP
4.	1161	8.87	59.26	NPHD	1801	13.29	62.14	NPHD
5.	1053	8.04	67.30	OD	895	6.61	68.75	OD
6.	822	6.28	73.58	A	792	5.85	74.59	A
7.	734	5.61	79.19	CS	671	4.95	79.55	SU
8.	575	4.39	83.58	SU	555	4.10	83.64	CS
9.	407	3.11	86.69	NPPO	482	3.56	87.20	NPPR
10.	271	2.07	88.76	NPPR	379	2.80	90.00	NPPO
11.	253	1.93	90.69	ELE	250	1.85	91.84	AJHD
12.	246	1.88	92.57	DTPS	246	1.82	93.66	DEFUNC
13.	159	1.21	93.78	AJHD	137	1.01	94.67	MVB
14.	152	1.16	94.94	DEFUNC	106	0.78	95.45	CJ
15.	102	0.78	95.72	CJ	103	0.76	96.21	DTPS
16.	76	0.58	96.30	MVB	98	0.72	96.94	ELE
17.	75	0.57	96.88	VB	82	0.61	97.54	VB
18.	67	0.51	97.39	PARA	51	0.38	97.92	P
19.	53	0.40	97.79	NOSU	43	0.32	98.24	PARA
20.	45	0.34	98.14	CO	39	0.29	98.52	NOSU
21.	36	0.27	98.41	AJPO	35	0.26	98.78	CO
22.	34	0.26	98.67	AVHD	31	0.23	99.01	AVHD
23.	25	0.19	98.86	DTCE	22	0.16	99.17	DTCE
24.	24	0.18	99.05	FNPPO	22	0.16	99.34	AJPO
25.	24	0.18	99.23	CT	19	0.14	99.48	CT
26.	23	0.18	99.40	P	11	0.08	99.56	FOC
27.	17	0.13	99.53	FOC	11	0.08	99.64	AJPR
28.	11	0.08	99.62	AJPR	9	0.07	99.70	FNPPO
29.	9	0.07	99.69	DTPE	7	0.05	99.76	OI
30.	8	0.06	99.75	DT	6	0.04	99.80	SBHD
31.	7	0.05	99.80	OP	6	0.04	99.84	DTPE
32.	6	0.05	99.85	NOOD	6	0.04	99.89	DT
33.	4	0.03	99.88	AVPO	4	0.03	99.92	OP
34.	3	0.02	99.90	SBHD	4	0.03	99.95	CF
35.	3	0.02	99.92	INDET	2	0.01	99.96	PMOD
36.	3	0.02	99.95	CF	2	0.01	99.98	NOOD
37.	2	0.02	99.96	OI	2	0.01	99.99	AVPR
38.	1	0.01	99.97	PMOD	1	0.01	100.00	PS

Table 9.11 (continued)

R	Speech				Writing			
	Freq	%	%%	Function	Freq	%	%%	Function
39.	1	0.01	99.98	DTPR				
40.	1	0.01	99.98	DISMK				
41.	1	0.01	99.99	COOR				
42.	1	0.01	100.00	AVPR				
	13,093				13,547			

Parsing Unit, is the most frequent in both speech and writing. The two modes of language production are also the same in the use of coordinations as prepositional complement (PC). However, utterance-level coordinations are significantly higher in speech, which account for 24.01% of all the coordinations found in speech. In contrast, writing has a much lower 18.42%. Conversely, speech has a lower use of coordinated constructions (13.40%) as the prepositional complement than writing (15.77%).

This observation coincides with our previous finding that a characteristic of speech lies in its higher preference for coordinated clauses, which emphasises the role of the clause as the basic unit of meaning expression. On the other hand, a relatively higher proportion of the prepositional complement (PC) found in writing confirms our previous observation that writing is different from speech because of its preference for NP constructions as the basic unit of meaning expression, which naturally include a higher proportion of coordinated NPs as the prepositional complement. Again, an unavoidable conclusion based on Table 9.11 is that, as far as coordination is concerned, speech is marked for its coordinated clauses while writing is marked by its preference for more complex coordinated NPs. To push the argument further, it can be hypothesised that this observation can be generally applied across registers; that is, higher registers tend to demonstrate a preference for coordinated NPs and lower registers are expected to exhibit a preference for coordinated utterance-level clauses, a hypothesis that was subsequently tested out with the sub-corpus of secondary data. See Table 9.12 for a summary of the results.

The sub-corpus, which is classed according to registers, shows that there is indeed a significant difference across the registers in terms of coordinations. First, untimed student essays, which have been shown to be the highest register, has the prepositional complement as the top-ranking function that involves coordination while the other three registers have the utterance as the most common function. Second, if we consider the second most common function across the registers, we see that spontaneous conversations and timed essays have a preference for coordinated predicate groups, which, like clauses, cover the scope of both the verb and the complement while prepared speech and untimed essays, which are higher in register, show a preference for coordinated prepositional complement and NP head (NPHD), both of which are directly related to the NP. It is therefore reasonable to draw the conclusion that based on both the primary data and the secondary data higher registers tend to prefer NP coordinations while lower registers are seen to prefer coordinations at the clause level.

Table 9.12 The syntactic functions of coordination across registers

Rank	Spontaneous Speech				Prepared Speech				Timed Essays				Untimed Essays			
	Freq	%	Cum%	Cat	Freq	%	Cum%	Cat	Freq	%	Cum%	Cat	Freq	%	Cum%	Cat
1.	1304	36.52	36.52	PU	469	15.98	15.98	PU	226	33.28	33.28	PU	128	18.39	18.39	PC
2.	419	11.73	48.25	PREDGP	469	15.98	31.96	PC	115	16.94	50.22	PREDGP	126	18.10	36.49	NPHD
3.	348	9.75	57.99	PC	352	11.99	43.95	PREDGP	69	10.16	60.38	PC	97	13.94	50.43	PREDGP
4.	322	9.02	67.01	OD	312	10.63	54.58	NPHD	60	8.84	69.22	NPHD	64	9.20	59.63	PU
5.	237	6.64	73.65	NPHD	217	7.39	61.98	SU	45	6.63	75.85	OD	45	6.47	66.09	OD
6.	235	6.58	80.23	CS	212	7.22	69.20	OD	35	5.15	81.00	CS	43	6.18	72.27	SU
7.	193	5.40	85.63	A	166	5.66	74.86	A	35	5.15	86.16	A	35	5.03	77.30	CS
8.	133	3.72	89.36	ELE	136	4.63	79.49	CS	21	3.09	89.25	SU	31	4.45	81.75	NPPR
9.	88	2.46	91.82	SU	124	4.22	83.71	NPPR	16	2.36	91.61	ELE	24	3.45	85.20	AJHD
10.	51	1.43	93.25	NPPO	119	4.05	87.77	NPPO	10	1.47	93.08	NPPR	19	2.73	87.93	A
11.	45	1.26	94.51	DTPS	68	2.32	90.09	DEFUNC	10	1.47	94.55	NPPO	18	2.59	90.52	NPPO
12.	35	0.98	95.49	PARA	55	1.87	91.96	DTPS	10	1.47	96.02	AJHD	13	1.87	92.39	CJ
13.	34	0.95	96.44	CJ	51	1.74	93.70	AJHD	7	1.03	97.05	MVB	8	1.15	93.53	DEFUNC
14.	22	0.62	97.06	DEFUNC	26	0.89	94.58	ELE	5	0.74	97.79	DEFUNC	6	0.86	94.40	DTPS
15.	18	0.50	97.56	NPPR	24	0.82	95.40	VB	5	0.74	98.53	CJ	5	0.72	95.11	VB
16.	16	0.45	98.01	MVB	24	0.82	96.22	MVB	2	0.29	98.82	DTPS	5	0.72	95.83	MVB
17.	15	0.42	98.43	AJHD	18	0.61	96.83	CO	2	0.29	99.12	AJPO	4	0.57	96.41	ELE
18.	13	0.36	98.80	NOSU	17	0.58	97.41	CJ	1	0.15	99.26	PARA	4	0.57	96.98	CO
19.	10	0.28	99.08	VB	10	0.34	97.75	AJPO	1	0.15	99.41	P	4	0.57	97.56	AVHD
20.	7	0.20	99.27	CO	9	0.31	98.06	CT	1	0.15	99.56	NOSU	3	0.43	97.99	P
21.	6	0.17	99.44	AJPO	8	0.27	98.33	PARA	1	0.15	99.71	FOC	2	0.29	98.28	PARA
22.	4	0.11	99.55	FNPPO	8	0.27	98.60	AVHD	1	0.15	99.85	FNPPO	2	0.29	98.56	FOC
23.	4	0.11	99.66	AVHD	7	0.24	98.84	P	1	0.15	100.00	AVHD	2	0.29	98.85	DT

Table 9.12 (continued)

Rank	Spontaneous Speech				Prepared Speech				Timed Essays				Untimed Essays			
	Freq	%	Cum%	Cat	Freq	%	Cum%	Cat	Freq	%	Cum%	Cat	Freq	%	Cum%	Cat
24.	3	0.08	99.75	NOOD	6	0.20	99.05	NOSU					2	0.29	99.14	AJPO
25.	2	0.06	99.80	FOC	6	0.20	99.25	FNPPO					1	0.14	99.28	NOSU
26.	1	0.03	99.83	SBHD	6	0.20	99.45	DTCE					1	0.14	99.43	DTPE
27.	1	0.03	99.86	P	4	0.14	99.59	FOC					1	0.14	99.57	DTCE
28.	1	0.03	99.89	OP	3	0.10	99.69	AJPR					1	0.14	99.71	CT
29.	1	0.03	99.92	OI	2	0.07	99.76	DTPE					1	0.14	99.86	CF
30.	1	0.03	99.94	DTCE	2	0.07	99.83	AVPO					1	0.14	100.00	AJPR
31.	1	0.03	99.97	DT	1	0.03	99.86	SBHD								
32.	1	0.03	100.00	CT	1	0.03	99.90	OI								
33.					1	0.03	99.93	NOOD								
34.					1	0.03	99.97	DT								
35.					1	0.03	100.00	COOR								
	3571				2935				679				696			

9.5   Conclusion

Following Chap. 8, this chapter described a second study to illustrate the syntactic characteristics of different text genres and registers. While the first in Chap. 8 concerns the use and distribution of adverbial clauses across a set of text categories with different degrees of the register, the second in this chapter examined the occurrence of coordinated constructions across the same set of texts. The overall finding is that these two syntactic constructions demonstrate a significant correlation with registerial degrees. The use of coordinated constructions showed a more complex situation than adverbial clauses: while coordination at the clause level is found to be more frequent with texts of a lower register, coordination of nouns is found to be a preferred construction in texts of a higher register, thus producing more evidence in support of complex NPs as an important characteristic of formal discourse. A subsequent look at the syntactic functions of the coordinated constructions led to the observation that informal discourse seems to show a preference for coordinated clauses and utterances. Formal discourse, on the other hand, demonstrated a more frequent use of coordinated constructions as prepositional complements. This finding provided further empirical backing of the clause and the complex NP as the two preferred units of expression, respectively, in informal and formal discourse.

Chapter 10
Semantic Features and Authorship Attribution

The language of poetry is different from that employed in other categories of writing. 'Defined from a linguistic perspective, poetry represents a variant form of language, different from speech and common writing, unique in its own way as a linguistic system' (Yuan 1989, p. 2). This is particularly true of classical Chinese poetry, which, because of its formal restrictions in terms of syllables, tonal variations and rhyming patterns, commands a language system that appears to be delicately concise, finely rich and immensely rhetorical. It is thus linguistically complex, requiring a high degree of creativity to produce, sophisticated interpretation to read and often a significant level of difficulty to understand. A major difference between poetic language and other types of writing typically exists in its intentionally polysemous readings through the creative use of imagery as part of the poet's artistic conception. Poetic imagery refers to the mental image that gets conjured up when we read poems, relating to the experience of the five senses, giving rise to some of the most frequently used rhetorical devices such as metaphor, simile, allegory and personification. According to Brown (1927, pp. 1–2), imageries are 'words or phrases denoting a sense-perceptible object, used to designate not that object but some other object of thought belonging to a different order of being'. The term imagery is often used interchangeably with image. Here, imagery is differentiated from image in the sense that imagery denotes a system with component parts while image tends to be monolithic and undividable. To quote *The Concise Oxford Dictionary of Literary Terms* (Baldick 2004),

> imagery, a rather vague critical term covering those uses of language in a literary work that evoke sense-impressions by literal or figurative reference to perceptible or 'concrete' objects, scenes, actions, or states, as distinct from the language of abstract argument or exposition. The imagery of a literary work thus comprises the set of images that it uses; these need not be mental 'pictures', but may appeal to senses other than sight. The term has often been applied particularly to the figurative language used in a work, especially to its metaphors and similes. Images suggesting further meanings and associations in ways that

An earlier version of this chapter was previously published as Fang, A. C., W.-Y. Li, and J. Cao. 2011. In search of poetic discourse of classical Chinese poetry: An imagery-based stylistic analysis of Liu Yong and Su Shi. *Chinese Language and Discourse* 2 (2): 232–249. We would like to acknowledge Dr W.-Y. Li for her computational assistance in the preparation of Sect. 10.2.

A. C. Fang, J. Cao, *Text Genres and Registers: The Computation of Linguistic Features*,
DOI 10.1007/978-3-662-45100-7_10

go beyond the fairly simple identifications of metaphor and simile are often called symbols. The critical emphasis on imagery in the mid–twentieth century, both in New Criticism and in some influential studies of Shakespeare, tended to glorify the supposed concreteness of literary works by ignoring matters of structure, convention, and abstract argument: thus Shakespeare's plays were read as clusters or patterns of 'thematic imagery' according to the predominance of particular kinds of image (of animals, of disease, etc.), without reference to the action or to the dramatic meaning of characters' speeches.

In this chapter, the term *imagery* will be used as a generic name subsuming individual images functioning in metaphors and similes as well as in symbols[1]. The same term is preferred also because of the structure that it entails, thus coinciding with the structured analysis of imageries this study intends to propose.

Robert Burns's famous line *My love is like a red, red rose* is a good example of the creation of a simile through the use of 'red rose' as an imagery, which instantly transfers its familiar qualities to 'my love'. Ezra Pound is also well remembered for his exploitation of images in his imagist poems, which were primarily inspired by classical Chinese poetry. According to Ezra Pound (1916, p. 93), 'every concept, every emotion, presents itself to the vivid consciousness in some primary form'. To illustrate the use of imagery in classical Chinese poetry, one readily available example can be found in *Meditations in Autumn* (《秋思》) by Ma Zhi-yuan (馬致遠, 1270–1330 AD), translated by C. A. Fang.

[1]　枯藤老樹昏鴉。　　　Withered vines, old trees, muddled crows,
　　　小橋流水人家。　　　Small bridge, flowing water, dwelling house.
　　　古道西風瘦馬。　　　Ancient road, westerly wind, bony horse.
　　　夕阳西下，　　　　　The sun is setting in the west,
　　　斷腸人在天涯。　　　And a nostalgic man despairing in a far-away land.

As can be seen in [1], the first three lines contain six imageries, namely, vines, trees, crows, bridge, water and house. They are juxtaposed without the usual connection established via verbs, prepositions and coordinators, leaving the cognitive space open to the reader for all possible combinations and mental associations[2]. The use of natural scenes and concrete objects by Chinese poets to incur different associative readings dates much further back than the fourteenth-century Yuan Dynasty.

---

[1] According to personal communication, Prof. Edwin Thomboo distinguishes between the literal and the figurative and prefers the use of figurative as a first-order term to subsume all the elements of figurative language, including images, metaphors, similes and symbols.

[2] For smooth reading and rhyming effects, the first three lines are alternatively translated with added verbs in Liu (1962, p. 41) as

Withered vines, aged trees, twilight crows.
Beneath the little bridge by the cottage the river flows.
On the ancient road and lean horse the west wind blows.

Writing in the early sixth-century China, Liu Xie (刘勰), an important literary critic, says in his famous *The Literary Mind and the Carving of Dragons* (《文心雕龍》; Liu 1959, p. 246)[3].

> In responding to things, the Ancient Poets operated on the principle of endless association of ideas. They lost themselves in the myriads of things, completely absorbed in the visual and auditory sensations. On the one hand, they depicted the atmosphere and painted the appearances of things in perfect harmony with their changing aspects; and on the other, the linguistic and tonal patterns they used closely corresponded with their perceptions.

Indeed, indirect expressions of the intended meaning and its expected interpretation through natural objects remain pretty much the norm in classical Chinese poetry throughout history, from the *Book of Poems* (《詩經》) compiled over 2500 years ago[4] to the beginning of the twentieth century before the rise of the so-called 'free-style poems' written in vernacular Chinese.

This study concerns itself with the challenging issue of identifying differentiating features in poetic discourse as indicators of stylistic differences between poets. It describes research that methodologically focuses on the detection and extraction of such stylistic features from literary texts and the application of such features to automatic authorship attribution. In particular, it reports experimental results from a comparative study of the lyric songs (*ci*; 詞) written by Liu Yong (柳永) and Su Shi (蘇軾), two well-known poets active in the Middle Ages in China in the tenth and eleventh centuries. This issue concerning imagery-based poetic discourse analysis is of a much wider interest that bears on comparative genre and registerial studies in general and literary stylistic appraisal in particular. The study reported in this chapter explores the intriguing question whether texts, either written by different authors or grouped according to a taxonomy of genres and registers, exhibit 'fingerprints' of some kind that unambiguously point to the source of the text. What is of particular interest is the question whether such fingerprints can be pinpointed, extracted and then modelled to account for other unseen poetic works.

Obviously, such a perspective on poetic discourse necessarily entails a computational framework and methodology through which patterns of imagery use as stylistic features of various kinds can be automatically identified, rigorously evaluated and then usefully formalised as a model. For this work, the current research has adopted computational techniques central to the area of automatic text

---

[3] Volume 46: The Physical World: '是以詩人感物, 聯類不窮, 流連萬象之際, 沉吟視聽之區; 寫氣圖貌, 既隨物以宛轉; 屬采附聲, 亦與心而徘徊。(*shi yi shi ren gan wu, lian lei bu qong, liu lian wan xiang zhi ji, chen yin shi ting zhi qu; xie qi tu mao, ji sui wu yi wan zhuan; shu cai fu sheng, yi yu xin er pai huai.*)' As a matter of fact, this piece of text can be alternatively translated as 'Thus the poet takes inspirations from natural objects and acquires everlasting associations therefrom. He lingers in a world of ten thousand images and immerses himself in a realm of visions and sounds. He describes atmospheres and portrays appearances, in harmony with the physical world; he chooses colours and mimics different sounds, in accordance with his own heart.' (translated by the first author)

[4] See Sampson (2006) for a recent translation of some of the love songs selected from the anthology.

classification. While a vast amount of research and an ample body of knowledge already exist for the automatic classification of contemporary texts for practical tasks such as opinion mining and document retrieval, relatively little effort has been made on the automatic authorship attribution of classical Chinese literary works such as poems. Compared with other types of textual data, classical Chinese poetry demonstrates particular complexity due to restrictive conventions on rhyming schemes and metrical feet as well as the creative use of language by individual writers. The current study is an extension of Fang et al. (2009) , which proposes a computational framework that attempts to explore the creative use of imageries as a major differentiating factor between poets. Within this framework, imageries are categorised into primary, complex and compound imageries. The same study also proposes that stylistic differences are likely to be highlighted against such a background of imagery systems. A major emphasis of Fang et al. (2009) is on the association between imageries and linguistic constructions, which in a nutshell can be represented in Fig. 10.1.

A central idea outlined in Fig. 10.1 is that there is a direct association between the imagery system and the linguistic system. While the primary imagery corresponds to the head of a noun phrase (NP) structure, the complex imagery involves a premodifying adjective phrase (AJP). The extended imagery comprises multiple NPs that are related to each other via a predicate (marked as pred in Fig. 10.1). Syntactically, the extended imagery therefore corresponds to a clause (CL), where

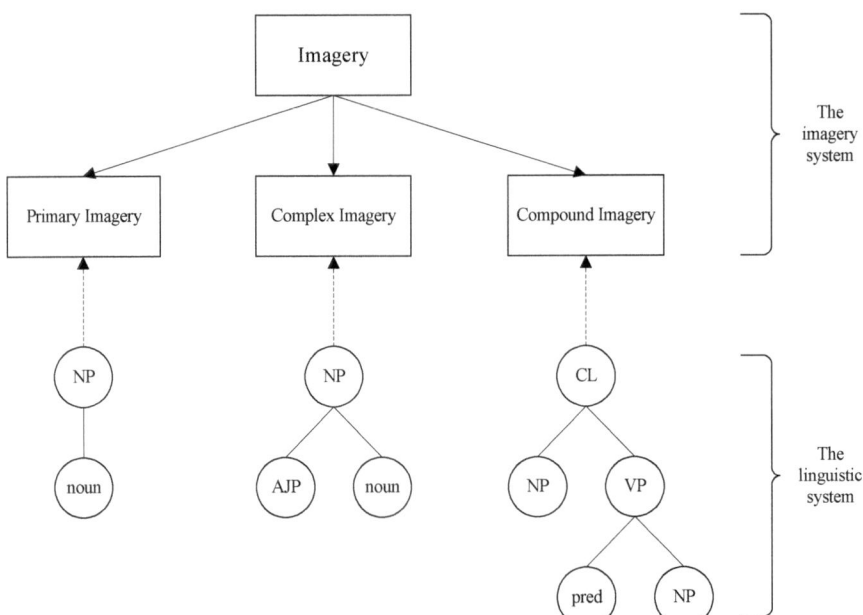

Fig. 10.1 The association between the imagery system and the linguistic system. (In Fang et al. 2009)

the component arguments, or NPs, are predicated in such a way that expresses the intended articulation of poetic meaning. This is where literary stylistic criticism can be integrated closely with a strictly structured syntactic analysis. Additionally, such a linguistically oriented approach to the imagery system also affords the benefit of the direct application of natural language processing (NLP) techniques for word segmentation, part-of-speech (POS) tagging and syntactic parsing. For research described in Fang et al. (2009) , the afore-mentioned NLP technologies were applied to the poems. Empirical results show rather drastic differences between the poems in their preference for linguistic constructions, suggesting that linguistic properties at the clausal level carry good potentials for stylistic differences.

The current study focuses on the imagery system and intends to acquire some initial empirical indication whether or not patterns of imagery use offer good potentials for the uncovering of stylistic differences between the two poets concerned in the study. The rest of the chapter is organised as follows: Section 10.1 describes the corpus of lyric songs used in the study along with a description of the ontological annotation of the poems. Section 10.2 discusses the use of machine learning techniques for the extraction of differentiating features. Section 10.3 evaluates the proposed method based on empirical results and concludes the work with discussions.

10.1 Corpus Annotated with Ontological Knowledge

The corpus contains a total of 597 lyric songs, with a component set of 218 written by Liu Yong (柳永; AD 987–1053) and a set of 379 by Su Shi (蘇軾; AD 1035–1101). Each poem in the corpus is segmented into word tokens that comprise one or more character tokens. Table 10.1 is a statistical summary of the two sets in the corpus. Accordingly, we observe that in terms of both word and character tokens, Liu Yong's poems tend to be generally longer than those written by Su Shi. In terms of vocabulary content as measured by the type-token ratio[5], Su Shi is observed to have a more varied vocabulary with 2363 unique character types and 7087 word types, compared with 2080 unique character types and 5798 word types used in the poems written by Liu Yong. These numbers indicate that Liu Yong uses a simpler language in his poems and thus partially explains the popularity of his lyric songs amongst the lower class.

To help with the extraction of imageries from the corpus, the ontological resource described in Lo (2008) is used to annotate each segmented word token. The ontol-

---

[5] The type-token ratio (TTR) is a measure of vocabulary size expressed as the number of unique word types per 100 word tokens. A higher TTR indicates a more varied vocabulary. Mathematically, it is calculated as the number of word types over the number of word tokens multiplied by 100. This measure is sensitive to sample size. The larger the sample, the lower the ratio and vice versa. In the case of Liu and Su here, the set of poems by Su represents a higher TTR as well as a larger sample size in terms of tokens than the set by Liu, thus emphasising the interpretation that Su's vocabulary is more varied than Liu's.

Table 10.1 Summary information about the two sets of poems in the corpus

	Liu Yong	Su Shi
Poems	218	379
Character tokens	18,399	21,124
Character tokens per song	84.39	55.74
Character types	2080	2363
Type-token ratio for characters (%)	11.30	11.18
Word tokens	10,669	12,416
Word tokens per song	48.94	32.76
Word types	5798	7087
Type-token ratio for words (%)	54.34	57.08

ogy is designed specifically for the study of classical Chinese poetry. As indicated in Fig. 10.2, the ontology is a hierarchy comprising six major conceptual groups: human, affair, time, space, object and miscellany. Each conceptual group is in turn a cluster of component entities named in various ways. The human group, for instance, contains 14 entities such as names, emperors, immortals, etc.

According to Lo (2008), the ontology has been applied to a complete collection of 51,170 poems written by 2821 poets from the Tang dynasty and is therefore fully tested in terms of coverage. The word tokens of all the poems in the corpus are annotated according to the ontological structure in Fig. 10.2. Each annotated word token is described by a set of four ontological descriptors with an occasional fifth one. As an example, the first line in *Gui Cao Huan* (歸朝歡; A Happy Return to Court) by Liu Yong contains seven characters.

[2]   別   岸   扁   舟   三   兩   隻
      bié   *àn*   *biǎn*   *zhōu*   *sān*   *liǎng*   *zhī*
      departure bank   small   boat   three   two   piece

The same line of seven characters in [2] is segmented into four word tokens:

[3]   別岸   扁舟   三兩   隻
      bié àn   *biǎn zōu*   *sān liǎng*   *zhī*
      departure bank   small boat   three or two   piece

Each word token in [3] is then annotated according to the ontological hierarchy represented in Table 10.2.

We thus see a gradient of change in granularity. Each level leads to a sub-level until it reaches the leaf node in the hierarchy, namely, the head of original word token in the poem. In a majority of the situations, Level 4 refers directly to the linguistic expression of the intended imagery while the higher levels typically define the conceptual classes of the imageries. This example here also serves to

Fig. 10.2 An ontology of conceptual descriptors for classical Chinese poetry

illustrate how we intend to approach differences in poetic discourse in this study: We say that stylistic differences can be found in significant differences in patters of use of imageries against the ontological structure outlined in Fig. 10.2; we are thus interested to find out whether the two lyric song writers under question exhibit any significant differences at the various ontological levels. In other words, author-

Table 10.2 Different levels of ontological description for [3]

Word	English	Level 1	Level 2	Level 3	Level 4
別岸	departure bank	地	自然景觀	沙洲島嶼	岸
		location	natural scene	wetland and island	bank
扁舟	small boat	物	器物	交通工具(水路)	舟
		object	artifact	means of transport (on water)	boat
三兩	three or two	其他	數詞	概量數詞	三兩
		miscellany	numeral	inexact numeral	three or two
隻	piece	其他	單位詞	個體量詞	隻
		miscellany	unit noun	countable unit noun	piece

ship attribution methodologically boils down to the automatic classification of the two sets of lyric songs through the use of ontological annotations as differentiating features. Different from other automatic text classification tasks, however, we are more interested in the set of differentiating descriptors as tell-tale stylistic markers.

There are altogether six descriptors at Level 1, namely, affair, human, miscellany, location, time, and object. Table 10.3 is a summary of the occurrences of these descriptors in the two sets of lyric songs.

According to Table 10.3, we have the following observations: While both poets show considerable similarity in the use of the six descriptors, they nonetheless demonstrate significant differences. Although both make the highest use for the human descriptor, it accounts for 42.78 % of the word tokens in Liu, 2.02 % higher than in Su. Conversely, with object as the second highest use of the object descriptor, it accounts for 27.7 % of the word tokens in Su but only 25.56 in Liu, 2.14 % lower. In addition, the location descriptor is nearly 2 % higher in Su than in Liu. These observations suggest that Liu is perhaps more concerned with human-related references in his poems such as emotions. Su definitely demonstrates a preference for more objective references such as location and object. With an expansion to the descriptors at lower levels, further significant and telling differences can be observed about the two poets. Word tokens described by the descriptor general emotion account for

Table 10.3 A Comparative summary of descriptor occurrences across Liu Yong and Su Shi

	Liu Yong		Su Shi	
	Frequency	Percent	Frequency	Percent
Incident	589	6.30	739	6.47
Human	3997	42.78	4654	40.76
Miscellany	797	8.53	1021	8.94
Location	923	8.62	1203	10.54
Time	650	6.96	638	5.59
Object	2388	25.56	3163	27.70
Total	9344	100.00	11,418	100.00

4.1 % in Liu but only 1.3 % in Su, a finding that confirms our earlier intuitive explanation. By the same token, Su makes a higher use of descriptors for natural scenes, climates and seasons than Liu, revealing a stylistic preference for impersonalised perspective in his poems. These observations have generally confirmed previous stylistic critiques of the two poets that Liu is more devoted to the direct expressions of emotions by women in love and that Su is more delineated to appraisals of natural beauty and in doing implicitly expressing the emotions of officials who have lost favour by the imperial court.

While initial indications have shown promising contributions of imagery towards stylistic differences between the two poets, it still remains a question to what extent imageries or patterns of imageries can be used to differentiate the two poets. Given a set of 100 poems by Liu and a set of characteristic patterns, as an example, how many can be unambiguously attributed to Liu and how many would be wrongly attributed to Su? This question is an important one since it addresses the need for empirical evidence in the conventionally impressionistic literary criticism. The question is also important in that it forces the necessary implementation of an evaluative procedure in the conventional discourse analysis whereby impressionistic hypothesis and postulations inherited from conventional wisdom can be rigorously tested and verified for their validity. In the following section of this chapter, we shall aim to introduce machine learning techniques for two purposes: First, we wish to see whether it is possible to automatically, and hence objectively, extract differentiating features that can be used to separate the poems written by Liu from those by Su. Second, we wish to verify the explanatory power of the set of extracted features by measuring, empirically, their accuracy of differentiation. The same section will describe an experiment that was designed to help answer these questions and present the results of the experiment.

10.2   Selection and Evaluation of Stylistic Features

This section concerns the identification and selection of imageries and imagery patterns as stylistic features that can be used to separate the two sets of poems concerned in the study. It also concerns itself with the evaluation of the feature set so that its performance, in terms of accuracy, can be empirically tested and verified. For the former, techniques for text classification are adopted. For our purposes, the stylistic attribution of poems is also seen as a specialised task in text classification: the poems from the corpus are classified according to the two poets, namely, Liu Yong and Su Shi. Different features have been used and tested in past research, including the use of words and/or their related grammatical information such as parts of speech. In this study, we propose the use of ontological knowledge for authorship attribution of classical Chinese poems. The use of ontologies has been attempted before for the classification of documents (Cumbo et al. 2004; Melo and Siersdorfer 2007; Janik and Kochut 2008; Netzer et al. 2009). For the current task, however, we believe that it represents a first attempt to apply ontologies to stylistic analysis of classical Chinese poems.

The corpus of poems is preprocessed by segmenting the character tokens into word tokens and linking each word token to a set of concept levels in the ontology. Thus, each poem p_i is represented as a collection of the features f_m as below

$$pi = \{f1, f2, f3, ..., fm\} \tag{10.1}$$

where m denotes the frequency of feature f in pi. The candidate features are formed of word tokens (BoW), wi, and/or the mapped ontological descriptors, Ok, j, at different levels ($k = 1.5$) with respect to the j classes under each level. Ontological descriptors $\{\forall jOkj\}$ are saved over all poems based on each ontological level k. For example, the six types of ontological descriptors under the first level $O1 = \{O1j\}$ ($j = 1.6$) over all the poems by the two poets are stored separately from the ones at other levels. To evaluate the effectiveness of the ontological descriptors Ok, j at different levels, feature sets from all the combinations of the five levels are constructed.

bié àn (location, natural scene, wetland and island, bank)

Altogether, 62 sets of different combinations were generated and then tested in the experiment, which are categorised into three different sets: (1) word tokens only, (2) word tokens annotated with ontological descriptors at different levels, and (3) ontological descriptors only at different levels. To thoroughly evaluate the impact of different ontological types from Levels l1 to l5, a combination of the three sets, which yields a total of 62 such feature combinations, will be tested. The evaluation of each ontological type is conducted by sorting according to performance against Liu, Su, and overall, which is a weighted average over both Liu and Su. The performance evaluation scheme includes precision, recall and F-score defined as in (3.3) in Chap. 3.

Figure 10.3 shows the overall performance (for both Liu and Su) of top 30 feature combinations measured in terms of precision, recall and F-score. The Y-axis represents performance and the X-axis represents the top 30 different feature sets sorted in descending order according to F-score.

According to Fig. 10.3, the use of word tokens alone (BoW) is ranked as the 19th best performing feature set, with an F-score of just above 87%, meaning that 87% of the poems can be correctly attributed to either Liu or Su through the use of word tokens. The best performing feature set is BowO1O4O5, a set that combines the word token, the first, the fourth and the fifth ontological descriptors, achieving an accuracy of over 89%, 2% better than BoW. As a general observation, word tokens combined with ontological descriptors at various levels outperform the use of bare word tokens.

Figure 10.4 presents a more detailed look at the performance of the top 30 features sets, showing the F-score separately for Liu, Su and both. First of all, it shows that the F-score variation pattern holds consistent with respect to Liu, Su, and over-

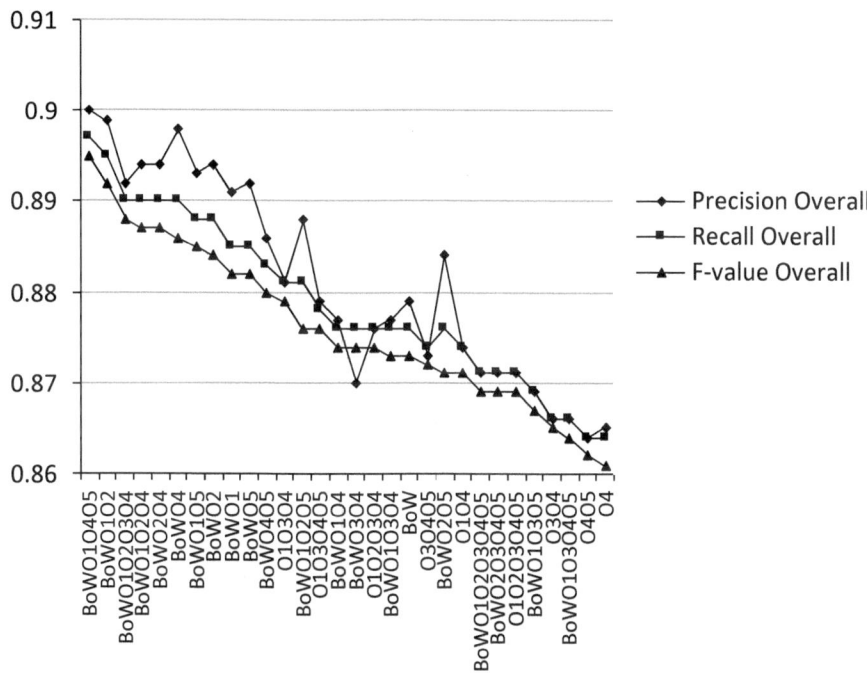

Fig. 10.3 Overall performance for top 30 feature sets sorted according to F-score

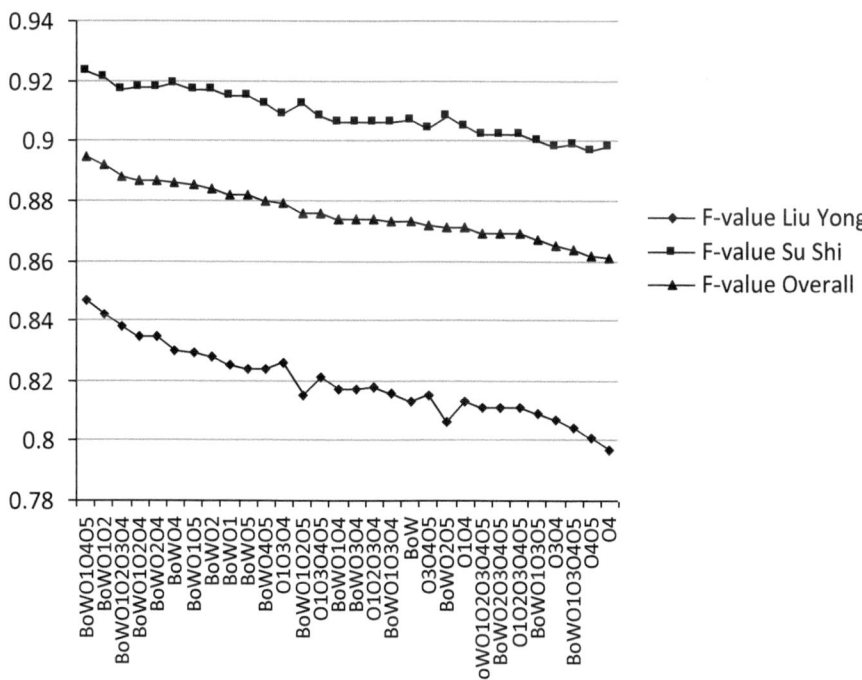

Fig. 10.4 F-score for the top 30 feature sets sorted according to overall F-score

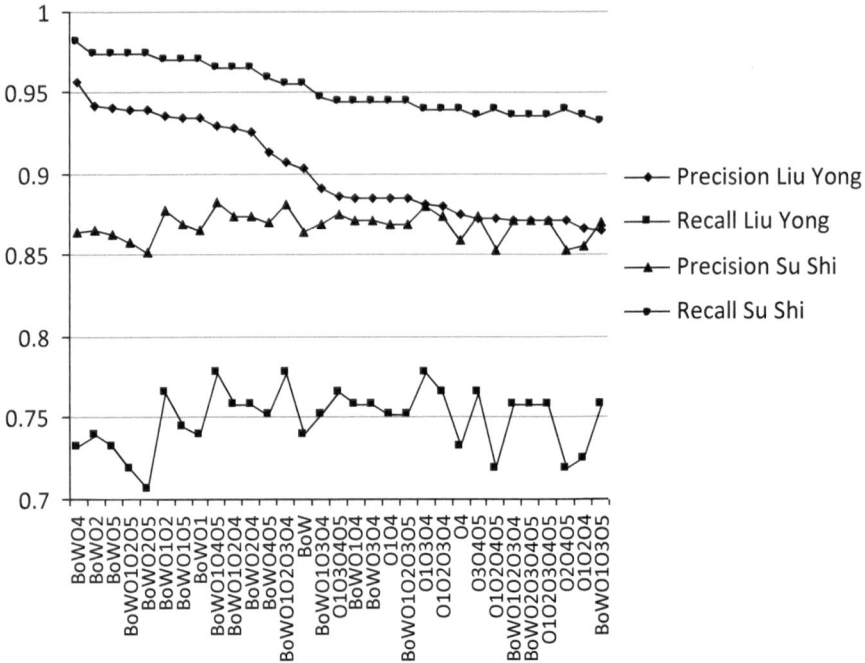

Fig. 10.5 Precision and recall sorted according to precision for Liu Yong

all performance. More interestingly, it is observable that the same features perform much better with Su than with Liu. Consider the feature BoW. It achieved over 90 % accuracy with Su but just over 81 % with Liu, a considerable difference of nearly 10 %. The best performing feature, *BowO1O4O5*, as another example, achieved an accuracy of over 92 % with the task of attributing Su's poems. When it comes to Liu, in comparison, this feature achieved just under 85 %, yet again showing a considerable difference of 7 %. While this phenomenon requires an in-depth study in the future, Fig. 10.4, along with Figs. 10.5 and 10.6, demonstrates that BoW in combination with ontological annotations performed consistently better with both Liu and Su than BoW alone without the ontological annotations, arguing strongly in favour of the contribution of ontological information to the task of stylistic attribution of authorships. As a matter of fact, a most important finding here is the observation that additional information related to imageries is shown to outperform features based on BoW alone, arguing forcefully that characteristic poetic discourse stylistically typical of a poet is better described in terms of imageries than in terms of lexical preferences.

From the empirical results observed and analysed above, *BowO1O4O5* as a feature set is verifiably the best feature set compared with the baseline feature set,

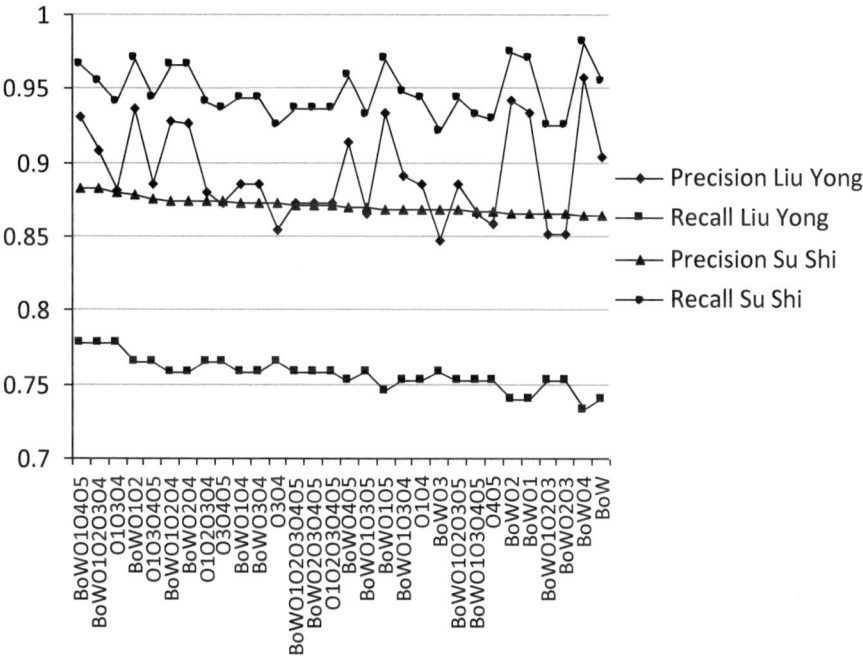

Fig. 10.6 Precision and recall sorted according to precision for Su Shi

Table 10.4 Performance gains of BoW combined with ontological annotations *O1O4O5*

	Liu Yong	Su Shi	Overall
Precision (%)	2.6	1.9	2.1
Recall (%)	3.9	1.1	2.1
F-score (%)	3.4	1.6	2.2

BoW. Table 10.4 is a summary of the performance gains when BoW is combined with ontological annotations *O1O4O5*.

Finally, Table 10.5 lists the top 20 feature combinations separately sorted in descending order according to the *F*-score for Liu, Su, and both respectively. The first eight of such combinations overlap in the three sorted lists with only slight differences. Specifically, BoW combined with ontological annotations from Levels 1, 4 and 5 (BowO1O4O5) consistently produces the best performance, while the integrated features of BoW and ontological annotations in Levels l1 and l2 yield the second best performance in our experiments.

Table 10.5 Top 20 feature sets sorted in descending order according to F-score

Rank	Liu Yong	Su Shi	Overall
1	$BoWO_1O_4O_5$	$BoWO_1O_4O_5$	$BoWO_1O_4O_5$
2	$BoWO_1O_2$	$BoWO_1O_2$	$BoWO_1O_2$
3	$BoWO_1O_2O_3O_4$	$BoWO_4$	$BoWO_1O_2O_3O_4$
4	$BoWO_1O_2O_4$	$BoWO_1O_2O_4$	$BoWO_1O_2O_4$
5	$BoWO_2O_4$	$BoWO_2O_4$	$BoWO_2O_4$
6	$BoWO_4$	$BoWO_1O_2O_3O_4$	$BoWO_4$
7	$BoWO_1O_5$	$BoWO_1O_5$	$BoWO_1O_5$
8	$BoWO_2$	$BoWO_2$	$BoWO_2$
9	$O_1O_3O_4$	$BoWO_1$	$BoWO_1$
10	$BoWO_1$	$BoWO_5$	$BoWO_5$
11	$BoWO_5$	$BoWO_4O_5$	$BoWO_4O_5$
12	$BoWO_4O_5$	$BoWO_1O_2O_5$	$O_1O_3O_4$
13	$O_1O_3O_4O_5$	$O_1O_3O_4$	$BoWO_1O_2O_5$
14	$O_1O_2O_3O_4$	$O_1O_3O_4O_5$	$O_1O_3O_4O_5$
15	$BoWO_1O_4$	$BoWO_2O_5$	$BoWO_1O_4$
16	$BoWO_3O_4$	BoW	$BoWO_3O_4$
17	$BoWO_1O_3O_4$	$BoWO_1O_4$	$O_1O_2O_3O_4$
18	$BoWO_1O_2O_5$	$BoWO_3O_4$	$BoWO_1O_3O_4$
19	$O_3O_4O_5$	$O_1O_2O_3O_4$	BoW
20	BoW	$BoWO_1O_3O_4$	$O_3O_4O_5$

10.3   Discussions and Conclusion

In this chapter, we described an experiment that was aimed at the use of ontological knowledge for the task of automatic stylistic authorship attribution of classical Chinese poems. This work was motivated by the understanding that the creative language use by different authors (hence the stylistic features pertaining to works by different authors) could be captured through their creative use of imageries as a form of poetic discourse. A corpus of lyric songs written by Liu Yong and Su Shi in the Song Dynasty was used, which is word segmented and ontologically annotated. Different feature sets were constructed that represent all the possible combinations of word tokens and their ontological annotations. Machine learning techniques were used to extract the characteristic patterns of imagery use, which were subsequently evaluated for their performance in terms of attribution accuracy. Empirical results show that word tokens alone could be used to achieve an accuracy of 87 % in the task of authorship attribution between Liu Yong and Su Shi. The high performance by lexical units alone suggests the highly distinctive use of lexical expressions by the two lyric song writers. More interestingly, ontological knowledge was shown to produce significant performance gains when combined with word tokens. This was reinforced by the observation that most of the feature sets with ontological annotation outperformed the use of bare word tokens as features. Specifically, our empirical experiment shows that word tokens combined with ontological annotations at l1, l4 and l5 levels produced the best performance, achieving an overall 89% F-sore, 2% higher than word tokens. In other words, nearly 90% of the poems can be accurately attributed to either Liu Yong or Su Shi.

The experimental results presented in this chapter have given rise to interesting and forceful suggestions. For one, our empirical observation that lexical features based on BoW alone produced generally poorer performance than those augmented with ontological descriptors, an observation that has lent empirical backing to the suggestion that imageries can be used as a powerful indicator of the poetic discourse characteristic of specific poets. This finding is significant: Ontological annotations at l1 and l4 levels refer directly to classes of imageries with l4 pinpointing the primary imagery and l5 providing more detailed information about the imagery if the word unit in question represents a nominal unit. In *Nan Ge Zi* (南歌子) written by Su Shi, the fourth line contains three word tokens that correspond to three different complex imageries (細草軟沙溪路; tender grass, soft sand and brook-side trail). The ontological annotation at l4 level explicitly identifies their primary imageries as *grass* (草), *sand* (沙) and *trail* (路) while l1 provides their ontological classification, namely, object for grass, object for sand and location for trail. The empirical results from our study confirm that ontological knowledge about poetic imageries provides valuable background knowledge for the identification of characteristic features for stylistic authorship attribution. The most important finding in our study is the observation that additional information related to imageries is shown to outperform features based on lexical expressions alone, arguing forcefully that characteristic poetic discourse stylistically typical of a poet is better described in terms of imageries than in terms of poetic diction deployed by the poets in question.

Our study has also raised interesting issues. One in particular has to do with the observation that ontological knowledge appeared to perform much better with the poems by Su Shi than those by Liu Yong, which suggests the hypothesis that Su Shi's poetry is probably more 'imagery-based' while Liu Yong's poetry is probably more based on some other linguistic property. While this hypothesis deserves a separate study on its own in the future, it nonetheless suggests that stylistic authorship attribution is a complex matter. Any attempt at a coherent framework or methodology will need to view literary works as a systemic network of different paradigms instead of a monolithic discourse pattern, some preferring the use of imageries, some the use of lexical devices such as reiterative locution (複疊詞), and others a combination of both. As far as our current plan is concerned, we intend to move further into the imagery as a system of structured linguistic expressions and to investigate whether different poets exhibit a distinguishing preference for and hence a unique pattern of imagery types.

Chapter 11
Pragmatics and Dialogue Acts

This chapter is intended to report our investigation into the pragmatic aspect of conversation. While discourse analysis of conversations has manifested intense interest in issues concerning power, inequality and ideology, the main stream of pragmatic analyses has been focusing on pragmatic markers such as interjections (e.g. Norrick 2009), conversational fillers (e.g. Beňuš et al. 2011), topic orientation markers (e.g. Fraser 2009) and closing devices (e.g. Park 2010; Wright 2011). More significantly, studies in pragmatics have begun to demonstrate their practical value through man-machine dialogue systems that have been put to real use in everyday life. The emergence of such real-world applications has called for systematic frameworks of pragmatic interpretations suited for such practical tasks as well as a more comprehensive understanding of human conversation. The analysis of dialogue acts (DAs) is good case. Most studies for the application purpose have concentrated how to improve the performance of automatic DA identification and annotation for better application to dialogue systems, and yet some more fundamental issues have been generally overlooked, that is, whether the predefined DA types are capable of capturing the salient communicative functions of the naturally occurring utterances, defined by each other as modulating contexts and recorded in a sizable corpus, and whether there is a palpable distinction between the predefined DA types for easy recognition and practical application.

As a matter of fact, many of the DA schemes (cf. Sect. 11.2) as interpretive frameworks were initially proposed and designed for task-specific applications and projects and thus unavoidably include some ad hoc treatments which eventually affect their applicability. Therefore, we attempt to revisit the taxonomy of DA types and explore the core issue of problematic DA types. To be more specific, it will be based on the taxonomy of DA types designed for the SWBD-DAMSL project. There are three reasons: first, although originally designed for a specific project, the targeted DA scheme is now publically available and also widely used for both practical application and academic research. Second, the Switchboard corpus itself contains a large number of dialogues that are essentially 'task-free', which is different from the task-oriented dialogues found in many other spoken resources, thus 'giving few external constraints on the definition of DA categories' (Stolcke et al.

© Springer-Verlag Berlin Heidelberg 2015

183

A. C. Fang, J. Cao, *Text Genres and Registers: The Computation of Linguistic Features*,
DOI 10.1007/978-3-662-45100-7_11

2000, p. 5). Thus, the SWBD-DAMSL is considered domain-independent, the use of which is expected to lead to more generic findings. Third, the chosen DA scheme has served as the basis for other annotation frameworks including the ICSI MRDA scheme (Shriberg et al. 2004). Different from conventional pragmatic studies, the current corpus-based study will draw on machine-learning techniques from the paradigm of artificial intelligence to identify the easily confusable DA types. More significantly, the study intends to set up a methodology of research in pragmatics that uses statistical probabilities to measure the fuzzy distinctions between DA types as an empirical and, hence, objective basis for subsequent theoretical discussions.

11.1 Corpus Resource

The Switchboard Dialogue Act (SWB-DA) corpus (Jurafsky et al. 1997), which is used in the current study, contains 1155 5-min conversations, orthographically transcribed in about 1.5 million word tokens. There is a large range of different subjects covered in these conversations, from care of the elderly, weather and vacation to gun control, family life and job benefits. The whole corpus has been analysed according to a DA scheme and each unit of analysis is annotated with a DA tag. The minimal unit of analysis for DA annotation in the SWB-DA corpus is called *slash unit* (Meteer and Taylor 1995), defined as 'maximally a sentence, but can be smaller unit' (p. 16), and 'slash-units below the sentence level correspond to those parts of the narrative which are not sentential but which the annotator interprets as complete' (p. 16). The corpus comprises 223,606 slash-units, each marked up with one SWBD DAMSL DA tag. Consider Example [1] below taken from the conversation sw_0002_4330.utt, where qy is the code for 'yes/no question'.

[1]   qy   A.1 utt1:   *{D Well, } {F uh, } does the company you work for test for drugs? /*

SWBD-DAMSL is a version of DAMSL (Dialogue Act Markup in Several Layers; Allen and Core 1997) that was specially adapted for the annotation of a subset of the Switchboard corpus. Altogether a total of 303 different DA tags can be found in the SWB-DA corpus. These tags can be clustered into 59 DA tags with the secondary tags conflated (see Fang et al. 2013). Table 11.1 is a complete list of the DA types, together with their corresponding codes, frequency, relative percentage and cumulative percentage.

First of all, we see that the SWBD-DAMSL taxonomy of DA tags intends to capture and wide range of conversational functions in fairly good detail, including statements, questions and answers as the major subdivisible types along with many other minor entities of interest such as hedges, self-talk, sympathy and offer. Since the corpus produces the absolute frequency of occurrence for each of the DA tags,

Table 11.1 Basic statistics of the SWB-DA Corpus

SWBD-DAMSL			Utterances		
DA types		Codes	Freq.	%	Cum%
1	Statement-non-opinion	sd	84,339	37.72	37.72
2	Acknowledge (backchannel)	b	38,484	17.21	54.93
3	Statement-opinion	sv	31,502	14.09	69.02
4	Abandoned	% -	12,986	5.81	74.82
5	Accept	aa	11,273	5.04	79.87
6	Yes-no-question	qy	4827	2.16	82.02
7	Appreciation	ba	4764	2.13	84.15
8	Non verbal	X	3730	1.67	85.82
9	Uninterpretable	%	3131	1.40	87.22
10	Yes answer	ny	3044	1.36	88.58
11	Conventional-closing	fc	2661	1.19	89.77
12	Statement expanding y/n answer	sd^e, sv^e	2240	1.00	90.78
13	Wh-question	qw	2083	0.93	91.71
14	No answer	mm	1381	0.62	92.33
15	Declarative yes-no-question	qy^d	1377	0.62	92.94
16	Acknowledge-answer	bk	1311	0.59	93.53
17	Hedge	H	1277	0.57	94.10
18	Summarize/reformulate	bf	1096	0.49	94.59
19	Backchannel in question form	bh	1068	0.48	95.07
20	Quoted material	^q	1058	0.47	95.54
21	Affirmative non-yes answer	na	892	0.40	95.94
22	Action-directive	ad	824	0.37	96.31
23	Other	o	820	0.37	96.67

Table 11.1 (continued)

SWBD-DAMSL		Codes	Utterances		
DA types			Freq.	%	Cum%
24	Completion	`2	813	0.36	97.04
25	Repeat-phrase	b^m	702	0.31	97.35
26	Open-question	qo	680	0.30	97.66
27	Rhetorical question	qh	659	0.29	97.95
28	Transcription errors slash units	@	649	0.29	98.24
29	Hold before answer/agreement	^h	577	0.26	98.50
30	Reject	ar	356	0.16	98.66
31	Negative non-no answer	ng	312	0.14	98.80
32	Signal-non-understanding	br, br^m	307	0.14	98.93
33	Other answer	no	298	0.13	99.07
34	Or-question	qr	276	0.12	99.19
35	Or-clause	qrr	230	0.10	99.29
36	Conventional-opening	fp	225	0.10	99.39
37	Dispreferred answer	nd	201	0.09	99.48
38	Exclamation	fe	136	0.06	99.55
39	3rd-party-talk	t3	118	0.05	99.60
40	Downplayer	bd	107	0.05	99.65
41	Self-talk	t1	106	0.05	99.69
42	Tag-question	^g	94	0.04	99.74
43	Declarative Wh-question	qw^d	91	0.04	99.78
44	Apology	fa	79	0.04	99.81
45	Thanking	ft	79	0.04	99.85
46	Offer	co	71	0.03	99.88

Table 11.1 (continued)

SWBD-DAMSL			Utterances		
DA types		Codes	Freq.	%	Cum%
47	Accept-part	aap	61	0.03	99.91
48	Maybe	am	46	0.02	99.93
49	Commit	cc	41	0.02	99.94
50	Double quote	"	27	0.01	99.96
51	Reject-part	arp	25	0.01	99.97
52	Sympathy	by	20	0.01	99.98
53	Correct misspeaking	bc	14	0.01	99.98
54	Explicit-performative	fx	9	0.00	99.99
55	Open-option	oo	9	0.00	99.99
56	No plus expansion	nn^e	7	0.00	99.99
57	Other forward function	fo	6	0.00	100.00
58	You're-welcome	fw	4	0.00	100.00
59	Yes plus expansion	ny^e	3	0.00	100.00
Total			*223,606*	*100.00*	*100.00*

we are able to estimate their relative importance in everyday conversation about
unrestricted subjects. According to Table 11.1, which is sorted in descending order
according to frequency of occurrence, there is an uneven distribution of the 59 DAs,
ranging from 84,339 occurrences of the top-ranking statement-non-opinion to yes-
plus-expansion, which occurred only four times in the whole corpus of 1.5 million
word tokens. See Jurafsky et al. (1997) for a detailed account of definitions and
examples of the DA types. The column % in the table lists the proportion of the DA
tag amongst all the tag occurrences, where we see that the top-ranking statement-
non-opinion accounts for 37.72 % of all the DA tags. The column Cum% lists the
cumulative proportion, where we see that the top 12 DA types alone account for
90.78 % of the whole corpus, suggesting again the uneven occurrence of DA types
in the corpus and hence the disproportional use of communicative functions in conversational discourse.

11.2   Related Research on the SWBD-DAMSL Scheme

The SWB-DA corpus has been mainly used as a test bed for DA modelling and
dialogue understanding, especially in the field of automatic DA annotation and
classification. Previous studies on automated DA modelling have focused on the
extraction of various features from the corpus for lexical, prosodic and acoustic
information (e.g. Stolcke et al. 1998). These past studies are especially interested in testing different machine-learning algorithms with the corpus without much
reference to the issue of confusability of the DA types found within the annotation scheme. Among them only Stolcke et al. (2000) referred back to the SWBD-
DAMSL scheme itself. They tested an integrated approach for DA modelling on
the SWB-DA corpus and the data revealed that 'the only DA types with higher
uncertainty were BACKCHANNELS and AGREEMENTS, which are easily confused with each other without acoustic cues' (Stolcke et al. 2000, p. 6), although
no significant difference is found between labelling with and without acoustic information. Unfortunately, Stolcke et al. (2000) did not further explore why or how
the two DA types (i.e. *backchannel* and *agreement*) are problematic. Most discussions about the SWBD-DAMSL taxonomy come from comparisons with other annotation schemes including the ICSI-MR DA scheme (Popescu-Belis 2004), the
Meeting Recorder DA (MRDA) scheme (Dhillon et al. 2004) and the ADAMACH
DA scheme (Quarteroni et al. 2008). Popescu-Belis (2004) critically reviewed the
SWBD-DAMSL scheme among other DA schemes when proposing the ICSI-MR
DA tagset. Two main issues were brought up. A major issue is that 'the resulting set
of tags seems to label properties that are sometimes remote from dialog functions'
(Popescu-Belis 2004, p. 17). The tag '^q' (meaning 'quotes') was the case in point
since 'the information it encodes is of a very specific nature' which is not really related to dialogue acts per se (Popescu-Belis 2004, p. 17). A second issue is that not
all the DA types were mutually exclusive as supposed. To be more specific, since
each utterance is annotated with only one DA type, the DA types are expected to
be mutually exclusive. However, Popescu-Belis argued that the DA tags belonging

to agreement (e.g. *accept, maybe,* etc.) and those belonging to answer (e.g. *yes answer*) in the SWBD-DAMSL scheme could not be mutually exclusive. However, the study pointed out the potentially problematic issues but stopped short of performing further empirical analysis.

Dhillon et al. (2004) proposed the MRDA scheme derived from the SWBD-DAMSL scheme. In this work, three observations can be made in relation to the SWBD-DAMSL tags: (1) Human annotators cannot distinguish between *statement-opinion* and *statement-non-opinion* in the SWBD-DAMSL scheme. As a result, the two DAs are combined into one (i.e. *statement*) in the MRDA tagset. (2) The DA types of *yes answer* and *agreement* in the SWBD-DAMSL scheme are merged as the DA type of *agreement* in the MRDA tagset. (3) The DA type of *hedge* in the SWBD-DAMSL 'is not included in the MRDA tagset due to lack of use and ambiguity as to what sort of utterance would be labelled as a hedge as opposed to another label' (Dhillon et al. 2004, p. 121). Once again, however, other than the decision made in mapping from the SWBD-DAMSL to MRDA, there is no empirical evidence to show why those particular DA types are especially problematic.

Quarteroni et al. (2008) compared the ADAMACH DA scheme with the SWBD-DAMSL scheme. An apparent difference is that the SWDB-DAMSL greatly outnumbers the ADAMACH scheme in terms of DA types (i.e. 59 vs. 16). The reduction of the DA taxonomy in the ADAMACH DA type echoes the treatment in Dhillon et al. (2004) in the following two ways. First of all, they both performed some kind of merging the SWBD-DAMSL tags into one. For instance, *statement-non-opinion*, *statement-opinion* and *open-option* in the SWBD-DAMSL were merged into *inform* in the ADAMACH. Second, some SWBD-DAMSL DA types are simply dropped in the ADAMACH scheme such as *explicit-performative*.

From the cursory review of some of the past studies, it is clear that the DA taxonomy found in SWB-DA corpus has been taken for granted and used as a basis for computational modelling. Most of the studies so far have largely ignored the other significant use of the SWB-DA corpus, that is, to use it as empirical data to evaluate the confusability of the DA entities included in the taxonomy. Such an evaluation is important. It provides for better insight into the question whether a subjectively designed DA scheme can be scaled up to describe the large number of utterances stored in a sizable corpus. A second related importance is that the evaluation will throw up problematic cases for further consideration and hence for continued enhancement of the interpretive scheme. With the development of computational modelling of linguistic phenomena, the state-of-art NLP techniques such as machine-learning techniques could be used to measure the fuzzy relations between different DA entities and to spot potentially problematic DA types as a basis for further theoretical elaboration. In addition, the existing discussions of the SWBD-DAMSL scheme have shown a similar pattern in handling certain DA types, the conflation of *statement-non-opinion* and *statement-opinion* for example. Again, the descriptions of the rearrangements are not supported with statistical evidence. Therefore, the current study is envisaged to explore the SWBD-DAMSL taxonomy through quantitative and qualitative analyses. More importantly, the current corpus-based study will draw on machine-learning techniques to identify the easily confused DA types for more detailed analysis.

11.3 Methodology

11.3.1 Machine Learning Techniques

As mentioned earlier, the current corpus-based study also draws on machine-learning techniques for the analysis of DA taxonomy. As Witten and Frank (2005, p. 96) pointed out, '[r]epeatedly in machine-learning people have eventually, after an extended struggle, obtained good results using sophisticated learning methods only to discover years later that simple methods such as Naïve Bayes do just as well—or even better'. Therefore, the current study employed the Naïve Bayes Multinomial Classifier, which is available from Waikato Environment for Knowledge Analysis, known as Weka (Hall et al. 2009). The experimental results are obtained from stratified ten-fold cross validation. To be more specific, 'the data is divided randomly into ten parts in which the class is represented in approximately the same proportions as in the full dataset. Each part is held out in turn and the learning scheme trained on the remaining nine tenths' (Witten and Frank 2005, p. 150). The machine-learning techniques in Weka were used because the standard output not only includes precision, recall and F-score (F_1), three indicators for classification performance, but more importantly, it also produces a confusion matrix. The confusion matrix, also known as a contingency table or an error matrix (Stehman 1997), is a specific table that presents visualization of the performance (see Sect. 11.4 for more details), which makes it easy to see if one DA type has been mislabelled as other types.

11.3.2 Data Preprocessing

In a machine-learning task, different types of features can be used to relate linguistic phenomena to a certain class. For example, lexical information, parts of speech and syntactic structures can be used to identify correlations between an utterance and a communicative function. Here, we are concerned with the recognition of utterances as belonging to a certain DA entity in the SWBD-DAMSL taxonomy. As Král and Cerisara (2010, p. 231) have pointed out, 'the DA of an utterance can be partly deduced from the lists of words that form this utterance' and '[l]exical information is typically captured by words unigrams'. The unigrams of each DA type in the SWBD-DAMSL scheme were used as features and extracted for automatic clustering according to DA types. Since there is an uneven distribution of DA types across the corpus (cf. Table 11.1), the top 15 DA types were chosen for the current study to ensure adequate cases. Furthermore, DA types that do not relate to dialogue acts, such as *abandoned*, *double labels* and *uninterpretable*, were removed from the list.

We thus derive Table 11.2 for the revised list of top 15 SWBD-DAMSL DA types. As can be noted, the revised list accounts for 85.72 % of the SWB-DA corpus with a cumulative proportion of 93.19 % of the whole corpus in terms of tokens.

Since the current study would consider lexical unigram as the classification feature, the top 15 DA types may well be adequate for the experiment.

11.3.3   Research Questions

As can be noted in Table 11.2, among the final list of top 15 DAs, the most discussed pair (i.e. *statement-non-opinion* and *statement-opinion*) and the often unlabelled DA type *hedge* are included. Given the different decisions on the choice of DA types in previous studies, the current study attempts to explore the empirical evidence behind those decisions. In particular, with the top 15 DA types in the SWBD-DAMSL scheme, we expect to answer the following three research questions:

- Is *hedge* a difficult function to identify? In what way it may cause confusions? More specifically, how often is it confused with other functions? Or which function is most likely to be mixed up with *hedge*?
- How different is *statement-non-opinion* from *statement-opinion*? Is it plausible to keep or ignore the distinction between these two DA types?
- Which DA would be the most distinctive to be identified?

11.4   Classification Results

The automatic classification of the top 15 SWBD-DAMSL DA types in Table 11.2 was then performed with ten-fold cross validation and the results evaluated in terms of precision, recall and F-score (F_l). See Table 11.3 for the results, where the DA types are arranged according to the F-score in descending order.

Table 11.3 presents the standard output of classification performance, in which *precision* represents the number of correct labelling divided by the number of all returned labelling results for a certain DA type, *recall* refers to the number of correct labelling divided by the number of results that should have been returned, and *F-score* is the weighted harmonic mean of precision and recall. It should also be mentioned that a precision value does not indicate how many instances of the given DA type has not been labelled correctly, whereas the recall value does not indicate how many other DA types have been incorrectly labelled as the given DA. Therefore, the interpretation of mere precision value or recall value cannot show the true picture of the performance, and that is where F-score comes in. The higher the F-score is, the better the classification result.

According to Table 11.3, the DA type of *acknowledge (backchannel)* achieved the best performance, with the highest F-score of 0.846. The value of precision (i.e. 0.751) shows that about 25 % of the DAs labelled as *acknowledge (backchannel)* belong to other DA types, and the value of recall (i.e. 0.967) shows that a slightly over 96 % of all the DAs functioning as *acknowledge (backchannel)* have

Table 11.2 Revised list of top 15 SWBD-DAMSL types

SWBD-DAMSL DA types	Utterances			Tokens		
	Freq	%	Cum%	Freq	%	Cum%
Statement-non-opinion	84,339	37.72	37.72	872,759	57.16	57.16
Acknowledge (backchannel)	38,484	17.21	54.93	40,951	2.68	59.84
Statement-opinion	31,502	14.09	69.02	364,791	23.89	83.73
Accept	11,273	5.04	74.06	21,186	1.39	85.12
Yes-no-question	4827	2.16	76.22	37,191	2.44	87.56
Appreciation	4764	2.13	78.35	14,366	0.94	88.50
Yes answer	3044	1.36	79.71	3537	0.23	88.73
Conventional-closing	2661	1.19	80.90	9442	0.62	89.35
Statement expanding y/n answer	2240	1.00	81.90	15,549	1.02	90.37
Wh-question	2083	0.93	82.83	14,953	0.98	91.35
No answer	1381	0.62	83.45	1649	0.11	91.46
Declarative yes-no-question	1377	0.62	84.07	10,908	0.71	92.17
Acknowledge-answer	1311	0.59	84.66	2048	0.13	92.30
Hedge	1277	0.57	85.23	5920	0.39	92.69
Summarize/reformulate	1096	0.49	85.72	7609	0.50	93.19
Total	191,659	85.72	85.72	1,422,859	93.19	93.19

Table 11.3 Results from automatic classification

SWBD-DAMSL DA types	Precision	Recall	F-score
Acknowledge (backchannel)	0.751	0.967	0.846
Statement-non-opinion	0.732	0.857	0.790
Appreciation	0.856	0.530	0.654
Statement-opinion	0.548	0.567	0.557
Conventional-closing	0.984	0.371	0.539
Accept	0.555	0.244	0.339
Wh-question	0.864	0.165	0.277
Yes-no-question	0.658	0.170	0.270
Hedge	0.375	0.005	0.009
No answer	0.357	0.004	0.007
Yes answer	0.087	0.001	0.001
Statement expanding y/n answer	0.016	0.000	0.001
Declarative yes-no-question	0.000	0.000	0.000
Acknowledge-answer	0.000	0.000	0.000
Summarize/reformulate	0.000	0.000	0.000
Weighted avg.	0.663	0.704	0.663

been correctly identified. Meanwhile, three DA types, namely, *declarative yes-no-question, acknowledge-answer, summarize/reformulate,* can be considered to be the most difficult to identify since the values of all the indicators are zero.

It can also be seen in Table 11.3 that the DA type of *statement-non-opinion* achieved the second best performance, with an *F*-score of 0.790, almost 25 % higher than the performance of *statement-opinion* (i.e. 0.557), indicating that *statement-non-opinion* could be easier to identify than *statement-opinion*. The DA type of *hedge* ranks No. 9 with an *F*-score as low as 0.009.

So far the classification results in Table 11.3 pinpoint the most distinctive DA type among the top 15, that is, *acknowledge (backchannel)*, but they could not tell in what way *statement-non-opinion* and *statement-opinion* are confused or what DA types are often confused with *hedge*.

Fortunately, the confusion matrix offers a more detailed quantitative description (see Fig. 11.1). To be more specific, each column of the matrix lists the instances labelled as a predicted DA type, while each row shows how the instances in a known DA type have been labelled. Take *statement-non-opinion* for example. According to second row, 72,294 instances have been correctly labelled, accounting for 85.7% of the 84,339 instances, which is the same as the recall value. As for the remaining 12,045 instances, for instance, 286 instances have been incorrectly labelled as *acknowledge (backchannel)* and 11,127 instances as *statement-opinion*. In addition, according to the first column, it can be noted that 1039 instances functioning as *acknowledge (backchannel)* has been incorrectly classified as *statement-non-opinion*, and that 13,075 instances functioning as *statement-opinion* have been classified as *statement-non-opinion* instead.

To sum up, the DA type of *acknowledge (backchannel)* is identified as the most distinctive type, and the confusion matrix provides informative data for the quantitative analysis as being discussed in the next section.

11.5   Qualitative Analysis

11.5.1   Hedge

In the SWBD-DAMSL scheme (Jurafsky et al. 1997, p. 57), *hedge* (h) is used when the speaker 'diminish the confidence or certainty with which she/he makes a statement or answers a question'. For example,

[2]	sd	B.6 utt1: I think it usually does. /
	ad	B.6 utt2: You might try, {F uh, } /
	h	**B.6 utt3: I don't know, /**
	ad	B.6 utt4: hold it down a little longer, /

(Conversation sw_0001_4325.utt)

	a	b	c	d	e	f	g	h	i	j	k	l	m	n	o	Classified as
a	72294	286	11127	199	210	100	12	5	56	29	5	6	0	9	1	a = statement-non-opinion
b	1039	37233	23	160	2	26	0	1	0	0	0	0	0	0	0	b = acknowledge (backchannel)
c	13075	78	17874	181	67	209	2	4	2	6	1	2	0	1	0	c = statement-opinion
d	1424	6568	494	2754	4	24	4	1	0	0	0	0	0	0	0	d = accept
e	2797	70	1052	53	819	19	0	1	1	14	1	0	0	0	0	e = yes-no-question
f	835	413	571	414	3	2524	2	1	0	1	0	0	0	0	0	f = appreciation
g	10	2995	0	37	0	0	2	1	0	0	0	0	0	0	0	g = yes answer
h	913	570	145	19	3	23	0	988	0	0	0	0	0	0	0	h = conventional-closing
i	1930	11	270	18	5	2	1	0	1	2	0	0	0	0	0	i = statement expanding y/n answer
j	1274	8	367	3	87	1	0	0	0	343	0	0	0	0	0	j = wh-question
k	134	135	2	2	0	2	0	0	0	0	5	0	0	0	0	k = no answer
l	1027	28	283	2	21	11	0	1	2	0	2	0	0	0	0	l = declarative yes-no-question
m	154	1142	1	10	1	3	0	0	0	0	0	0	0	0	0	m = acknowledge-answer
n	1182	3	84	2	0	0	0	0	0	0	0	0	0	6	0	n = hedge
o	683	25	344	11	23	6	0	2	0	2	0	0	0	0	0	o = summarize/reformulate

Fig. 11.1 Confusion matrix

In this excerpt, B was telling A how to make the recorder work. Since B was not sure about the exact situation on the other side of the phone, a hedge was used in B.6_utt3 to show the lack of certainty. It seems quite clear for a human annotator to mark out such a pragmatic phenomenon—*hedge*.

However, we notice that the clearly defined definition is not easy to follow as we expected. For example, a conflict between the annotation guidelines and the actual mark-up has been spotted. The only example given in the manual shows that *hedge* could occur before a statement as presented in Example [3].

[3]   br   A.19 utt1: # The accuracy? # /
         h   *A.19 utt2: I don't know. /*
         h   *A.19 utt3: I don't know. /*
         sd   A.19 utt4: {C But, } I know there are a lot of things that can in-
                   fluence them /
         sv   A.19 utt5: {C and } I think that a person deserves a second
                   chance with it or something because most things will stay in
                   your system for a long time. /

As can be noted, both utterances A.19_utt2 and A.19_utt3 in the manual are annotated as *hedge*, whereas in actual marking of the corpus both turned out to be annotated as *other answers* (no). See Example [4].

[4]   qy   B.18 utt2: [Are they, + {E I mean, } is there] a # margin of
                   error? # /
         br   A.19 utt1: # The accuracy? # /
         no   *A.19 utt2: I don't know. /*
         no^r   *A.19 utt3: I don't know. /*
         sd   A.19 utt4: {C But, } I know there are a lot of things that can in-
                   fluence them /
         sv   A.19 utt5: {C and } I think that a person deserves a second
                   chance with it or something because most things will stay in
                   your system for a long time. /
                                                    (Conversation sw_0516_4618.utt)

We include one more preceding utterance here in this excerpt. From the context, it is not difficult to see that A really did not know if there is a margin of error or how accurate it is, a question raised by B, although she could name some factors that would cause errors (as said in A.19_utt4). This case shows that although *hedge* may be used to answer questions, but not all the answers with the tokens of 'I don't know' are hedges, which give rise to confusion as to the correct annotation.

According to Jurafsky et al. (1997), the most commonly used *hedge* in the corpus is standing-free 'I don't know'. As in Example [2], utterance B.6 utt3 is coded as h (*hedge*), and the tokens 'I don't know' is segmented as a single slash unit. The data shows that among the 1277 utterances that are annotated as *hedge* (cf. Table 11.1), 730 utterances are single slash units of 'I don't know' (with the discourse markers ignored), which accounts for 57.17% of the total number of hedges in the corpus. Therefore, a close look at those prototype hedges (i.e. 'I don't know') would reveal the issues of ambiguity. We will next examine this kind of hedges from two aspects: (1) when *hedge* is used to answer a question and (2) when *hedge* is used to make a statement.

In addition, the confusion matrix in the current study (see Fig. 11.1) also shows that, based on the lexical features, about 92.56% of hedges in the corpus have been classified as *statement-non-opinion*, which directs us to examine how *hedge* and *statement-non-opinion* have been mixed up in the two aspects.

Issue 1: *Hedge* used to answer a question According to the manual, if the speaker said 'I don't know' together with some second utterance to 'indicate knowledge', then 'I don't know' is annotated as *hedge* (Jurafsky et al. 1997, p. 58). See Examples [5] and [6] where *hedge* is used to answer a yes-no question and a Wh-question respectively.

[5] qy   A.15 utt6: do you know? /
     qy   A.15 utt7: Are there some set guidelines, like only under these circumstances? /
     h   ***B.16 utt1: I don't know.*** /
     sv   B.16 utt2: I believe it's, {F uh, } at the discretion of the judge or jury. /

                                          (Conversation sw_0826_2981.utt)

[6] sd   B.15 utt7: I don't have a lot of crafty type things I do. /
     b   A.16 utt1: Uh-huh. /
     qw   B.17 utt1: {C But, } {F uh, } <<pause>> what are some other things you enjoy? /
     h   ***A.18 utt1: I don't know.*** /
     sd   A.18 utt2: [My, + my] father is [in the, + in the] antique business. /

                                          (Conversation sw_1049_2889.utt)

In Example [5], A was asking B whether the state of Texas has certain restrictions on capital punishment. 'I don't know' in B.16_utt1 is annotated as *hedge* because B was trying to diminish the certainty of his own opinion expressed in B.16_utt2. The topic in Example [6] is HOBBIES AND CRAFTS. B was asking A what other things A would do besides playing the trumpet or cutting out things with his daughter. A answered by saying 'I don't know' and then started to talked about his father's antique business and how he once repaired some stuff there. Since the tokens of 'I don't know' are followed by further explanation, the utterance is annotated as *hedge*.

With the help of the confusion matrix, it would be easier to identify that the tokens of 'I don't know' in similar situations, nevertheless, have been annotated as *statement-non-opinion* (sd). See Examples [7], [8] and [9].

[7]   qw   B.14 utt1: {D Now, } how long does it take for your contribu-
             tion to vest? /
      sd   *A.15 utt1: {D God, } I don't know. /*
      sv   A.15 utt2: <laughter> It's probably a long time <laughter>. /
      sd   A.15 utt3: I'm sure it's not till {D like } twenty-five years, thirty
             years. /
                                          (Conversation sw_0007_4171.utt)

[8]   qo^t   A.1 utt1: {D Well, } how did you like that topic? /
      sd   *B.2 utt1: {F Uh, } I don't know, /*
      sd^t   B.2 utt2: I've got mixed feelings about the topic. /
      qy   @A.3 utt1: Do you? /
                                          (Conversation sw_0187_3242.utt)

[9]   qw   B.66 utt2: <<Back to phone>> [wh-, + where] do they get it?
             <Laughter>. /
      sd   *A.67 utt1: {D Well, } I don't know, /*
      sv   A.67 utt2: I guess they don't have it at home, /
                                          (Conversation sw_0226_3081.utt)

In Example [7], A and B were talking about job benefits. A just told B that the retirement plan in his company was not bad because the company offered a match-up to his own amount. Then to answer B's question in B.14_utt1, A said 'I don't know' and then expressed his own guess that it would be a long time before he could get the money back. The tokens of 'I don't know' indicate a sense of uncertainty, and yet it was annotated as a statement.

In Example [8], the topic is DRUG TESTING and the two speakers were expected to discuss how they felt about companies testing employees on drug. When A asked B about her opinion, B answered 'I don't know' and then admitted that she had mixed feelings. The tokens of 'I don't know' apparently suggest a certain degree of uncertainty or vagueness.

In Example [9], the topic is RECIPES/FOOD/COOKING. A just told B that when she took some guacamole salad she made to a pool party, her friends said they never made guacamole. To answer B's question in B.66_utt12, A first said 'I don't know' and then made a guess. Again, here the tokens of 'I don't know' seem to have a similar function as that in Example [5].

As can be noticed here, the function of the tokens of 'I don't know' in Examples [7]–[9] is in line with the definition of *hedge* in the manual, and yet in all the three cases they are annotated as *statement-non-opinion*. This observation reveals that human annotators are not always consistent in how to annotate the two DA types (i.e. *hedge* and *statement-non-opinion*).

Issue 2: *Hedge* used to make a statement   When *hedge* is used in making a statement, it is expected to 'soften utterances by signalling imprecision and noncommitment' (Behnam and Khaliliaqdam 2012, p. 76). For example,

[10]   sv   A.89 utt2: {C but, } I know that, {D you know, } the further we
                 go from Adam the worse the food is for you, /

        sv   A.89 utt3: {C but } God still somehow makes us all be able to
                 still live. /

        sv   A.89 utt4: I think it's a miracle we're all still alive after so many
                 generations, /

        sd   A.89 utt5: {D well } the last couple of processed foods, - /

        h   ***A.89 utt6: {D you know, } {E I mean, } {C but, } <lipsmack> I
                 don't know. /***

                                                    (Conversation sw_0815_2354.utt)

In Example [10], A made some comments on the food (from A.89_utt2 to A.89_utt4) and then added a hedge (i.e. A.89_utt6) to diminish the certainty of his statements.

However, we also observed some cases where the single slash-unit 'I don't know' used in making statements has been mistakenly annotated as *statement-non-opinion*. See Examples [11]–[13].

[11]   sd   B.10 utt1: -- I'm not sure if we know what to do in terms of cur-
                 ing some who has already gotten polio. /

        sd   A.11 utt1: {D Well, } that might be the difference. /

        sd   ***A.11 utt2: I don't know. /***

                                                    (Conversation sw_0032_4333.utt)

In this excerpt, A and B were talking about the cure for polio. Earlier A told B that he believed that the cure for polio was founded, and then B was wondering about the people who had already gotten the disease. A admitted that there might be a difference and also added the tokens of 'I don't know' to further soften the statement in A.11_utt1.

[12]   sd   A.71 utt1: -- {C and then } they check you out and make sure
                you don't have a record {D you know } and things like that. /
        sd   A.71 utt2: I think that's a pretty good idea. /
        %   A.71 utt3: {F Uh, } {C and } that's, - /

In this excerpt, A was describing the gun control in Florida, and he believed that the
checking is 'pretty good idea' (in A.71_utt2). After saying that, B tried to soften the
assertion by adding 'I don't know' and also revised the statement from 'pretty good
idea' (in A.71_utt2) to 'not a bad idea' (in A.71_utt5). Apparently, the tokens of 'I
don't know' indicate that B was trying to diminish the confidence, in the way that a
hedge works rather than a statement-non-opinion.

sd   ***A.71 utt4: I don't know, /***
sv   A.71 utt5: that's not a bad idea, /
                                    (Conversation sw_0630_4080.utt

In this excerpt, the topic is SPACE FLIGHT AND EXPLORATION, and A thought
we would gain a lot from space flight and exploration. In A.47_utt1, he made it clear
that it was his personal opinion, and then added 'I don't know' with laughter. He
said, 'I don't know, but I think…'. The tokens of 'I don't know' in both utterances
in this turn do have an effect of softening A's personal opinion.
    In addition to being a single slash-unit, the tokens of 'I don't know' can also be
followed by objective clauses. We observed cases where such a pattern is annotated
either as *hedge* or as *statement-non-opinion*. See the following four examples.

[13]   sv   A.43 utt1: Any of that stuff from the Jetsons, from that cartoon,
                that you would never imagine would [come, + become] possi-
                ble, and now [you, + we] have a lot of those, /
        %   A.43 utt2: {D so, }-/
        b   B.44 utt1: Uh-huh./
        sv   A.45 utt1: {C So } you never know [what, + what] may occur,
                /
        sd   A.45 utt2: {C but } --
        b   B.46 utt1: Yeah. /
        +/sd   A.47 utt1: -- as far as me seeing it, {D you know, }
        x   B.48 utt1: <Laughter>.
        +/sd   ***A.49 utt1: I don't know <laughter>. /***
        sd   ***A.49 utt2: I don't know, /***
        sv   A.49 utt3: {C but } I think it's real vital important for the future,
                {D you know } --
        b   B.50 utt1: Uh-huh. /
                                    (Conversation sw_0096_3580.utt)

[14]   sd   A.85 utt5: {C And, } {F um, } I'm pretty sure I saw, yeah, stuff
                in Ohio and [Indi-, + Indiana] about it and [Pennsylvania, +
                maybe Pennsylvania,] /

        sd   A.85 utt6: I don't remember for sure now. /

        h   ***B.86 utt1: {C And } I don't know about your part of the coun-
                try, /***

        sd   B.86 utt2: {C but, } {F uh, } down here in the last, {F oh, } year
                plus, {A [I, + it] was [las-, + beginning with last] year's Earth
                Day }--

                                            (Conversation sw_0148_2604.utt)

In Example [14], the two speakers were talking about environmental concerns.
When B tried to describe the situation in her place, she used hedge (in B.86_utt1)
to be modest about her statement (in B.86_utt2). In Example [15], the two speakers were talking about the actor Dustin Hoffman. When B claimed that she thought
Dustin Hoffman played the character so well that she believed it (in B.85_utt1),
she continued to say that it was only a personal opinion and that it may not be true
for anyone else (in B.85_utt2). Although B.85_utt2 is annotated as *statement-non-
opinion* (sd), it is actually a hedge (h).

[15]   sd   A.82 utt1: He will do that, to research it and to be able to mimic
                a person, {F uh, } {F uh, } with the kinds of problems that he
                had. /

        ^2   B.83 utt1: And to make it believable. /

        aa   A.84 utt1: Yes. /

        sd   B.85 utt1: {E I mean } [I was, + I was] believing it, /

        sd   ***B.85 utt2: I don't know about any body else /***

        sv   B.85 utt3: {C but } [I was, + it was] great. /

                                            (Conversation sw_0084_2109.utt)

[16]   sd   B.34 utt5: some people are really afraid to recycle the fuel be-
                cause they're afraid it could become, {F uh, } bomb quality.
                <sigh> /

        sv   B.34 utt6: {C But, } that's the only sensible thing to do, is recy-
                cle and reuse the fuel and not store it down in the ground. As
                far as I'm concerned, where it could eventually, perhaps, there's
                some problem, {F uh, } pollute the groundwater. /

        h   ***B.34 utt7: {C So, } I don't know what the answer is. /***

        sv   B.34 utt8: The best answer, of course, would be solar or, {F uh,
                } <static> fusion, or something clean <laughter>. /

                                            (Conversation sw_0230_3148.utt)

[17]   +/sv   B.60 utt1: -- in the future, I think, maybe to help in some ways.
                /
        sd   B.60 utt2: It may not in all ways. /
        sd   B.60 utt3: Maybe they'll come up with fusion. <Lipsmack> {D
                You know, } [con-, + be able to control] it. /
        sd   ***B.60 utt4: I don't know how long that'll take, /***
        sv   B.60 utt5: {C but, } <laughter> one of these days, - /
        sv   B.60 utt6: {C because } that's perfectly clean. /
                                            (Conversation sw_0230_3148.utt)

The above examples show that hedges are very often mixed up with statement-non-opinions, and even the human annotators are not consistent when identify what a hedge is.

Moreover, we have also noticed an issue with the segment of slash units. See the following example.

[18]   %   B.198 utt2: [[I, + I] was just, + {D you know, } it just seems
                ] -/
        sd(^q)^t B.198 utt3: [like I, + as I] said when I heard [the, +] what
                the subject was, I thought {F oh, } gosh I haven't thought
                about, {F uh, } what I went through at that other house in so
                long. /
        sd   B.198 utt4: I've been so busy. /
        h   ***B.198 utt5: {C But, } {F uh, } I don't know /***
        sd   B.198 utt6: *of everything that I did*, I guess I enjoyed proba-
                bly wallpapering the most /
        sd   B.198 utt7: {C and } I thought that would be the hardest thing
                to do. /
                                            (Conversation sw_0117_2837.utt)

In the excerpt, it is not difficult to notice that 'I don't know' in B.198_utt5 is not an independent sentence. Instead, it should be 'I don't know of...'.

To sum up, the analysis did confirm what the confusion matrix has revealed, that is, *hedge* and *statements-non-opinion* are often confused. The discussed examples show that even with the manual, it is not as easy for a human annotator to distinguish *hedge* from *statement-non-opinion* as we expected. To some extent, the corpus evidence support the chosen made by previous researchers in that when a DA type is difficult for human annotators to identify it may not be practical for the machine to automatically identify or to build a model for dialogue systems.

11.5.2   *Statement-non-Opinion Vs. Statement-Opinion*

The second case study is about the distinction between *statement-non-opinion* and *statement-opinion*. According to the confusion matrix, 11,127 instances (or 13.19%) of *statement-non-opinion* have been incorrectly identified as *statement-opinion*, while 41.5% of *statement-opinion* has been mistakenly labelled as *statement-non-opinion*. The results do call for a closer look at the definition of the two DA types and their annotations.

According to the SWBD-DAMSL manual, pragmatically speaking, statements in the corpus have been divided into two mutually exclusive categories, namely, *statement-non-opinion* (sd) and *statement-opinion* (sv). *Statement-non-opinion* includes three sub-types:

- Descriptive
- Narrative
- Personal statements

Statement-opinion is defined to refer to 'other-directed opinion statements'. It can be noticed here that the definitions do give rise to issues such as how to determine a personal statement, and how to tell the difference between the fuzzy sub-type 3) of *statement-non-opinion* and *statement-opinion*.

The manual explains that the subtle difference can be observed by determining whether the topic is personal or general to the speaker. In other words, if the speaker is expert on the statement, such a statement should be marked as *statement-non-opinion* (sd); otherwise, it is *statement-opinion* (sv). For example, in Example [18], speaker A is talking about his/her opinion on war, a topic anyone may be 'expert' on. As a result, the two utterances are coded as *statement-opinion* (sv).

[19]   sv   A.25 utt8: {C and } I believe that the real warfare is not with Saddam Hussein, or the North Vietnamese, /
       sv   A.25 utt9: {C but } it's in spiritual kingdoms, and that the real warfare is done, {D you know, } in your prayer closet, on your knees.

The sample provided in the manual seems to suggest that judging whether a topic is general could be helpful for human annotators to differentiate *statement-non-opinion* from *statement-opinion*. However, contradictory cases have been found in the actual annotations. See example [20].

[20]   sv   B.32 utt2: I guess that's a problem too for people. Wait lists and
                all. /
        b   A.33 utt1: Yeah, /
        h   A.33 utt2: # I guess. # /
        %   B.34 utt1: # That, {F uh, } - /
        sv   B.34 utt2: # you can't always get in when you want too /
        sd   ***B.34 utt3: {C and } of course, you can't just sit around and
                wait. /***
        aa   A.35 utt1: Right. /

                                        (Conversation sw_0005_4646.utt)

Topic in this extract is CARE OF THE ELDERLY. Both speakers were not old
people, and they were discussing how to take care of the elderly and about nursing
homes. Therefore, according to the manual, their statements should be considered
as *statement-opinion*. From the context, we may notice that both B.34_utt2 and
B.34_utt3 were talking about the difficulty old people would encounter. 'You' in
both utterances clearly refers to impersonal 'you', and hypothetically, both would
serve the same function in the communication. However, B.34_utt2 is annotated as
statement-opinion while B.34_utt3 is annotated as *statement-non-opinion*, which is
not consistent with the coding manual. The example indicates that to know that a
topic is general may not result in the right annotation.

Another tricky issue coming from the definition is how to determine what a personal statement is. See the following two examples from the corpus.

[21]   sv   A.23 utt3: {C and } [I, + I] know that any statement in abso-
                luteness is not necessarily true, {F uh, } /
        sv   A.23 utt4: only the guns were in the hands of the criminals, /
        %   A.23 utt5: {C but } how many times, - /
        sv   ***A.23 utt6: I guess I have never heard of [a, + a] robbery be-
                ing foiled or spoiled because the person who's being robbed
                had a gun. /***

                                        (Conversation sw_0275_2540.utt)

[22]   sd   B.26 utt3: I used to have a (( )) Chevy. /
        b   A.27 utt1: # Uh-huh. # /
        sd   B.28 utt1: # With a # three fifty in it. /
        b   A.29 utt1: Yeah. /
        sd   B.30 utt1: {C And, } {F uh, } I really liked working on it. {F
                Uh, } cause it was pretty easy too. /
        sd   B.30 utt2: It was about a nineteen seventy. /
        sd   B.30 utt3: {C So } I'm kind of, {F uh, } biased in that /
        sv   ***B.30 utt4: {C and, } {D you know, } I want a car that I can
                work on because I think it just costs too much even to get the
                oil changed anymore. /***

                                        (Conversation sw_0010_4356.utt)

Example [21] is about GUN CONTROL. In the last utterance (A.23_utt6), A was talking about his own experience, and yet it is annotated as *statement-opinion*. The topic in Example [22] is BUYING A CAR and the two speakers were talking about what kind of car they may buy next. In the last utterance (B.30_utt4), B was explaining his own criteria for his next car, which he himself is expected to be the 'expert' on. Again, contrary to the manual, the utterance is annotated as *statement-opinion* instead.

In addition, some personal statements do possess strong opinions, which may present challenges to the definition of 'personal statement' and 'other-directed opinion'. See the following example, and again the topic is BUYING A CAR.

[23]   sd   B.7 utt3: I just bought mine, {F uh, } /
       sd   B.7 utt4: it will be a year in August. /
       b   A.8 utt1: Yeah. /
       sd   B.9 utt1: I love it though. /
       sd   ***B.9 utt2: I love Hondas. /***
                                              (Conversation sw_0173_25 48.utt)

As can be seen in Example [23], utterance B.9_utt2 shows that B not only likes his car but has special feelings for products of the brand name 'Honda', which suggests a very strong opinion. Examples like this would make people to wonder whether the definition of *statement-non-opinion* in the SWBD-DAMSL scheme is reasonable.

Still, another issue is that in daily conversation, people would often relate to their personal experience when discussing a general topic. For instance, in Example [24], the topic is about TAXES and speaker B was speaking of his own experience in Massachusetts, which he would be 'expert' on.

[24]   sd   B.28 utt4: {C and, } {F uh, } I lived in Massachusetts for a while
                   /
       sd   B.28 utt5: {C and, } {F uh, } when Dukakis vetoed certain
                   things, there was a big uproar and wasn't necessarily so popular.
                   /
       b   A.29 utt1: Yeah, /
       sv   A.29 utt2: {C but } Massachusetts [wasn't, + {A when Dukakis
                   was there, anyway, } wasn't] in that great shape financially. /
       %   B.30 utt1: D-, - /
       sv   B.30 utt2: at least at the end. /
       b   A.31 utt1: Uh-huh. /
       h   A.31 utt2: {E I mean, } I don't know, /
       %   A.31 utt3: I, -/
       b   B.32 utt1: Yeah, /
       sv   ***B.32 utt2: [[i-, + i-,] + they] were very good at first, /***
       sv   ***B.32 utt3: they were in very good financials at first /***
       sv   ***B.32 utt4: {C and, } {F uh, } that's part of the reason he be-***
                   came a nominee is because things went so well. /
                                              (Conversation sw_0032_4333.utt)

The first two utterances in this extract (B.28_utt4 and B.28_utt5) show that B was talking about the situation of Massachusetts from his own experience since he once lived there. Later on in the turns from B.32_utt2 to B.32_utt4, he continued to talk about the situation there. According to the manual, given the fact that he lived there during that specific time (i.e. when Dukakis was there), what he said would be considered as personal statements, which should be coded as *statement-non-opinion*. Nevertheless, the actual annotation is *statements-opinion* instead.

Another example is with the topic WOMEN'S ROLE. The two speakers in Example [25] were discussing the changes in the roles of women in American society over the past generation or two.

[25]	qo	B.170 utt1: How do you feel your career has gone? /
	sd	A.171 utt1: [I don't, + I don't] feel for the most part that I've been discriminated against. /
	bh	B.172 utt1: You don't. /
	ba	B.172 utt2: That's good. /
	nn	A.173 utt1: No. /
	sd^e	A.173 utt2: I was a department chairman. /
	sd	A.173 utt3: [I, + {C but } I] don't like administration. /
	bk	B.174 utt1: Oh. /
	sv	*A.175 utt1: {D So } then I'm, {F uh, } {F uh, } probably a poor example, although, {D you know, } I was an administrator and could still be I suppose. /*

(Conversation `sw_0904_2767.utt`)

To sum up, the examples discussed in this subsection show that even with the definitions and examples given in the manual, human annotators might still fail to follow the coding rules. The inconsistent annotations in the corpus would make people to wonder whether the definition of *statement-non-opinion* in the SWBD-DAMSL scheme is reasonable and whether the distinction made between *statement-non-opinion* and *statement-opinion* is reasonable. When human annotators find hard to follow, how well could one expect automatic dialogue systems to work.

11.5.3 Acknowledge (Backchannel)

As mentioned earlier, the experimental results suggest that *acknowledge (backchannel)* (b) is comparatively easier to identify due to its highest *F*-score (0.846). The results also show that the recall is as high as 96.7%, suggesting that 96.7% of backchannels can be identified. However, the precision is only 75.1%, indicating that there are some 'noises' in the retrievals. In other words, some utterances functioning as other DA types have been mistakenly retrieved as backchannels. With the help of the confusion matrix, the top three noise-types can be identified, namely, *yes answer* (error rate of 98.39 %), *acknowledge-answer* (error rate of 87.11 %), and *accept* (error rate of 58.26 %). Next, a brief introduction of *acknowledge (backchannel)* will be made before the discussion of the three problematic DA pairs.

In the SWB-DA Corpus, *acknowledge (backchannel)* is annotated for two aspects: Firstly, the basic 'b' is a continuer, according to the manual (p. 42), which means that the utterance 'performs primarily a function of encouraging the teller to continue' (Drummond and Hopper 1993, p. 163). Therefore, the utterance is 'short, on topic, and the floor shifts quickly and unequivocally back to prior speaker' (Drummond and Hopper 1993, p. 170). See Example [26].

[26]   sv   B.50 utt2: [{C and } you, + {C and } you] don't always even
                know if [it's, + it's] going to be the right place or not. /
        b   *A.51 utt1: Uh-huh. /*
        sv   B.52 utt1: Anything, I guess, could happen. /
        b   *A.53 utt1: Uh-huh. /*
        qy^d   B.54 utt1: [{C Because } after, + I guess after] he, {D you
                know, } gets to a certain age she's going to have to take him to a
                day care. /

                                            (Conversation sw_0001_4325.utt)

As can be seen in Example [26], a continuer merely takes 'the turn, not the floor' (Drummond and Hopper 1993, p. 159). Therefore, the first type is also called 'free-standing acknowledgement' (Drummond and Hopper 1993, p. 167).

Secondly, after the acknowledgement, the speaker still holds the floor, and may go on with a related topic. For instance,

[27]   sd   B.66 utt1: I think she has problems with that, too. /
        b   *A.67 utt1: Uh-huh. /*
        qy   *A.67 utt2: {D Well, } when you have kids, will you work? /*
        qy   *A.67 utt3: Do you --*
        no   B.68 utt1: I don't know -- /
                                            (Conversation sw_0001_4325.utt)

In this excerpt, the topic is CHILD CARE. A showed her understanding in A.67_ utt1, and then moved on to a related but new topic when she asked what B would do when having kids.

In the SWB-DA Corpus, when ignoring the discourse markers and fillers, the most commonly used ten utterances for *acknowledge (backchannel)* account for over 96 % of all the backchannels. See Table 11.4.

Table 11.4 Top ten utterances functioning as acknowledge (backchannel)

	Utterance	Freq.	%
1	Uh-huh	13,963	38.55
2	Yeah	13,486	37.23
3	Right	3408	9.41
4	Oh	1206	3.33
5	Okay	773	2.13
6	Yes	667	1.84
7	Huh	429	1.18
8	Sure	359	0.99
9	Really	346	0.96
10	Huh-uh	277	0.76
Total		34,914	96.39

Acknowledge (Backchannel) Vs. Yes Answer According to the manual (Jurafsky et al. 1997, p. 51), *yes answer* (ny) is used to code utterances that only contains 'yes', 'yeah', 'yep', 'uh-huh' and other variations of 'yes', with filled pauses and discourse markers ignored.

For example:

[28]   qy   B.28 utt2: Do they have a death penalty in California?<child_
                talking>. /
       ny   *A.29 utt1: Yes. /*

Table 11.5 Top three utterances functioning as yes answer

	Utterance	Freq	%
1	Yeah	1948	63.99
2	Yes	620	20.37
3	Uh-huh	420	13.80
Total		2988	98.16

In the corpus, the top three utterances of *yes answer* (ny) are summarized in Table 11.5.

As can be noted in the table, the top three utterances account for 98.16% of the total number of utterances in *yes answer*. It can also be noted that there are only three unique tokens (i.e. yeah, uh-huh, yes), with the discourse marker (i.e. oh) ignored. Furthermore, the three unique tokens also occur frequently in the DA type of *acknowledge (backchannel)*, accounting for 77.62%. Therefore, it is understand-able that based solely on the unigram feature, it would be difficult for the classifier to learn a distinctive feature/pattern when the majority of features overlap with another DA type. However, such an ambiguity can be avoided when the previous utterance is considered.

Acknowledge (Backchannel) Vs. Acknowledge-Answer Jurafsky et al. (1997) defines
acknowledge-answer as 'acknowledgements of answers to questions' (p. 44), and
an essential feature is that there is always 'a preceding question + answer pair'
before an acknowledge-answer. For instance,

[29]   qy   A.5 utt1: Have you ever served on a jury before? /
       na   B.6 utt1: {F Uh, } I have twice. /
       bk   ***A.7 utt1: {F Oh, } okay. /***

                                          (Conversation `sw_0017_4036.utt`)

   In this excerpt, there is a sequence of 'qy + na + bk' (*yes-no-question + affirma-*
tive non yes answer + acknowledge-answer).

   Nevertheless, such a particular sequence cannot be observed in all the annotations. For instance, in Examples [30]–[32], utterances with tokens of 'Okay' or '{F
Oh, } okay' are annotated *acknowledge-answer* as although there is no 'question +
answer' pattern in the preceding conversation.

[30]   sv   A.45 utt1: I think maybe those people that really do need to
                work, both parents, just to <sigh> survive. - /
       sv   A.45 utt2: # {C And # --
       b   B.46 utt1: # Yeah. # /
       sv   A.47 utt1: -- then } there, [th-, +] [is, + is] that other group #
                that is # --
       b   B.48 utt1: # Uh-huh. # /
       sv   A.49 utt1: -- working to maintain a standard of living --
       bk   ***B.50 utt1: Okay. /***
       sv   A.51 utt1: -- that, {F uh, } they think [is, + is] surviving
                <laughter> which is really more luxuries. /

                                          (Conversation `sw_0012_4360.utt`)

[31]   sd   A.39 utt3: {C But } I'd want to be with a skilled sailor <laugh-
                ter>. /
       aa   B.40 utt1: Yeah, /
       aa   B.40 utt2: really. /
       %   A.41 utt1: {C But } it, -/
       sd   B.42 utt1:   {D Well, } they offer classes out at, {F uh, } Ray
                Hubbard. /
       b   A.43 utt1: Yeah, /
       sd   A.43 utt2: {D well, } [I, + I've] always thought I'd like to. /

sd	A.43 utt3: I've never \<noise\> wanted to bad enough to make any effort to do it, {D you know. } /
b	B.44 utt1: Yeah. /
sd	A.45 utt1: {C And, } at this stage of the game, I'm not that interested in it anymore. /
bk	**B.46 utt1: {F Oh, } okay. /**

(Conversation <code>sw_0125_3306.utt</code>)

Table 11.6 Top five utterances functioning as acknowledge-answer

	Utterance	Freq	%
1	*Okay*	831	63.39
2	*Oh*	163	12.43
3	*I see*	125	9.53
4	*Uh-huh*	49	3.74
5	*Yeah*	41	3.13
Total		1209	92.22

These examples indicate that human annotators are not always consistent when following the coding principles.

In addition, the tokens in the utterances of *acknowledge-answer* have a close infinity with those in *acknowledge (backchannel)*. For instance, the top five most commonly used utterances in *acknowledge-answer* are listed in Table 11.6. It can be noted that the top five utterances account for 92.22% of the total number of *acknowledge-answer*. Thus, similar to the case of *yes answer*, it would be easy for machine to mix up *acknowledge (backchannel) vs. acknowledge-answer* based on the uni-gram lexical feature.

Acknowledge (Backchannel) Vs. Accept (aa) A close look at the actual annotations in the corpus shows that there are two possible reasons why 58.26% of utterances originally annotated as *accept* has been mistakenly identified as *acknowledge (backchannel)*. One possible reason is the similarity in the use of tokens. Table 11.7 lists the top ten most commonly used utterances in *accept*, when ignoring the discourse markers.

It would not be difficult to notice that these utterances share a high resemblance in tokens (e.g. yeah, right, yes, uh-huh) with those of *acknowledge (backchannel)*.

A second reason is that the confusion could be created by the definition of *accept* in the SWBD-DAMSL scheme. *Accept* (aa) in the SWBD-DAMSL is quite a broad category since it covers situations when a speaker 'accepts some previous proposal,

Table 11.7 Top ten utterances functioning as accept

	Utterance	Freq.	%
1	*Yeah*	3476	33.97
2	*Right*	1003	9.80
3	*Yes*	705	6.89
4	*That's right*	608	5.94
5	*No*	505	4.94
6	*That's true*	438	4.28
7	*Uh-huh*	391	3.82
8	*Exactly*	327	3.20
9	*I know*	271	2.65
10	*I agree*	171	1.67
Total		7895	77.15

plan, opinion, or statement' (Jurafsky et al. 1997, p. 37). Different from Allen and Core (1997), the SWBD-DAMSL scheme applies *accept* also to reactions to statements of the previous speaker, which would cause the ambiguity. See the following two sets of examples.

Set I

a. *Exactly* annotated as *acknowledge (backchannel)*

[32]	sd	B.6 utt1: # {C So } # I was used to the heat, out here right now, /
	b	A.7 utt1: # Yeah. # /
	sd	B.8 utt1: # {F Gosh, } # it gets to about [seventies, + high seventies] /
	sd	B.8 utt2: {C and } it gets very cold at night. /
	b	A.9 utt1: Uh-huh. /
	sd	B.10 utt1: {C And } Monterey it's, {F um, } right on the coast. /
	sd	B.10 utt2: {C And, } I don't know if your familiar with California coastline, / *[[your -> you're]]
	sd	B.10 utt3: {C but } [we're + we're] [about two hours, + about a two hour drive] south of San Francisco, /
	bk	***A.11 utt1: {F Oh, } okay. /***

(Conversation sw_0151_2772.utt)

[33]	sd	A.27 utt2: We have a little path that we do.
	b	B.28 utt1: Uh-huh. /
	+	A.29 utt1: [{C And, } + {F uh, } except] if it's raining or real cold --
	b	B.30 utt1: Yeah. /
	+	A.31 utt1: -- which it hasn't been -- /
	b	*B.32 utt1: Exactly. /*

(Conversation sw_0979_3181.utt)

[34]	sd	A.15 utt2: Usually when we entertain we do something really simple, because I like to visit with my company,
	b	B.16 utt1: Yeah. /
	+	A.17 utt1: and not be scurrying around in the kitchen, /
	sd	A.17 utt2: {C so, }
	b	*B.18 utt1: Exactly. /*

(Conversation sw_1070_3013.utt)

In Example [33] (topic: EXERCISE AND FITNESS), B (in B.32_utt1) seemed to agree with A that it hasn't been raining or real cold; while in Example [34] (topic: RECIPES/FOOD/COOKING), B (in B.18_utt1) agreed with A that they often prefer not to be just scurrying around in the kitchen.

b. *That's true* annotated as *acknowledge (backchannel)*

[35]	sd	A.97 utt1: -- {C and } we spend weekends [at the, + in the] country with them – -
	b	B.98 utt1: Uh-huh. /
	+/sd	A.99 utt1: -- quite a bit, /
	sd	A.99 utt2: {C but } --
	b@	B.100 utt1: {F Uh. }
	+/sd	A.101 utt1: -- as far as doing any activity, now that the grand kids are here, we all just stay around the house mostly. /
	+/b@	B.102 utt1: {F Oh, } yeah /
	b	*B.102 utt2: <laughter>. That's true. /*
	sv	A.103 utt1: <Laughter> It's too much effort to go somewhere with all the kids. /
	aa	B.104 utt1: {F Oh, } yes, /
	aa	B.104 utt2: {F oh, } yes. /

(Conversation sw_0836_3326.utt)

[36] sd   A.231 utt2: {E I mean, } usually a (( )) of elderly people [like
              to, + they like to,] {F uh, } share their experiences [with the, +
      b   B.232 utt1: # Uh-huh. # /
      +/sd   A.233 utt1: # with # the] younger children. /
      sd   A.233 utt2: They'll be telling them all kinds of stories.
      b   B.234 utt1: # Yeah. # /
      +/sd   A.235 utt1: # that # they don't even know what they mean. /
      b   *B.236 utt1: That's true. /*
      sv   A.237 utt1: {D You know, } they feel like they've lived life /
      sv   A.237 utt2: {C so } they need to share it. /
      b   B.238 utt1: Yeah. /

(Conversation sw_0866_2768.utt)

In Example [35] (topic: FAMILY LIFE), it would not be difficult to notice that when
B was showing that she was listening (in B.102_utt2), the laughter and the tokens
of 'That's true' also suggests that she would agree with the idea that to go out with a
large group of children would not be easy. Similarly, in Example [36] (topic: CARE
OF THE ELDERLY), B in B.236_utt1 was showing she was listening, but also she
agreed with A that what the elderly people would usually do.

As shown in the above four examples, some utterances seem to have more than
one function.

Set II The following examples show that in the actual DA annotations, human
annotators would make misjudgements on identifying an *accept* or an *acknowledge*
(backchannel).

[37] sd   B.22 utt1: {C So } you don't see too many thrown out around
              the <laughter> streets.
      b   A.23 utt1: Really <laughter>. /
      +/sd   B.24 utt1: Or even bottles. /
      x   A.25 utt1: <Laughter>.
      sv   B.26 utt1: {D You know, } all kinds of bottles [[they, + they,]
              + they] really charge people [to, +] I guess when you purchase
              them [{C and, } + {C and then }] when you turn them back in. /
      b   *A.27 utt1: Right. /*
      sd   B.28 utt1: [I n-, + I] remember the old days as a kid where bot-
              tle was a nickel. /
      aa   *A.29 utt1: Right. /*
      sv   A.29 utt2: {C And } [now, + now] most of them are throwa-
              way. /
      b   *B.30 utt1: Right. /*
      x   A.31 utt1: <Laughter>.

(Conversation sw_0009_4329.utt)

In this excerpt, the two speakers were talking about RECYCLING. It can be noted that although A said 'right' in A.27_utt1 and A.29_utt1, the first one is annotated as *acknowledge-(backchannel)* while the second as *accept*. The only difference between them is that A.29_utt1 is followed by a further statement. Nevertheless, the token 'Right' in A.29_utt1 seems to function as acknowledgement and a change to a related topic, because in the following utterance A went on to describe what happened now.

[38]	ba	A.11 utt2: that's good. /
	sd	A.11 utt3: [I, + I] used to watch them a lot when they were playing the big [iron curtain, +
	aa	***B.12 utt1: # That's right. # /***
	+/sd	A.13 utt1: # {E or } steel curtain.] # /
	qw	B.14 utt1: How about your favorite team? /

(Conversation sw_0016_3389.utt)

In this excerpt where the topic is FOOTBALL, A described what he used to do (in A.11_utt3). B responded to what A said (in B.12_utt1) but did not hold the floor since A continued to finish what he started in A.11_utt3. In fact, B in B.12_utt1 and A in A.13_utt1 were speaking at the same time (as coded with #). Given the context, B in B.12_utt1 was just acknowledging what A just said because A was talking about his own experience, and it would not be reasonable for B to agree with that.

11.6   Conclusions

The study reported in this chapter attempted to revisit the taxonomy of DA types based on the well-known SWB-DA corpus. Different from other pragmatic studies, the study drew on the state-of-the-art machine-learning techniques to explore the core issue of problematic DA types. To be more specific, the DA types of the SWBD-DAMSL scheme will be chosen as the research subject. The automatic classification of the top 15 SWBD-DAMSL DA types was then performed using the Naïve Bayes Multinomial Classifier. The automatic classification data shows that *acknowledge (backchannel)* has the highest *F*-score (0.846), indicating that such a DA type is comparatively easier to identify. The resulting confusion matrix table was used for further analysis of the targeted DA types. The investigation shows that a majority of the DA type of *hedge* (about 92.56 %) tend to be easily confused with *statement-non-opinion* based on lexical features. The analysis also reveals that *statement-non-opinion* and *statement-opinion* are difficult to distinguish even by human annotators, raising reasonable doubts as to the definition of *statement-non-opinion* and the applicability of the distinction between the two DA types (i.e.

statement-non-opinion and *statement-opinion*). Meanwhile, further analysis of *acknowledge (backchannel)* illustrates that the most distinctive DA is very likely to be confused with *yes answer, acknowledge-answer* and *accept* based on lexical information. The results of the current study suggest that techniques of artificial intelligence could benefit linguistic research. The observations here also call for a more systematic and comprehension investigations of DA taxonomy.

Chapter 12
The Future

This book originated from a fundamental interest in literary stylistics and contains a set of chapters that report various corpus-based investigations into the interaction between the external and the internal dimension of language. It seeks to demonstrate that, given linguistically informed annotation of an appropriately designed corpus with balanced text categories, empirically verifiable correlations can be observed between the two dimensions: between the choice of linguistic forms and the designated genre which often implicitly entails a specific register. A primary focus of the various studies collected in this book is the identification of the linguistic features characteristic of such genres and registers. They range from etymology, parts of speech and syntax to ontological knowledge and the pragmatics of dialogue acts. These studies reflect a concerted effort that attempts to combine linguistics, computation and artificial intelligence to identify an analytical framework within which linguistic features in general and stylistic features in particular could be extracted and verified according to the external dimensions pertaining to text genres and registers.

This endeavour is part of a broader interest in a better understanding of and a deeper insight into the complex relationships between meaning and linguistic forms. While a lot of progress has been made in the areas of linguistic annotation and mathematical algorithms to discover the salient features characteristic of different text categories, new challenges and new demands have arisen, commercially, politically and intellectually.

Commercial factors are perhaps the most important driving force that has singled out corpus-based computational linguistics from amongst other branches of linguistic studies as the one that has a direct bearing on commercial applications such as machine translation and question answering systems. A fundamental driving force behind this development is the fact that new knowledge is generated and published at an ever increasing speed. We are now in an era where there is simply too much published literature to read but much of the published information is vital to timely application and sustained development. In the area of biomedical engineering, for instance, the published literature grows exponentially and huge amounts of scientific information such as protein property and gene function are widely hidden in

© Springer-Verlag Berlin Heidelberg 2015
A. C. Fang, J. Cao, *Text Genres and Registers: The Computation of Linguistic Features*,
DOI 10.1007/978-3-662-45100-7_12

prohibitively large collections of text. For example, the literature in PubMed grows at a speed of two printed pages per second (Xia et al. 2014). As a result, it is practically impossible to manually curate experimental results from texts. In recent years, there has been a more and more urgent task to implement automatic systems to understand natural language to pinpoint specific knowledge sets in vast amounts of published literature. Most recently, the emphasis has been placed on sophisticated applications that perform knowledge engineering on texts to facilitate the generation of new knowledge. One such example in the area of biomedical engineering is the processing of published literature to identify hidden patterns of side effects that might eventually help with the repurposing of drugs. As yet another example, while named entity recognition has been exploited as a powerful approach to effective information extraction, there has recently been an increased interest to find more complex structural information and more abundant knowledge in documents (Faiz et al. 2014). Hence, as a more recent development, moving beyond named entity recognition, the GENIA task in the BioNLP 2009/2011 shared tasks (Kim et al. 2009, 2011) was set to identify and extract biomedical events from GENIA-based corpus texts (Kim et al. 2008), including gene expression, transcription, protein catabolism, localization, binding, phosphorylation, regulation, positive regulation and negative regulation. Tasks such as this one have called for sophisticated linguistic analysis as well as expert domain knowledge to produce in-depth annotation of the source text in support of subsequent information retrieval.

Additionally, new computer technologies combined with fast Iinternet access have engendered a growing range of social media that allow for on-the-move communication amongst everyday users. We have not only seen the Facebook, Twitter, MSN, blogs and micro-blogs, which combine images and texts for speedy broadcasting of personal writings but also the most recent popularity of WeChat, a smart phone-based social media platform designed by Tencent based in Beijing, China, which allows for the seamless transmission and sharing of texts, images, videos and voice amongst friends and chat groups. Here, these computer mediated communication methods are no longer restricted to the written language but have created a novel, multi-modal norm within which our traditional linguistic behaviour has been most forcefully impacted on. Information is no longer transmitted in the written words only but the proper understanding of the transmitted message necessarily involves access to the accompanying smileys, sounds, images and often videos. Brandwatch, a company based in Brighton, UK, specialises in the development of a web-based platform to monitor social media. It collects data important to businesses and organisations from various forms of social media such as blogs, Facebook, forums, news, reviews and Twitter. To provide interested clients with the sort of data they are in need of, the software system needs to perform intelligent analysis of not only the written language, but images, sounds and also videos.

Politically, we have seen several government and public-sector initiatives that have undoubtedly changed our linguistic behaviour. Most notably, these include the various plain language movements to promote the use of simpler language in official, legal and commercial writing (as in forms, contracts, business letters and descriptions of products) and medical usage (including labels on medicinal products). Among them is Plain English Campaign, which started in the late 1980s in the UK and has campaigned over the years for language of clear information. The Campaign has now evolved into an influential service with thousands of clients with its crystal mark. It explicitly promotes a simpler English with short sentences, a preference for active verbs and an avoidance of nominalisations. In the USA, as a direct result of the Charrows' campaign for clear instructions within the judicial system, the 'Plainer English' version of the California Criminal Code was approved in 2006 and adopted by the Florida Court in 2013. On 1 June 1998, US President Bill Clinton issued a memorandum and directed US federal departments and agencies to use plain language in order to make government 'more responsive, accessible and understandable in its communications with the public.' According to the memorandum, 'Plain language saves the Government and the private sector time, effort and money' (Clinton 1998). In 2010, Obama signed the Plain Writing Act, which requires all federal agencies to use plain writing in every covered document that the agency issues or substantially revises and to establish a process for overseeing the agency's compliance with this Act. As is easily conceivable, these initiatives strive for a simpler, clearer expression of meaning that will have a direct impact on the choice of linguistic forms of expression. In addition, the increasing prominence of 'World Englishes' has also admitted more regional varieties into the family and accelerated the changes, pushing towards a simpler and plainer form of the language that is known as 'International English'.

The commercial and political factors have thus created a trend towards a period of drastic changes to our conventional linguistic behaviour. The scenario right now has thus grown more complex than before: We are witnessing a global trend towards a simpler language for effective communication, within which there is a fast relaxation of the stylistic features that used to be characteristic of specific genres and registers; we are also seeing the increasing availability of novel multi-modal social media facilitated and enabled by the Internet which will undoubtedly engender novel linguistic expressions; and, most important of all, we are faced with the need to transmit and express more and more specialised and sophisticated knowledge across countless different domains at an ever increasing speed.

Intellectually speaking, as a result, the future is not going to be easier but there is an even greater urgency within the linguistic research community to help resolve the challenging issues. The corpus-based computational approach to language has assumed a particularly heavy task to propose linguistically sound theories that will eventually deliver in terms of commercial applications. While a lot has been achieved in the past, an important task in the near future seems to be an automatable annotation formalism that takes the text from deep linguistic analysis to sound semantic representation of meaning. Obviously, this is exactly what the NLP community have been trying to do. However, what has been done in the past is largely *ad hoc* and dependent on projects, knowledge domains and, often, personal skills and preferences. The new requirement calls for an underlying generic design that can be incrementally developed and enriched by different teams across different disciplines. This requirement entails 'standards' of various sorts to ensure interoperability and data reusability amongst the participants. Technical Committee 37 of the International Organisation for Standardisation has recently published a series of standards for the annotation of morpho-syntactic structures, semantic roles and dialogue acts amongst many others, which is paving the way for the future. A particularly useful step is to see these standards adopted and automated for informative annotation of texts.

After all, whatever happens in the future, linguistic research always will be an ongoing quest into language as a window into human cognition. The corpus-based computational approach will prove to be an even more lively testbed of different linguistic theories and natural language processing techniques.

Appendix A

A List of ICE Part-of-Speech Tags

`ADJ(comp)`	Adjective, comparative
`ADJ(edp)`	Adjective, *-ed* participle
`ADJ(ge)`	Adjective, general
`ADJ(ingp)`	Adjective, *-ing* participle
`ADJ(sup)`	Adjective, superlative
`ADV(add)`	Adverb, additive
`ADV(excl)`	Adverb, exclusive
`ADV(ge)`	Adverb, general
`ADV(ge,comp)`	Adverb, comparative
`ADV(ge,sup)`	Adverb, superlative
`ADV(inten)`	Adverb, intensifier
`ADV(inten,comp)`	Adverb, intensifier, comparative
`ADV(inten,sup)`	Adverb, intensifier, superlative
`ADV(partic)`	Adverb, particularizer
`ADV(phras)`	Adverb, phrasal
`ADV(rel)`	Adverb, relative
`ADV(wh)`	Adverb, *wh*-adverb
`ART(def)`	Article, definite
`ART(indef)`	Article, indefinite
`AUX(do,imp)`	Auxiliary, *do* imperative
`AUX(do,imp,neg)`	Auxiliary, *do* imperative, negative
`AUX(do,past)`	Auxiliary, *do*, past
`AUX(do,past,neg)`	Auxiliary, *do*, past, negative
`AUX(do,pres)`	Auxiliary, *do*, present
`AUX(do,pres,encl)`	Auxiliary, *do*, present, enclitic
`AUX(do,pres,neg)`	Auxiliary, *do*, present, negative
`AUX(do,pres,procl)`	Auxiliary, *do*, present, proclitic

© Springer-Verlag Berlin Heidelberg 2015

A. C. Fang, J. Cao, *Text Genres and Registers: The Computation of Linguistic Features,*
DOI 10.1007/978-3-662-45100-7

`AUX(let,imp)`	Auxiliary, *let* imperative
`AUX(modal,past)`	Auxiliary, modal, past
`AUX(modal,past,encl)`	Auxiliary, modal, past, enclitic
`AUX(modal,past,neg)`	Auxiliary, modal, past, negative
`AUX(modal,pres)`	Auxiliary, modal, present
`AUX(modal,pres,encl)`	Auxiliary, modal, present, enclitic
`AUX(modal,pres,neg)`	Auxiliary, modal, present, negative
`AUX(pas,edp)`	Auxiliary, passive, *-ed* participle
`AUX(pas,imp)`	Auxiliary, passive, imperative
`AUX(pas,infin)`	Auxiliary, passive, infinitive
`AUX(pas,ingp)`	Auxiliary, passive, *-ing* participle
`AUX(pas,past)`	Auxiliary, passive, past
`AUX(pas,past,neg)`	Auxiliary, passive, past, negative
`AUX(pas,pres)`	Auxiliary, passive, present
`AUX(pas,pres,encl)`	Auxiliary, passive, present, enclitic
`AUX(pas,pres,neg)`	Auxiliary, passive, present, negative
`AUX(pas,subjun)`	Auxiliary, passive, subjunctive
`AUX(pas,subjun,neg)`	Auxiliary, passive, subjunctive, negative
`AUX(perf,infin)`	Auxiliary, perfect, infinitive
`AUX(perf,infin,encl)`	Auxiliary, perfect, infinitive, enclitic
`AUX(perf,ingp)`	Auxiliary, perfect, *-ing* participle
`AUX(perf,past)`	Auxiliary, perfect, past
`AUX(perf,past,encl)`	Auxiliary, perfect, past, enclitic
`AUX(perf,past,neg)`	Auxiliary, perfect, past, negative
`AUX(perf,pres)`	Auxiliary, perfect, present
`AUX(perf,pres,encl)`	Auxiliary, perfect, present, enclitic
`AUX(perf,pres,neg)`	Auxiliary, perfect, present, negative
`AUX(prog,edp)`	Auxiliary, progressive, *-ed* participle
`AUX(prog,infin)`	Auxiliary, progressive, infinitive
`AUX(prog,ingp)`	Auxiliary, progressive, *-ing* participle
`AUX(prog,past)`	Auxiliary, progressive, past
`AUX(prog,past,neg)`	Auxiliary, progressive, past, negative
`AUX(prog,pres)`	Auxiliary, progressive, present
`AUX(prog,pres,encl)`	Auxiliary, progressive, present, enclitic
`AUX(prog,pres,neg)`	Auxiliary, progressive, present, negative
`AUX(prog,subjun)`	Auxiliary, progressive, subjunctive
`AUX(semi,edp)`	Semi-auxiliary, *-ed* participle
`AUX(semi,edp,disc)`	Semi-auxiliary, *-ed* participle, discontinuous
`AUX(semi,ellipt)`	Semi-auxiliary, elliptical
`AUX(semi,ellipt,disc)`	Semi-auxiliary, elliptical, discontinuous
`AUX(semi,imp)`	Semi-auxiliary, imperative
`AUX(semi,imp,disc)`	Semi-auxiliary, imperative, discontinuous
`AUX(semi,infin)`	Semi-auxiliary, infinitive
`AUX(semi,infin,disc)`	Semi-auxiliary, infinitive, discontinuous
`AUX(semi,ingp)`	Semi-auxiliary, *-ing* participle

AUX(semi,ingp,disc)	Semi-auxiliary, -*ing* participle, discontinuous
AUX(semi,past)	Semi-auxiliary, past
AUX(semi,past,disc)	Semi-auxiliary, past, discontinuous
AUX(semi,past,ellipt)	Semi-auxiliary, past, elliptical
AUX(semi,past,encl)	Semi-auxiliary, past, enclitic
AUX(semi,past,encl, disc)	Semi-auxiliary, past, enclitic, discontinuous
AUX(semi,past,neg)	Semi-auxiliary, past, negative
AUX(semi,past,neg, disc)	Semi-auxiliary, past, negative, discontinuous
AUX(semi,past,neg, ellipt)	Semi-auxiliary, past, negative, elliptical
AUX(semi,pres)	Semi-auxiliary, present
AUX(semi,pres,disc)	Semi-auxiliary, present, discontinuous
AUX(semi,pres,ellipt)	Semi-auxiliary, present, elliptical
AUX(semi,pres,encl)	Semi-auxiliary, present, enclitic
AUX(semi,pres,encl, disc)	Semi-auxiliary, present, enclitic, discontinuous
AUX(semi,pres,neg)	Semi-auxiliary, present, negative
AUX(semi,pres,neg, disc)	Semi-auxiliary, present, negative, discontinuous
AUX(semi,pres,neg, ellipt)	Semi-auxiliary, present, negative, elliptical
AUX(semi,procl)	Semi-auxiliary, proclitic
AUX(semi,subjun)	Semi-auxiliary, subjunctive
AUX(semi,subjun,neg)	Semi-auxiliary, subjunctive, negative
AUX(semip,edp)	Semi-auxiliary, -*ed* participle
AUX(semip,edp,disc)	Semi-auxiliary, -*ed* participle, discontinuous
AUX(semip,imp)	Semi-auxiliary, imperative
AUX(semip,imp,disc)	Semi-auxiliary, imperative, discontinuous
AUX(semip,infin)	Semi-auxiliary, infinitive
AUX(semip,infin,disc)	Semi-auxiliary, infinitive, discontinuous
AUX(semip,ingp)	Semi-auxiliary, -*ing* participle
AUX(semip,ingp,disc)	Semi-auxiliary, -*ing* participle, discontinuous
AUX(semip,past)	Semi-auxiliary, past
AUX(semip,past,disc)	Semi-auxiliary, past, discontinuous
AUX(semip,pres)	Semi-auxiliary, present
AUX(semip,pres,disc)	Semi-auxiliary, present, discontinuous
AUX(semip,subjun)	Semi-auxiliary, subjunctive
CONJUNC(coord)	Conjunction, coordinating
CONJUNC(subord)	Conjunction, subordinating

CONJUNC(subord,disc)	Conjunction, subordinating, discontinuous
CONJUNC(subord,ellipt)	Conjunction, subordinating, elliptical
CONNEC(appos)	Connective, appositive
CONNEC(appos,disc)	Connective, appositive, discontinuous
CONNEC(ge)	Connective, general
CONNEC(ge,disc)	Connective, general, discontinuous
EXTHERE	Existential there
FRM	Formulaic expression
GENM	Genitive marker
INTERJEC	Interjection
N(com,plu)	Noun, common, plural
N(com,sing)	Noun, common, singular
N(prop,plu)	Noun, proper, plural
N(prop,sing)	Noun, proper, singular
NADJ(comp,plu)	Nominal adjective, comparative, plural
NADJ(comp,sing)	Nominal adjective, comparative, singular
NADJ(edp,plu)	Nominal adjective, -ed participle, plural
NADJ(edp,sing)	Nominal adjective, -ed participle, singular
NADJ(ingp,plu)	Nominal adjective, -ing participle, plural
NADJ(plu)	Nominal adjective, plural
NADJ(prop,plu)	Nominal adjective, proper, plural
NADJ(prop,sing)	Nominal adjective, proper, singular
NADJ(sing)	Nominal adjective, singular
NADJ(sup,plu)	Nominal adjective, superlative, plural
NADJ(sup,sing)	Nominal adjective, superlative, singular
NUM(card,plu)	Numeral, cardinal, plural
NUM(card,sing)	Numeral, cardinal, singular
NUM(frac,plu)	Numeral, fraction, plural
NUM(frac,sing)	Numeral, fraction, singular
NUM(hyph)	Numeral, hyphenated number
NUM(mult)	Numeral, multiplier
NUM(ord)	Numeral, ordinal
NUM(ord,plu)	Numeral, ordinal, plural
NUM(ord,sing)	Numeral, ordinal, singular
PREP(ge)	Preposition, general
PREP(ge,disc)	Preposition, general, discontinuous
PREP(ge,ellipt)	Preposition, general, elliptical
PREP(inter)	Preposition, interrogative
PREP(phras)	Preposition, phrasal
PROFM(conjoin)	Proform, conjoin
PROFM(one,plu)	Proform, one, plural
PROFM(one,sing)	Proform, one, singular
PROFM(so)	Proform, so
PRON(antit)	Anticipatory it
PRON(antit,procl)	Anticipatory it, proclitic

PRON(ass)	Pronoun, assertive
PRON(ass,sing)	Pronoun, assertive, singular
PRON(cleft)	Pronoun, cleft
PRON(cleft,procl)	Pronoun, cleft, proclitic
PRON(dem)	Pronoun, demonstrative
PRON(dem,plu)	Pronoun, demonstrative, plural
PRON(dem,sing)	Pronoun, demonstrative, singular
PRON(neg)	Pronoun, negative
PRON(neg,sing)	Pronoun, negative, singular
PRON(nonass)	Pronoun, nonassertive
PRON(nonas,sing)	Pronoun, nonassertive, singular
PRON(one,plu)	Pronoun, one, plural
PRON(one,sing)	Pronoun, one, singular
PRON(pers)	Pronoun, personal
PRON(pers,plu)	Pronoun, personal, plural
PRON(pers,plu,encl)	Pronoun, personal, plural, enclitic
PRON(pers,procl)	Pronoun, personal, proclitic
PRON(pers,sing)	Pronoun, personal, singular
PRON(pers,sing,procl)	Pronoun, personal, singular, proclitic
PRON(poss)	Pronoun, possessive
PRON(pos,plu)	Pronoun, possessive, plural
PRON(pos,sing)	Pronoun, possessive, singular
PRON(quant)	Pronoun, quantifying
PRON(quant,plu)	Pronoun, quantifying, plural
PRON(quant,sing)	Pronoun, quantifying, singular
PRON(recip)	Pronoun, reciprocal
PRON(ref,plu)	Pronoun, reflexive, plural
PRON(ref,sing)	Pronoun, reflexive, singular
PRON(rel)	Pronoun, relative
PRON(univ)	Pronoun, universal
PRON(univ,plu)	Pronoun, universal, plural
PRON(univ,sing)	Pronoun, universal, singular
PRON(wh)	Pronoun, *wh*
PRTCL(for)	Particle *for*
PRTCL(to)	Particle *to*
PRTCL(to,disc)	Particle *to*, discontinuous
PRTCL(with)	Particle *with*
REACT	Reaction signal
V(cop,edp)	Verb, copular, *-ed* participle
V(cop,edp,disc)	Verb, copular, *-ed* participle, discontinuous
V(cop,imp)	Verb, copular, imperative
V(cop,imp,disc)	Verb, copular, imperative, discontinuous
V(cop,infin)	Verb, copular, infinitive
V(cop,infin,disc)	Verb, copular, infinitive, discontinuous
V(cop,ingp)	Verb, copular, *-ing* participle

V(cop,ingp,disc)	Verb, copular, -*ing* participle, discontinuous
V(cop,past)	Verb, copular, past
V(cop,past,disc)	Verb, copular, past, discontinuous
V(cop,past,neg)	Verb, copular, past, negative
V(cop,pres)	Verb, copular, present
V(cop,pres,disc)	Verb, copular, present, discontinuous
V(cop,pres,encl)	Verb, copular, present, enclitic
V(cop,pres,neg)	Verb, copular, present, negative
V(cop,pres,procl)	Verb, copular, present, proclitic
V(cop,subjun)	Verb, copular, subjunctive
V(cop,subjun,disc)	Verb, copular, subjunctive, discontinuous
V(cop,subjun,neg)	Verb, copular, subjunctive, negative
V(cxditr,imp)	Verb, complex-ditransitive, imperative
V(cxditr,infin)	Verb, complex-ditransitive, infinitive
V(cxditr,ingp)	Verb, complex-ditransitive, -*ing* participle
V(cxditr,past)	Verb, complex-ditransitive, past
V(cxditr,pres)	Verb, complex-ditransitive, present
V(cxditr,subjun)	Verb, complex-ditransitive, subjunctive
V(cxtr,edp)	Verb, complex-transitive, -*ed* participle
V(cxtr,imp)	Verb, complex-transitive, imperative
V(cxtr,infin)	Verb, complex-transitive, infinitive
V(cxtr,ingp)	Verb, complex-transitive, -*ing* participle
V(cxtr,past)	Verb, complex-transitive, past
V(cxtr,past,encl)	Verb, complex-transitive, past, enclitic
V(cxtr,past,neg)	Verb, complex-transitive, past, negative
V(cxtr,pres)	Verb, complex-transitive, present
V(cxtr,pres,encl)	Verb, complex-transitive, present, enclitic
V(cxtr,pres,neg)	Verb, complex-transitive, present, negative
V(cxtr,subjun)	Verb, complex-transitive, subjunctive
V(dimontr,edp)	Verb, dimonotransitive, -*ed* participle
V(dimontr,imp)	Verb, dimonotransitive, imperative
V(dimontr,infin)	Verb, dimonotransitive, infinitive
V(dimontr,ingp)	Verb, dimonotransitive, -*ing* participle
V(dimontr,past)	Verb, dimonotransitive, past
V(dimontr,pres)	Verb, dimonotransitive, present
V(dimontr,subjun)	Verb, dimonotransitive, subjunctive
V(ditr,edp)	Verb, ditransitive, -*ed* participle
V(ditr,imp)	Verb, ditransitive, imperative
V(ditr,infin)	Verb, ditransitive, infinitive
V(ditr,ingp)	Verb, ditransitive, -*ing* participle
V(ditr,past)	Verb, ditransitive, past
V(ditr,pres)	Verb, ditransitive, present
V(ditr,subjun)	Verb, ditransitive, subjunctive
V(intr,edp)	Verb, intransitive, -*ed* participle
V(intr,imp)	Verb, intransitive, imperative

`V(intr,infin)`	Verb, intransitive, infinitive
`V(intr,ingp)`	Verb, intransitive, -*ing* participle
`V(intr,past)`	Verb, intransitive, past
`V(intr,past,neg)`	Verb, intransitive, past, negative
`V(intr,pres)`	Verb, intransitive, present
`V(intr,pres,encl)`	Verb, intransitive, present, enclitic
`V(intr,pres,neg)`	Verb, intransitive, present, negative
`V(intr,subjun)`	Verb, intransitive, subjunctive
`V(intr,subjun,neg)`	Verb, intransitive, subjunctive, negative
`V(montr,edp)`	Verb, monotransitive, -*ed* participle
`V(montr,imp)`	Verb, monotransitive, imperative
`V(montr,infin)`	Verb, monotransitive, infinitive
`V(montr,ingp)`	Verb, monotransitive, -*ing* participle
`V(montr,past)`	Verb, monotransitive, past
`V(montr,past,neg)`	Verb, monotransitive, past, negative
`V(montr,pres)`	Verb, monotransitive, present
`V(montr,pres,encl)`	Verb, monotransitive, present, enclitic
`V(montr,pres,neg)`	Verb, monotransitive, present, negative
`V(montr,subjun)`	Verb, monotransitive, subjunctive
`V(trans,edp)`	Verb, transitive, -*ed* participle
`V(trans,imp)`	Verb, transitive, imperative
`V(trans,infin)`	Verb, transitive, infinitive
`V(trans,ingp)`	Verb, transitive, -*ing* participle
`V(trans,past)`	Verb, transitive, past
`V(trans,past,neg)`	Verb, transitive, past, negative
`V(trans,pres)`	Verb, transitive, present
`V(trans,subjun)`	Verb, transitive, subjunctive

Appendix B

A List of LOB Part-of-Speech Tags

!	Exclamation mark
&FO	Formula
&FW	Foreign word
(	Left bracket
)	Right bracket
`*`	Begin quote
`**'`	End quote
`*-`	Dash
,	Comma
`---`	Beginning or end of sentence marker
.	Full stop
...	Ellipsis
:	Colon
;	Semicolon
?	Question mark
ABL	Pre-qualifier (quite, rather, such)
ABN	Pre-quantifier (all, half)
ABX	Pre-quantifier/double conjunction (both)
AP	Post-determiner (few, fewer, former, last, little, several, very, etc.)
AP$	*Other's*
APS	*Others*
APS$	*Others'*
AT	Singular article (*a*, *an*, *every*)
ATI	Singular or plural article (*the*, *no*)
BE	*Be*
BED	*Were*

A. C. Fang, J. Cao, *Text Genres and Registers: The Computation of Linguistic Features,*
DOI 10.1007/978-3-662-45100-7

BEDZ	*Was*
BEG	*Being*
BEM	*Am, 'm*
BEN	*Been*
BER	*Are, 're*
BEZ	*Is, 's*
CC	Coordinating conjunction (*and, and/or, but, nor, only, or, yet*)
CD	Cardinal (*two, three,* etc.; *hundred, thousand,* etc.; *dozen, zero*)
CD$	Cardinal + genitive
CD-CD	Hyphenated pair of cardinals
CD1	*One, 1*
CD1$	*One's*
CD1S	*Ones*
CDS	Cardinal + plural (*tens, millions, dozens,* etc.)
CS	Subordinating conjunction (*after, although,* etc.)
DO	*Do*
DOD	*Did*
DOZ	*Does, 's*
DT	Singular determiner (*another, each, that, this*)
DT$	Singular determiner + genitive (*another's*)
DTI	Singular or plural determiner (*any, enough, some*)
DTS	Plural determiner (*these, those*)
DTX	Determiner/double conjunction (*either, neither*)
EX	Existential *there*
HV	*Have*
HVD	*Had, 'd*
HVG	*Having*
HVN	*Had* (past participle)
HVZ	*Has, 's*
IN	Preposition (*about, above,* etc.)
JJ	Adjective attributive-only
JJB	Adjective (*chief, entire, main,* etc.)
JJR	Comparative adjective
JJT	Superlative adjective
JNP	Adjective with w.i.c. (*English, German,* etc.)
MD	Modal auxiliary (*'ll, can, could,* etc.)
NC	Cited word
NN	Singular common noun
NN$	Singular common noun + genitive
NNP	Singular common noun with w.i.c. (*Englishman, German,* etc.)
NNP$	Singular common noun with w.i.c. + genitive
NNPS	Plural common noun with w.i.c.
NNPS$	Plural common noun with w.i.c. + genitive
NNS	Plural common noun
NNS$	Plural common noun + genitive
NNU	Abbreviated unit of measurement unmarked for number (*hr, lb,* etc.)

NNU$	Possessive abbreviated neutral unit of measurement: e.g. *cwt's*
NNUS	Abbreviated plural unit of measurement (*gns, yds*, etc.)
NNUS$	Possessive abbrev. plural unit of measurement: e.g. *c.c.s'*
NP	Singular proper noun
NP$	Singular proper noun + genitive
NPL	Singular locative noun with w.i.c. (*Abbey, Bridge*, etc.)
NPL$	Singular locative noun with w.i.c. + genitive
NPLS	Plural locative noun with w.i.c.
NPLS$	Plural locative noun with w.i.c. + genitive
NPS	Plural proper noun
NPS$	Plural proper noun + genitive
NPT	Singular titular noun with w.i.c. (*Archbishop, Captain*, etc.)
NPT$	Singular titular noun with w.i.c. + genitive
NPTS	Plural titular noun with w.i.c.
NPTS$	Plural titular noun with w.i.c. + genitive
NR	Singular adverbial noun (*January, Sunday, east, today, downtown, home*)
NR$	Singular adverbial noun + genitive
NRS	Plural adverbial noun
NRS$	Plural adverbial noun + genitive
OD	Ordinal (*1st, first*, etc.)
OD$	Ordinal + genitive
PN	Nominal pronoun (*anybody, anyone, anything; everybody, everyone,* etc.)
PN$	Nominal pronoun + genitive
PP$	Possessive determiner (*my, your*, etc.)
PP$$	Possessive pronoun (*mine, yours*, etc.)
PP1A	Personal pronoun, 1st person singular nominative (*I*)
PP1AS	Personal pronoun, 1st person plural nominative (*we*)
PP1O	Personal pronoun, 1st person singular accusative (*me*)
PP1OS	Personal pronoun, 1st person plural accusative (*us, 's*)
PP2	Personal pronoun, 2nd person (*you, thou, thee, ye*)
PP3	Personal pronoun, 3rd person singular nominative + accusative (*it*)
PP3A	Personal pronoun, 3rd person singular nominative (*he, she*)
PP3AS	Personal pronoun, 3rd person plural nominative (*they*)
PP3O	Personal pronoun, 3rd person singular accusative (*him, her*)
PP3OS	Personal pronoun, 3rd person plural accusative (*them, 'em*)
PPL	Singular reflexive pronoun
PPLS	Plural reflexive pronoun, reciprocal pronoun
QL	Qualifier (*as, awfully, less, more, so, too, very*, etc.)
QLP	Post-qualifier (*enough, indeed*)
RB	Adverb
RB$	Adverb + genitive (*else's*)
RBR	Comparative adverb
RBT	Superlative adverb

RI	Adverb (homograph of preposition: *below*, *near*, etc.)
RN	Nominal adverb (*here*, *now*, *there*, *then*, etc.)
RP	Adverbial particle (*back*, *down*, *off*, etc.)
TO	Infinitival *to*
UH	Interjection
VB	Base form of verb
VBD	Past tense of verb
VBG	Present participle, gerund
VBN	Past participle
VBZ	3rd person singular of verb
WDT	*Wh*-determiner (*what*, *whatever*, *whatsoever*, interrogative *which*, *whichever*)
WP	*Wh*-pronoun, interrogative, nominative + accusative (*who*, *whoever*)
WP$	*Wh*-pronoun, interrogative, genitive (*whose*)
WPA	*Wh*-pronoun, nominative (*whosoever*)
WPO	*Wh*-pronoun, interrogative, accusative (*whom*, *whomsoever*)
WQL	*Wh*-degree adverb: e.g. *how*, *however*, in *how green*, *however well*
WRB	*Wh*-adverb (*how*, *when*, etc.)
XNOT	*Not, n't*
ZZ	Letter of the alphabet(*e*, *pi*, *x*, etc.)

Appendix C

A List of Penn Treebank Part-of-Speech Tags

,	Comma
:	Colon, semi-colon
.	Sentence-final punctuation
'	Right close single quote
``	Left open double quote
''	Right close double quote
"	Straight double quote
(	Left bracket character
)	Right bracket character
#	Pound sign
`	Left open single quote
$	Dollar sign
CC	Coordinating conjunction
CD	Cardinal number
DT	Determiner
EX	Existential there
FW	Foreign word
IN	Preposition/subordinating conjunction
JJ	Adjective
JJR	Adjective, comparative
JJS	Adjective, superlative
LS	List item marker
MD	Modal
NN	Noun, singular or mass
NNP	Proper noun, singular
NNPS	Proper noun, plural
NNS	Noun, plural

© Springer-Verlag Berlin Heidelberg 2015
A. C. Fang, J. Cao, *Text Genres and Registers: The Computation of Linguistic Features*,
DOI 10.1007/978-3-662-45100-7

PDT	Predeterminer
POS	Possessive ending
PP	Possessive pronoun
PRP	Personal pronoun
RB	Adverb
RBR	Adverb, comparative
RBS	Adverb, superlative
RP	Particle
SYM	Symbol (mathematical or scientific)
TO	*To*
UH	Interjection
VB	Verb, base form
VBD	Verb, past tense
VBG	Verb, gerund/present participle
VBN	Verb, past participle
VBP	Verb, non-3rd person singular present
VBZ	Verb, 3rd person singular present
WDT	*Wh*-determiner
WP	Possessive *wh*-pronoun
WP	*Wh*-pronoun
WRB	*Wh-adverb*

Appendix D

A List of ICE Parsing Symbols

A	Adverbial
AJHD	Adjective phrase head
AJP	Adjectve phrase
AJPO	Adjective phrase postmodifier
AJPR	Adjective phrase premodifier
AVB	Auxiliary verb
AVHD	Adverb phrase head
AVP	Adverb phrase
AVPO	Adverb phrase postmodifier
AVPR	Adverb phrase premodifier
CF	Focus complement
CJ	Conjoin
CL	Clause
CLOP	Cleft operator
CO	Object complement
COOR	Coordinator
CS	Subject complement
CT	Transitive complement
DEFUNC	Detached function
DISMK	Discourse marker
DISP	Disparate coordination
DT	Determiner
DTCE	Central determiner
DTDE	Deterred determiner
DTP	Determiner phrase
DTPE	Pre-determiner
DTPO	Determiner postmodifier

© Springer-Verlag Berlin Heidelberg 2015
A. C. Fang, J. Cao, *Text Genres and Registers: The Computation of Linguistic Features*,
DOI 10.1007/978-3-662-45100-7

DTPR	Determiner premodifier
DTPS	Post-determiner
ELE	Clause element
EXOP	Existential operator there
FOC	Focus
FRM	Formulaic expression
GENF	Genitive function
IMPOP	Imperative operator
INDET	Indetermined
INTOP	Interrogative operator
INVOP	Inversion operator
LIM	Limiter
LK	Linker
MVB	Main verb
NONCL	Non-clause
NOOD	Notional object
NOSU	Notional subject
NP	Noun phrase
NPHD	Noun phrase head
NPPO	Noun phrase postmodifier
NPPR	Noun phrase premodifier
OD	Direct object
OI	Indirect object
OP	Operator
P	Prepositional
PARA	Paratactic
PC	Prepositional complement
PMOD	Preposition premodifier
PP	Prepositional phrase
PRED	Predicate
PREDG	Predicate group
PROD	Provisional object
PRSU	Provisional subject
PS	Stranded preposition
PU	Parsing unit
SBMO	Subordinator phrase premodifier
SU	Subject
SUB	Subordinator
SUBHD	Subordinator phrase head
SUBP	Subordinator phrase
TO	Infinitive *to*
VB	Verbal
VP	Verb phrase

Appendix E

A List of Penn Treebank Parsing Symbols

⋆	"Understood" subject of infinitive or imperative
0	Zero variant of *that* in subordinate clauses
ADJP	Adjective phrase
ADVP	Adverb phrase
NP	Noun phrase
PP	Prepositional phrase
S	Simple declarative clause
SBAR	Subordinate clause
SBARQ	Direct question introduced by *wh-element*
SINV	Declarative sentence with subject-aux inversion
SQ	Yes/no questions and subconstituent of SBARQ excluding *wh*-element
T	Trace of *wh*-constituent
VP	Verb phrase
WHADVP	Wh-adverb phrase
WHNP	Wh-noun phrase
WHPP	Wh-prepositional phrase
X	Constituent of unknown or uncertain category

© Springer-Verlag Berlin Heidelberg 2015   237
A. C. Fang, J. Cao, *Text Genres and Registers: The Computation of Linguistic Features,*
DOI 10.1007/978-3-662-45100-7

Appendix F

A List of Adverbial Subordinators in Speech

Rank	Subordinate	Frequency	Percentage (%)	Accumulative Frequency	Accumulative percentage (%)
1	*if*	1408	25.39	1408	25.39
2	*because*	964	17.38	2372	42.77
3	*when*	889	16.03	3261	58.80
4	*as*	723	13.04	3984	71.84
5	*cos*	155	2.79	4139	74.63
6	*although*	142	2.56	4281	77.19
7	*before*	120	2.16	4401	79.35
8	*that*	115	2.07	4516	81.43
9	*so that*	107	1.93	4623	83.36
10	*while*	104	1.88	4727	85.23
11	*until*	74	1.33	4801	86.57
12	*once*	61	1.10	4862	87.67
13	*as far as*	60	1.08	4922	88.75
14	*since*	58	1.05	4980	89.79
15	*so*	57	1.03	5037	90.82
16	*unless*	54	0.97	5091	91.80
17	*though*	50	0.90	5141	92.70
18	*after*	50	0.90	5191	93.60
19	*whereas*	41	0.74	5232	94.34
20	*whether*	29	0.52	5261	94.86
21	*than*	28	0.50	5289	95.37
22	*as soon as*	26	0.47	5315	95.83
23	*as if*	21	0.38	5336	96.21

© Springer-Verlag Berlin Heidelberg 2015
A. C. Fang, J. Cao, *Text Genres and Registers: The Computation of Linguistic Features*,
DOI 10.1007/978-3-662-45100-7

Rank	Subordinate	Frequency	Percentage (%)	Accumulative Frequency	Accumulative percentage (%)
24	*like*	17	0.31	5353	96.52
25	*where*	16	0.29	5369	96.81
26	*as long as*	15	0.27	5384	97.08
27	*in that*	13	0.23	5397	97.31
28	*whilst*	12	0.22	5409	97.53
29	*till*	10	0.18	5419	97.71
30	*provided*	10	0.18	5429	97.89
31	*as though*	9	0.16	5438	98.05
32	*so far as*	8	0.14	5446	98.20
33	*now that*	8	0.14	5454	98.34
34	*in case*	8	0.14	5462	98.49
35	*whenever*	6	0.11	5468	98.59
36	*except*	6	0.11	5474	98.70
37	*in so far as*	5	0.09	5479	98.79
38	*given that*	5	0.09	5484	98.88
39	*so long as*	4	0.07	5488	98.95
40	*now*	4	0.07	5492	99.03
41	*no matter*	4	0.07	5496	99.10
42	*whether or not*	3	0.05	5499	99.15
43	*supposing*	3	0.05	5502	99.21
44	*such that*	3	0.05	5505	99.26
45	*if only*	3	0.05	5508	99.31
46	*even though*	3	0.05	5511	99.37
47	*wherever*	2	0.04	5513	99.40
48	*providing*	2	0.04	5515	99.44
49	*insofar as*	2	0.04	5517	99.48
50	*in order that*	2	0.04	5519	99.51
51	*in as far as*	2	0.04	5521	99.55
52	*for*	2	0.04	5523	99.59
53	*except that*	2	0.04	5525	99.62
54	*even if*	2	0.04	5527	99.66
55	*considering that*	2	0.04	5529	99.69
56	*but*	2	0.04	5531	99.73
57	*suppose*	1	0.02	5532	99.75
58	*such*	1	0.02	5533	99.77
59	*soon as*	1	0.02	5534	99.78
60	*seeing as how*	1	0.02	5535	99.80
61	*rather than*	1	0.02	5536	99.82
62	*other than*	1	0.02	5537	99.84

Rank	Subordinate	Frequency	Percentage (%)	Accumulative Frequency	Accumulative percentage (%)
63	*in order to*	1	0.02	5538	99.86
64	*in order so*	1	0.02	5539	99.87
65	*in as much*	1	0.02	5540	99.89
66	*however*	1	0.02	5541	99.91
67	*given*	1	0.02	5542	99.93
68	*ere*	1	0.02	5543	99.95
69	*considering*	1	0.02	5544	99.96
70	*as opposed to*	1	0.02	5545	99.98
71	*any more than*	1	0.02	5546	100.00

Appendix G

A List of Adverbial Subordinators in Writing

Rank	Subordinate	Frequency	Percentage (%)	Accumulative Frequency	Accumulative percentage (%)
1	*if*	1025	24.26	1025	24.26
2	*as*	696	16.47	1721	40.73
3	*when*	641	15.17	2362	55.91
4	*because*	259	6.13	2621	62.04
5	*although*	212	5.02	2833	67.05
6	*while*	195	4.62	3028	71.67
7	*before*	116	2.75	3144	74.41
8	*so that*	103	2.44	3247	76.85
9	*though*	102	2.41	3349	79.27
10	*until*	95	2.25	3444	81.51
11	*since*	91	2.15	3535	83.67
12	*that*	67	1.59	3602	85.25
13	*once*	62	1.47	3664	86.72
14	*after*	60	1.42	3724	88.14
15	*whilst*	57	1.35	3781	89.49
16	*unless*	49	1.16	3830	90.65
17	*so*	43	1.02	3873	91.67
18	*as soon as*	37	0.88	3910	92.54
19	*whereas*	30	0.71	3940	93.25
20	*where*	28	0.66	3968	93.92
21	*as if*	28	0.66	3996	94.58
22	*whether*	25	0.59	4021	95.17

© Springer-Verlag Berlin Heidelberg 2015
A. C. Fang, J. Cao, *Text Genres and Registers: The Computation of Linguistic Features,*
DOI 10.1007/978-3-662-45100-7

Rank	Subordinate	Frequency	Percentage (%)	Accumulative Frequency	Accumulative percentage (%)
23	*in that*	21	0.50	4042	95.67
24	*whenever*	18	0.43	4060	96.09
25	*than*	15	0.36	4075	96.45
26	*as far as*	15	0.36	4090	96.80
27	*now that*	11	0.26	4101	97.07
28	*in case*	9	0.21	4110	97.28
29	*as though*	9	0.21	4119	97.49
30	*as long as*	8	0.19	4127	97.68
31	*for*	7	0.17	4134	97.85
32	*albeit*	6	0.14	4140	97.99
33	*so long as*	5	0.12	4145	98.11
34	*provided that*	5	0.12	4150	98.22
35	*provided*	5	0.12	4155	98.34
36	*like*	5	0.12	4160	98.46
37	*if only*	5	0.12	4165	98.58
38	*except*	5	0.12	4170	98.70
39	*wherever*	4	0.09	4174	98.79
40	*providing*	4	0.09	4178	98.89
41	*given that*	4	0.09	4182	98.98
42	*even though*	4	0.09	4186	99.08
43	*whether or not*	3	0.07	4189	99.15
44	*so far as*	3	0.07	4192	99.22
45	*rather than*	3	0.07	4195	99.29
46	*providing that*	3	0.07	4198	99.36
47	*except that*	3	0.07	4201	99.43
48	*but*	3	0.07	4204	99.50
49	*altho*	3	0.07	4207	99.57
50	*till*	2	0.05	4209	99.62
51	*now*	2	0.05	4211	99.67
52	*no matter*	2	0.05	4213	99.72
53	*in order that*	2	0.05	4215	99.76
54	*altho'*	2	0.05	4217	99.81
55	*supposing*	1	0.02	4218	99.83
56	*suppose*	1	0.02	4219	99.86
57	*such that*	1	0.02	4220	99.88
58	*other than*	1	0.02	4221	99.91
59	*in so far as*	1	0.02	4222	99.93
60	*if only because*	1	0.02	4223	99.95
61	*coz*	1	0.02	4224	99.98
62	*cos*	1	0.02	4225	100.00

Bibliography

Aarts, B. 2011. *Oxford modern English grammar*. Oxford: OUP.

Aarts, J., H. van Halteren, and N. Oostdijk. 1996. The TOSCA analysis system. In Proceedings of the first AGFL workshop, ed. C. Koster and E. Oltmans, 181–191. Nijmegen: CSI.

ACL/DCI. 1993. Linguistic data consortium, Philadelphia.

Advanced Research Projects Agency. 1994. *Proceedings of the 1994 ARPA Human Language Technology Workshop*, Princeton, New Jersey, March 1994. Morgan Kaufmann.

Alexandersson, J., B. Buschbeck-Wolf, T. Fujinami, M. Kipp, S. Koch, E. Maier, N. Reithinger, B. Schmitz, and M. Siegel. 1998. *Dialogue acts in VERBMOBIL-2 2nd ed*. Verbmobil Report 226: DFKI, Saarbrücken.

Allen, J., and M. Core. 1997. *DAMSL: Dialogue act markup in several layers (Draft 2.1)*. Technical report, multiparty discourse group. Discourse Resource Initiative, September/October 1997.

Alpaydin, E. 2010. *Introduction to machine learning*. 2nd ed. Cambridge: MIT Press.

American Heritage Dictionary of the English Language. 1969. Edited by William Morris. Boston: Houghton Mifflin.

Ananiadou, S., S. Albert, and D. Schuh-mann. 2000. Evaluation of automatic term recognition of nuclear receptors from MEDLINE. *Genome Informatics* 11:450–451.

Andersen, G., and K. Bech. 2013. *English corpus linguistics: Variation in time, space and genre: Selected papers from ICAME 32*. Amsterdam: Rodopi.

Andersson, E. 1985. On verb complementation in written English. Philadelphia: Coronet Books Inc.

Ang, J., Y. Liu, and E. Shriberg. 2005. Automatic dialogue act segmentation and classification in multiparty meetings. In Proceedings of IEEE international conference on acoustics, speech, and signal processing, March 19–23, 2005, Philadelphia, USA, 1061–1064.

Artstein, R., and M. Poesio. 2008. Inter-coder agreement for computational linguistics. *Computational Linguistics* 34 (4): 555–596.

Aston, G. 1998. Learning English with the British National Corpus. Presented at the 6th Jornada de Corpus, UPF, Barcelona, May 28–30, 1998. http://www.sslmit.unibo.it/~guy/barc.htm. Accessed 9 Dec 2014.

Athanaselis, T., S. Bakamidis, I. Dologlou, R. Cowie, E. Douglas-Cowie, and C. Cox. 2005. ASR for emotional speech: Clarifying the issues and enhancing performance. *Neural Networks* 18:437–444.

Atkins, S., C. J. Fillmore, and C. J. Johnson. 2003. Lexicographic relevance: Selecting information from corpus evidence. *International Journal of Lexicography* 16 (3): 251–280.

Aubin, S., and T. Hamon. 2006. Improving term extraction with terminological resources. In *FinTAL 2006, LNAI 4139*, 380–387.

Auwera, J., D. Noël, and A. Wit. 2012. The diverging need (to)'s of Asian Englishes, In *Mapping unity and diversity world-wide*, ed. M. Hundt and U. Gut, 55–76. Amsterdam: John Benjamins.

© Springer-Verlag Berlin Heidelberg 2015   245
A. C. Fang, J. Cao, *Text Genres and Registers: The Computation of Linguistic Features*,
DOI 10.1007/978-3-662-45100-7

Backlund, U. 1981. Restrictive adjective-noun collocations in English. *Umea studies in the humanities 23*. Stockholm: Almqvist & Wiksell.

Baker, C. F., and H. Sato. 2003. The FrameNet data and software. In Proceedings of 41st annual meeting of the Association for Computational Linguistics, 161–164.

Baker, C. F., C. J. Fillmore, and J. B. Lowe. 1998. The Berkeley FrameNet project. In Proceedings of the COLING-ACL, 86–90.

Baldick, C. 2004. *The concise Oxford dictionary of literary terms*. Oxford: Oxford University Press.

Banerjee, S., and T. Pedersen. 2002. An adapted lesk algorithm for word sense disambiguation using WordNet. In Proceedings of the third international conference on intelligent text processing and computational linguistics *(CICLING-02)*, Mexico City.

Banerjee, S., and T. Pedersen. 2003. Extended gloss overlaps as a measure of semantic relatedness. In Proceedings of the eighteenth international joint conference on artificial intelligence *IJCAI-2003*, Acapulco, Mexico.

Bar-Ilan, L., and R. A. Berman. 2007. Developing register differentiation: The Latinate–Germanic divide in English. *Linguistics* 45 (1): 1–35.

Bawakid, A., and M. Oussalah. 2010. A semantic-based text classification system. In Proceedings of 2010 IEEE 9th international conference on cybernetic intelligent systems (CIS), 1–6.

Becker, T., and T. Wilson. 2012. Language structure. In *Multimodal signal processing: Human interactions in meetings,* ed. S. Renals, H. Bourlard, J. Carletta, and A. Popescu-Belis, 125–154. Cambridge: Cambridge University Press.

Beers, S., and W. Nagy. 2011. Writing development in four genres from grades three to seven: Syntactic complexity and genre differentiation. *Reading and Writing* 24 (2): 183–202.

Bekkeerman, R., K. Eguchi, and J. Allan. 2006. Unsupervised non-topical classification of documents. Technical report IR-472, UMass Amherst.

Ben Aharon, R., I. Szpektor, and I. Dagan. 2010. Generating entailment rules from FrameNet. In Proceedings of the ACL 2010 conference short papers, 241–246, Uppsala, Sweden.

Beňuš, S., A. Gravano, and J. Hirschberg. 2011. Pragmatic aspects of temporal accommodation in turn-taking. *Journal of Pragmatics* 42:3001–3027.

Berber-Sardinha, T. 2011. Dimensions of variation in Brazilian Portuguese. In Proceedings of the 10th AACL, American Association for Corpus Linguistics, Atlanta, GA.

Bhardwaj, V., R. Passonneau, A. Salleb-Aouissi, and N. Ide. 2010. Anveshan: A framework for analysis of multiple annotators' labeling behavior. In Proceedings of the fourth linguistic annotation workshop (LAW IV), Uppsala, Sweden.

Biber, D. 1988. *Variation across speech and writing*. Cambridge: Cambridge University Press.

Biber, D. 1995. *Dimensions of register variation: A cross-linguistic perspective*. Cambridge: Cambridge University Press.

Biber, D. 2004. Conversation text types: A multi-dimensional analysis. In Proceedings of the 7th international conference on the statistical analysis of textual data, 15–34.

Biber, D., and J. Kurjian. 2006. Towards a taxonomy of web registers and text types: A multidimensional analysis. In *Corpus linguistics and the web,* ed. M. Hundt, N. Nesselhauf, and C. Biewer, 109–131. Amsterdam: Rodopi.

Biber, D., M. Davies, J. Jones, and N. Tracy-Ventura. 2006. Spoken and written register variation in Spanish: A multi-dimensional analysis. *Corpora* 1 (1): 1–37.

Biber, D., S. Conrad, and R. Reppen. 1998. *Corpus linguistics: Investigating language structure and use*. Cambridge: Cambridge University Press.

Biber, D., S. Conrad, R. Reppen, P. Byrd, and M. Helt. 2002. Speaking and writing in the university: A multi-dimensional comparison. *TESOL Quarterly* 36 (1): 9–48.

Boas, H. C. 2002. Bilingual FrameNet dictionaries for machine translation. In Proceedings of the third international conference on language resources and evaluation, vol. IV, 1364–1371, Las Palmas.

Boese E., and A. Howe. 2005. Effects of web document evolution on genre classification. In Proceedings of the CIKM'05. New York: ACM.

Bowie, J., and B. Aarts. 2013. Clause fragments in spoken English. In Book of abstracts of ICAME 34, 83.

Brent, M. 1991. Automatic acquisition of subcategorization frames from untagged text. In Proceedings of the 29th annual meeting of the association for computational linguistics, Berkeley, CA, 193–200.

Brill, E. 1995. Transformation-based error-driven learning and natural language processing: A case study in part-of-speech tagging. *Computational linguistics* 21 (4): 543–565.

Briscoe, T. 1990. English noun phrases are regular: A reply to Professor Sampson. In *Theory and practice in corpus linguistics,* ed. J. Aarts and W. Meijs, 45–60. Amsterdam: Rodopi.

Briscoe, T., and J. Carroll. 1993. Generalised probabilistic LR parsing for unification-based grammars. *Computational Linguistics* 19 (1): 25–60.

Briscoe, T., and J. Carroll. 1996. Automatic extraction of subcategorization from corpora. In Proceedings of ACL SIGDAT workshop on very large corpora, Copenhagen, 4 August 1996.

Brown, S. J. 1927. *The World of imagery.* London: Kegan Paul, Trench, Trubner.

Bunt, H. 1994. Context and dialogue control. *THINK Quarterly* 3 (1): 19–31.

Bunt, H. 2009. Multifunctionality and multidimensional dialogue semantics. In Proceedings of DiaHolmia workshop on the semantics and pragmatics of dialogue, Stockholm, 24–26 June 2009.

Bunt, H. 2011. Multifunctionality in dialogue and its interpretation. *Computer, Speech and Language* 25 (2): 225–245.

Bunt, H., J. Alexandersson, J. Carletta, J.-W. Choe, A. C. Fang, K. Hasida, K. Lee, V. Petukhova, A. Popescu-Belis, L. Romary, C. Soria, and D. Traum. 2010. Towards an ISO standard for dialogue act annotation. 2010. In Proceedings of the seventh international conference on language resources and evaluation. Valletta, MALTA, 17–23 May 2010.

Bunt, H., A. C. Fang, X. Liu, J. Cao, and V. Petukhova. 2013. Making Switchboard dialogue annotations ISO-compliant. In Proceedings of the 9th workshop on interoperable semantic annotation, Potsdam, 19–20 March 2013.

Burnard, L. 2007. Reference guide for the British National Corpus (XML Edition). http://www.natcorp.ox.ac.uk/XMLedition/URG/. Accessed 9 Dec 2014.

Burnard, L., and G. Aston. 1998. *The BNC handbook: Exploring the British National Corpus.* Edinburgh: Edinburgh University Press.

Campbell, J. A., and A. C. Fang. 1995. Automated alignment in multilingual corpora. In Proceedings of the 10th Pacific Asia conference on language, information and computation (PACLIC10), Hong Kong, 27–28 December 1995. 185–193.

Carletta, J., A. Isard, S. Isard, J. Kowtko, and G. Doherty-Sneddon. 1996. *HCRC dialogue structure coding manual.* Technical report HCRC/TR-82.

Carlson, Lynn, Daniel Marcu, and Mary Ellen Okurowski. 2002. RST Discourse Treebank LDC2002T07. Web download. Philadelphia: Linguistic Data Consortium.

Carroll, J.B., P. Davies, and B. Richman. 1971. *The American heritage word frequency book.* Boston: Houghton Mifflin.

Chafe, W. 1982. Integration and involvement in speaking, writing, and oral literature. In *Spoken and written language: Exploring orality and literacy,* ed. D. Tannen, 35–53. Norwood: Ablex.

Chafe, W., and J. Danielewicz. 1987. Properties of spoken and written language. In *Comprehending oral and written language,* ed. R. Horowitz and S. J. Samuels, 83–113. San Diego: Academic.

Chen, Y., H. Cao, Q. Mei, K. Zheng, and H. Xu. 2013. Applying active learning to supervised word sense disambiguation in MEDLINE. *Journal of the American Medical Informatics Association* 20 (5): 1001–1006.

Cheng, S. 2010. A corpus-based approach to the study of speech act of thanking. *Concentric: Studies in Linguistics* 36 (2): 254–274.

Choi, H. 2012. A linear regressional analysis of *With*-PPs in English. *Linguistic Research* 29 (1): 21–44.

Chow, I. C., and J. J. Webster. 2007. Integration of linguistic resources for verb classification: FrameNet, WordNet, VerbNet, and suggested upper merged ontology. In Proceedings of CICLing, Mexico City, 18–24 February 2007, 1–11.

Chujo, K. 2004. Measuring vocabulary levels of English textbooks and tests using a BNC lemmatized high frequency word list. In *Corpora under Japanese eyes English,* ed. J. Nakamura, 231–249. Amsterdam: Rodopi.

Clinton, W. 1998. Memorandum for the heads of executive departments and agencies. http://www.plainlanguage.gov/whatisPL/govmandates/memo.cfm. Accessed 9 Dec 2014.

Coates, J. 1983. *The semantics of the modal auxiliaries*. London: Croom Helm.

Coates, J., and G. N. Leech. 1980. The meanings of the modals in modern British and American English. *York Papers in Linguistics* 8:3–34.

Cohen, J. 1960. A coefficient of agreement of nominal scales. *Educational and Psychological Measurement* 20:37–46.

Collins, P., and X. Yao. 2012. Modals and quasi-modals in new Englishes, In *Mapping unity and diversity world-wide*, ed. M. Hundt and U. Gut, 35–54. Amsterdam: John Benjamins.

Collins, P., and X. Yao. 2012. In *Modals and quasi-modals in New Englishes*, ed. M. Hundt and U. Gut, 35–54.

Conrad, S., and D. Biber. 2001. *Variation in English: Multi-dimensional studies*. London: Longman.

Corbett, P., C. Batchelor, and T. Simone. 2007. Annotation of chemical named entities. In Proceedings of BioNLP 2007: Biological, translational, and clinical language processing, 57–64.

Core, M., and J. Allen. 1997. Coding Dialogs with the DAMSL Annotation Schema. AAAI fall symposium on communicative action in humans and machines, Boston, MA, 8–10 November 1997.

Couture, B. 1986. Effective ideation in written text: A functional approach to clarity and exigence. In *Functional approaches to writing: Research perspectives*, ed. B. Couture, 69–92. Norwood: Ablex.

Coyne, R., and O. Rambow. 2009. LexPar: A freely available English paraphrase lexicon automatically extracted from FrameNet. In Proceedings of the third IEEE international conference on semantic computing (ICSC 2009), Berkeley, California, 14–16 September 2009.

Crowhurst, Marion. 1983. Syntactic complexity and writing quality: A review. *Canadian Journal of Education* 8 (1): 1–16.

Crystal, D., and D. Davy. 1969. *Investigating English style*. Bloomington: Indiana University Press.

CSR-II (WSJ1) Complete LDC94S13A. 1994. *Web download*. Philadelphia: Linguistic Data Consortium.

Cuadros, M., G. Rigau, and L. Padró. 2006. An empirical study for automatic acquisition of topic signatures. In Proceedings of the 2nd international conference on WordNet, Jeju Island, Korea.

Culpeper, J., and P. Clapham. 1996. The borrowing of classical and romance words into English: A study based on the electronic Oxford English Dictionary. *International Journal of Corpus Linguistics* 1 (2): 199–218.

Cumbo, C., S. Iiritano, and P. Rullo. 2004. Combing logic programming and domain ontologies for text classification. In *Convegno Italiano di Logica Computazionale*, Parma, Italy.

Darmoni, S. J., L. F. Soualmia, C. Letord, M. C. Jaulent, N. Griffon, B. Thirion, and A. Névéol. 2012. Improving information retrieval using medical subject headings concepts: A test case on rare and chronic diseases. *Journal of Medical Library Association* 100 (3): 176–183.

de Forest, M., and E. Johnson. 2001. The density of Latinate words in the speeches of Jane Austen's characters. *Literary and Linguistic Computing* 16 (4): 389–401.

de Melo, G., and S. Siersdorfer. 2007. Multilingual text classification using ontologies. In Proceedings of the 29th European conference on information retrieval, Rome, 2–5 April 2007.

de Melo, G., C. F. Baker, N. Ide, R. Passonneau, and C. Fellbaum. 2012. Empirical comparisons of MASC word sense annotations. In Proceedings of the eighth language resources and evaluation conference, Istanbul, 23–25 May 2012.

Demetriou G., and R. Gaizauskas. 2003. Corpus resources for development and evaluation of a bio-logical text mining system. In Proceedings of the intelligent systems for molecular biology (ISMB) workshop on text mining (BioLINK2003), Berlin, 11 July 2003.

Dempsey, K. B., P. M. McCarthy, and D. S. McNamara. 2007. Using phrasal verbs as an index to distinguish text genres. In Proceedings of the twentieth International Florida Artificial Intelligence Research Society Conference. Menlo Park, California, 7–9 May 2007. 217–222.

Deuber, D. 2014. *English in the Caribbean: Variation, style and standards in Jamaica and Trinidad*. Studies in English Language. Cambridge: Cambridge University Press.

Deuber, D., C. Biewer, S. Hackert, and M. Hilbert. 2012. Will and would in selected new Englishes: General and variety-specific tendencies, In *Mapping unity and diversity world-wide,* ed. M. Hundt and U. Gut, 77–102. Amsterdam: John Benjamins.

Deutschmann, M. 2003. *Apologising in British English.* Umeå, Sweden: Umeå.

Dewdney, N., C. VanEss-Dykema, and R. MacMillan. 2001. The form is the substance: Classification of genres in text. In Proceedings of ACL workshop on human language technology and knowledge management, Toulouse, 6–7 July 2001.

Dhillon, R., S. Bhagat, H. Carvey, and E. Shriberg. 2004. *Meeting recorder project: Dialog act labeling guide.* ICSI Technical report TR-04-002.

Díaz-Galiano, M. C., M. T. Martín-Valdivia, and L. A. Ureña-López. 2009. Query expansion with a medical ontology to improve a multimodal information retrieval system. *Computers in Biology and Medicine* 39 (4): 396–403.

Diederich, J., J. L. Kindermann, E. Leopold, and G. Paaß. 2003. Authorship attribution with support vector machines. *Applied Intelligence* 19 (1/2): 109–123.

Dolbey, A. 2009. *BioFrameNet: A FrameNet extension to the domain of molecular biology.* California: UC Berkeley.

Dolbey, A., M. Ellsworth, and J. Scheffczyk. 2006. BioFrameNet: A domain-specific FrameNet extension with links to biomedical ontologies. In Proceedings of KR-MED, Baltimore, Maryland, 8 November 2006.

Domingos, P. 2012. A few useful things to know about machine learning. *Communications of the ACM* 55 (10): 78–87.

Dorr, B. J. 1997. Large-scale dictionary construction for foreign language tutoring and interlingual machine translation. *Machine Translation* 12 (1): 1–55.

Eissen S. M., and B. Stein. 2004. Genre classification of web pages: User study and feasibility analysis. In *KI 2004: Advances in Artificial Intelligence,* eds. S. Biundo, T. Fruhwirth, and G. Palm, 256–269. Berlin: Springer.

Elberrichi, Z., A. Rahmoun, and M. A. Bentaalah. 2008. Using WordNet for text categorization. *The International Arab Journal of Information Technology* 5 (1): 16–24.

Ellegård, A. 1978. *The syntactic structure of English texts. Gothenburg Studies in English 43.* Gothenburg: Acta Universitatis Gothoburgensis.

Faiz, R., M. Amami, and A. Elkhlifi. 2014. Semantic event extraction frombiological texts using a kernel-basedmethod. In *Advances in knowledge discovery and management,* ed. F. Guillet et al., 77–94. Berlin: Springer.

Fang, A. C. 1991. Applications of COMPAID. In *Text analysis in computer assisted language learning,* ed. J. Milton and K.S.T. Tong, 15–30. Hong Kong: Hong Kong University of Science and Technology.

Fang, A. C. 1994. ICE: applications and possibilities in NLP. In Proceedings of international workshop on directions of lexical research, 15–17 Aug 1994, Beijing, 23–44.

Fang, A. C. 1995. The distribution of infinitives of contemporary British English: A study based on the British ICE Corpus. *Literary and Linguistic Computing* 10 (4): 247–257.

Fang, A. C. 1996a. Automatically generalising a wide-coverage formal grammar. In *Synchronic corpus linguistics,* ed. C. Percy, C. Meyer, and I. Lancashire, 207–222. Amsterdam: Rodopi.

Fang, A. C. 1996b. The survey parser: Design and development. In *Comparing English world wide: The international corpus of English,* ed. S. Greenbaum, 142–160. Oxford: Oxford University Press.

Fang, A. C. 1996c. AUTASYS: Automatic tagging and cross-tagset Mapping. In *Comparing English world wide: The international corpus of English,* ed. S. Greenbaum ,110–124. Oxford: Oxford University Press.

Fang, A. C. 2000. From cases to rules and vice versa: Robust practical parsing with analogy. In Proceedings of the sixth international workshop on parsing technologies, 23–25 Feb 2000, Trento, Italy. 77–88.

Fang, A. C. 2006a. Evaluating the performance of the Survey Parser with the NIST scheme. In *Lecture notes in computer science 3878: Computational linguistics and intelligent text processing,* ed. A. Gelbukh, 168–179. Berlin: Springer.

Fang, A. C. 2006b. A corpus-based empirical account of adverbial clauses across speech and writing in contemporary British English. In *Lecture notes in artificial intelligence 4139: Advances in natural language processing,* ed. T. Salakoski, F. Ginter, S. Pyysalo, and T. Pahikkala, 32–43. Berlin: Springer.

Fang, A. C. 2007. *English corpora and automated grammatical analysis.* Beijing: The Commercial Press.

Fang, A. C., and G. Nelson. 1994. Tagging the survey corpus: A LOB to ICE experiment using AUTASYS. *ALLC Literary & Linguistic Computing* 9 (2): 189–194.

Fang, A. C., F. J. Lo, and C. Chinn. 2009a. A computational framework for syntax-driven structured analysis of imageries in Tang and Song poems. In Proceedings of the 4th China international symposium on tang and song poetry, 10–12 November 2009, Hangzhou, China, 289–300.

Fang, A. C., J. Cao, and Y. Song. 2009b. A new corpus resource for studies in the syntactic characteristics of terminologies in contemporary English. In Proceedings of the 8th terminology and artificial intelligence conference (TIA'09), Toulouse, France, 18–20 November 2009.

Fang, A. C., H. Bunt, J. Cao, and X. Liu. 2011. Relating the semantics of dialogue acts to linguistic properties: A machine learning perspective through lexical cues. In Proceedings of the 5th IEEE international conference on semantic computing, 18–21 Sept 2011, Stanford University, Palo Alto, CA, USA.

Fang, A. C., J. Cao, H. Bunt, and X. Liu. 2012. The annotation of the Switchboard Corpus with the new ISO standard for dialogue analysis. In Proceedings of the Eighth joint ACL-ISO workshop on interoperable semantic annotation, 3–5 Oct 2012, Pisa.

Fang, A. C., J. Cao, and X. Liu. 2013. SWBD-ISO: A corpus-based study of dialogue act annotation schemes. *Contemporary Linguistics* 15 (4): 1–21.

Federica, B. 2013. General extenders in American English: Cross-register and intra-register variation. In Proceedings of genre- and register-related text and discourse features in Multilingual Corpora International Conference, Brussels, 11–12 Jan 2013.

Fellbaum, C. 1990. English verbs as a semantic net. *International Journal of Lexicography* 3 (4): 278–301.

Fellbaum, C. 1995. Co-occurrence and antonymy. *International Journal of Lexicography* 8 (4): 281–303.

Fellbaum, C. 1996. The organization of verbs and verb concepts in a semantic net. In Proceedings of the workshop on predicative forms in natural language and lexical knowledge bases, Toulouse.

Fellbaum, C. 2004. Metaphors in the (Mental) Lexicon. In *proceedings of the second global WordNet Conference* , Brno, Czech Republic, 20–23 January 2004, 3–3.

Fellbaum, C., J. Grabowski, and S. Landes. 1998. Performance and confidence in a semantic annotation task. In *WordNet: An electronic lexical database,* ed. C. Fellbaum. Cambridge (Mass.): MIT Press, May 1998.

Fellbaum, C., M. Palmer, H. T. Dang, L. Delfs, and S. Wolf. 2001. Manual and automatic semantic annotation with WordNet. In Proceedings of the NAACL 2001 workshop on WordNet and other lexical resources, Pittsburgh, 3–4 June 2001.

Fillmore, C. J., and M. R. L. Petruck. 2003. Framenet Glossary. *International Journal of Lexicography* 16 (3): 359–361.

Finn, A., and N. Kushmerick. 2006. Learning to classify documents according to genre. In Proceedings of IJCAI-03 workshop on computational approaches to style analysis and synthesis.

Flank, S. 2000. Cross-language multimedia information retrieval. In Proceedings of the sixth conference on applied natural language processing (ANLP-2000), Seattle, Washington, 29 April–3 May 2000.

Flickinger, D., Y. Zhang, and V. Kordoni. 2012. DeepBank: A dynamically annotated Treebank of the Wall Street Journal. In Proceedings of the 11th international workshop on treebanks and linguistic theories, Lisbon, Portugal, 30 November–1 December 2012: Edições Colibri, 85–96.

Fliedner, G. 2004. Towards using FrameNet for question answering. In Proceedings of the LREC 2004 workshop on building lexical resources from semantically annotated corpora. Lisbon, Portugal, 30 May 2004.

Flowerdew, J., and L. Flowerdew. 2013. Discourse properties of signalling nouns in academic genres. In Proceedings of genre- and register-related text and discourse features in Multilingual Corpora International Conference, Brussels, 11–12 Jan 2013.

Francis, W. N., and H. Kučera. 1982. *Frequency analysis of English usage: Lexicon and grammar.* Boston: Houghton Mifflin.

Fraser, B. 2009. Topic orientation markers. *Journal of Pragmatics* 41:892–898.

Fung, P., and B. Chen. 2006. Robust word sense translation by EM learning of frame semantics. In Proceedings of the COLING/ACL 2006 main conference poster sessions. Sydney, 22 July 2006.

Garofolo, J., D. Graff, D. Paul, and D. Pallett. 1993. CSR-I (WSJ0) Complete LDC93S6A. Web download. Philadelphia: Linguistic Data Consortium.

Garside, R., G. Leech, and G. Sampson. eds. 1987. *The computational analysis of English: A corpus-based approach.* London: Longman.

Gildea, D., and D. Jurafsky. 2000. Automatic labeling of semantic roles. In Proceedings of ACL 2000, Hong Kong, 1–8 December 2000.

Gildea, D., and D. Jurafsky. 2001. Automatic labeling of semantic roles. ICSI Technical Report.

Gildea, D., and D. Jurafsky. 2002. Automatic labeling of semantic roles. *Computational Linguistics* 28 (3): 245–288.

Goyoh, Y., and S. Renals. 1999. Topic-based mixture language modeling. *Natural Language Engineering* 5 (4): 355–375.

Gramley, S., and K. M. Paetzold. 1992. *A Survey of modern English.* London : Routledge.

Gray, G. 2013. More than discipline: Uncovering multi-dimensional patterns of variation in academic research articles. *Corpora* 8 (2): 153–181.

Greenbaum, S. 1988. A proposal for an international corpus of English. *World Englishes* 7:315.

Greenbaum, S. 1992. A new corpus of English: ICE. In J. Svartvik (ed.), Direstions in corpus linguistics. Proceedings of the nobel symposium 82, Stockholm, 4–8 Aug 1991, Berlin, 171–179.

Greenbaum, S. 1992. *The ICE tagset manual.* London: Survey of English usage, University College London.

Greenbaum, S. 1993. In *The tagset for the international corpus of English,* ed. E. Atwell and C. Souter. 11–24.

Greenbaum, S. 1995. *The ICE tagset manual.* London: Survey of English usage, University College London.

Greenbaum, S. 1996a. *Comparing English world wide: The international corpus of English.* Oxford: Oxford University Press.

Greenbaum, S. 1996b. *The Oxford English grammar.* Oxford: Oxford University Press.

Greenbaum, S., and G. Nelson. 2009. *An introduction to English grammar,* 3rd ed. London: Pearson.

Greenbaum, S., and Y. Ni. 1994. Tagging the British ICE corpus: English word classes. In *Corpus-based research into language,* ed. N. Oostdijk and P. de Haan, 33–45. Amsterdam: Rodopi.

Greenbaum, S., and Y. Ni. 1996. Introducing ICE. In *Comparing English worldwide: The international corpus of English,* ed. S. Greenbaum, 3–12. Oxford: Clarendon.

Greene, B., and G. Rubin. 1971. *Automated grammatical tagging of English,* MA thesis. Providence: Brown University.

Grieve, J., D. Biber, E. Friginal, and T. Nekrasova. 2010. Variation among blogs: A multi-dimensional analysis. In *Genres on the Web: Computational models and empirical studies,* ed. A. Mehler, S. Sharoff, and M. Santini, 303–322. Dordrecht: Springer.

Gupta, R., and L. Ratinov. 2008. Text categorization with knowledge transfer from heterogeneous data sources. In Proceedings of the 23rd AAAI conference on artificial intelligence, Chicago, 13–17 July 2008, 842–847.

Gut, U. and L. Coronel. 2012. Relatives worldwide, In *Mapping unity and diversity world-wide,* ed. M. Hundt and U. Gut, 215–242. Amsterdam: John Benjamins.

Haase, C. 2004. Conceptualization specifics in East African English: Quantitative arguments from the ICE-East Africa corpus. *World Englishes* 23 (2): 261–268.

Hall, M., E. Frank, G. Holmes, B. Pfahringer, P. Reutemann, and I. H. Witten. 2009. The WEKA data mining software: An update. *SIGKDD Explorations* 11 (1): 10–18.

Halliday, M. A. K. 1978. Language as social semiotic. *The social interpretation of language and meaning*. London: Edward Arnold.

Halliday, M. A. K., and C. Matthiessen. 2004. *An introduction to functional grammar*. London: Arnold.

Harris, Z. 1951. *Structural linguistics*. Chicago: The University of Chicago Press.

Hasselgard, H. 2010. *Adjunct adverbials in English*. Cambridge: Cambridge University Press.

Hawkins, J. 1994. *A performance theory of order and constituency*. Cambridge: Cambridge University Press.

Hermerén, L. 1978. Testing the meanings of modals. *Studia Anglica Posnaniensia* 10:137–140.

Heylighen, F., and J. M. Dewaele. 1999. Formality of language: Definition, measurement and behavioral determinants. Internal Report, Center "Leo Apostel", Free University of Brussels.

Heylighen, F., and J. M. Dewaele. 2002. Variation in the contextuality of language: An empirical measure. *Context in Context: Special Issue Foundations of Science* 7 (3): 293–340.

Hilert, M., and M. Krug. 2012. Progressives in Maltese English: A comparison with spoken and written text types of British and American English, In *Mapping unity and diversity world-wide,* ed. M. Hundt and U. Gut, 103–136. Amsterdam: John Benjamins.

Hoffmann, S. 2009. Lexical change. In *English Language: Description, variation and context,* ed. J. Culpeper, F. Katamba, P. Kerwill, R. Wodak, and T. McEnery, 286–300. Basingstoke: Palgrave MacMillan.

Hofland, K., and S. Johansson. 1982. *Word frequencies in British and American English*. Bergen: Norwegian Computing Centre for the Humanities.

Höhn, N. 2012. "And they were all like 'What's going on?'": New quotatives in Jamaican and Irish English, In *Mapping unity and diversity world-wide,* ed. M. Hundt and U. Gut, 263–290. Amsterdam: John Benjamins.

Huddleston, R. 1971. *The sentence in written English: A syntactic study based on the analysis of scientific texts*. Cambridge: Cambridge University Press.

Hundt, M., and U. Gut. Eds. 2012. *Mapping unity and diversity world-wide: Corpus-based studies of new Englishes*. Amsterdam: Benjamins.

Hunt, Kellog. 1965. Grammatical structures written at three grade levels. NCTE Research report No. 3. Champaign, IL, USA: NCTE.

Hurmalainen, A., J. Gemmeke, and T. Virtanen. 2013. Compact long context spectral factorisation models for noise robust recognition of medium vocabulary speech. In Proceedings of the 2nd CHiME workshop, Vancouver, 1 June 2013, 13–18.

Ide, N., and K. Suderman. 2004. The American National Corpus first release. In Proceedings of the fourth language resources and evaluation conference (LREC), Lisbon, 26–28 May 2004, 1681–1684.

Ide, N., and K. Suderman. 2006. Merging Layered Annotations. In Proceedings of merging and layering linguistic information, Genoa, 24–26 May 2006.

Ikonomakis, M., S. Kotsiantis, and V. Tampakas. 2005. Text classification using machine learning techniques. *WSEAS Transactions on Computers* 4 (8): 966–974.

ISO 24617-2. 2012. Language resource management—Semantic annotation framework (SemAF), Part 2: Dialogue acts, Geneva

Jalali, V., and M. Borujerdi. 2011. Information retrieval with concept-based pseudo-relevance feedback in MEDLINE. *Knowledge and Information Systems* 29:237–248.

Janik, M., and K. J. Kochut. 2008. Wikipedia in action: Ontological knowledge in text categorization. In Proceedings of the 2nd international conference on semantic computing, Santa Clara.

Jeffery, C., and B. Van Rooy. 2004. Emphasizer now in colloquial South African English. *World Englishes* 23 (2): 269–280.

Jimeno-Yepes, A J., B. T. McInnes, and A. R. Aronson. 2011. Exploiting MeSH indexing in MEDLINE to generate a data set for word sense disambiguation. *BMC Bioinformatics* 12:223.

Johansson, S. 1978. Some aspects of the vocabulary of learned and scientific English. *Gothenburg Studies in English 42*. Gothenburg: Acta Universitatis Gothoburgensis.

Johansson, S. 1980. Corpus-based studies of British and American English. Papers from the Scandinavian Symposium on syntactic variation, Stockholm, 18–19 May 1979, ed. S. Jacobson, *Stockholm Studies in English 52,* 85–100, Stockholm: Almqvist & Wiksell.

Johansson, S., and K. Hofland. 1989. *Frequency analysis of English vocabulary and grammar: Based on the LOB corpus.* Oxford: Clarendon Press.

Johansson, S., and E. H. Norheim. 1988. The subjunctive in British and American English. *ICAME Journal* 12:27–36.

Johansson, S., and S. Oksefjell. 1996. Towards a unified account of the syntax and semantics of GET. In *Using corpora for language research: Studies in honour of geoffrey leech,* ed. J. Thomas & M. Short, 57–75. London: Longman.

Johansson, S., E. Atwell, R. Garside, and G. Leech. 1986. *The tagged LOB corpus: Users' manual.* Bergen: Norwegian Computing Centre for the Humanities.

Jucker, A. H., G. Schneider, I. Taavitsainen, and B. Breustedt. 2008. Fishing for compliments: Precision and recall in corpus-linguistic compliment research. In *Speech acts in the history of English,* ed. A. H. Jucker and I. Taavitsainen, 273–294. Amsterdam: Benjamins.

Jurafsky, D., E. Shriberg, and D. Biasca. 1997. Switchboard SWBD-DAMSL shallow-discourse-function annotation coders manual, Draft 13., Boulder: University of Colorado. Institute of Cognitive Science Technical report 97–02.

Kaatari, H. 2013. Adjectival complementation: Genre variation and meaning. In *Book of abstracts of ICAME* 34, 117.

Karlgren, J., and D. Cutting. 1994. Recognizing text genres with simple metrics using discriminant analysis. In Proceedings of the 15th international conference on computational linguistics *(COLING),* vol. 2, 1071–1075, Kyoto, 5–9 August 1994.

Kay, H., and Dudley-Evans, T. 1998. Genre: What teachers think. *ELT Journal* 52 (4): 308–314.

Kayaalp, M., A. R. Aronson, S. M. Humphrey, N. C. Ide, L. K. Tanabe, L. H. Smith, D. Demner, R. R. Loane, J. G. Mork, and O. Bodenrieder. 2003. Methods for accurate retrieval of MED-LINE citations in functional genomics. In *Notebook of the text retrieval conference (TREC),* 175–184.

Kehagias, A., V. Petridis, VG. Kaburlasos, and P. Fragkou. 2003. A comparison of word-and sense-based text categorization using several classification algorithms. *Journal of Intelligent Information Systems* 21 (3): 227–247.

Keller, F., and M. Lapata. 2003. Using the web to obtain frequencies for unseen bigrams. *Computational Linguistics* 29 (3): 459–484.

Kelly, C., B. Deverus, and A. Korhonen. 2010. Acquiring human-like feature-based conceptual representations from corpora. In Proceedings of the NAACL HLT 2010 first workshop on computational neurolinguistics, Los Angeles, California, 6 June 2010, 61–69.

Kerz, E., and F. Haas. 2009. The aim is to analyze NP: The function of prefabricated chunks in academic texts. In *Formulaic language: Vol 1: Distribution and historical change,* ed. R. Corrigan, E. Moravcsik, H. Ouali, and K. Wheatley, 97–116. Amsterdam: Benjamins.

Kessler, B., G. Nunberg, and H. Schütze. 1997. Automatic detection of genre. In Proceedings of the 35th annual meeting of the association for computational linguistics and the 8th meeting of the European chapter of the association for computational linguistics, Madrid, 7–12 July 1997, 32–38.

Kim, J. D., T. Ohta, and J. Tsujii. 2008. Corpus annotation for mining biomedical events from literature. *BMC Bioinformatics* 9:10

Kim, J. D., T. Ohta, S. Pyysalo, Y. Kano, and J. Tsujii. 2009. Overview of BioNLP '09 shared task on event extraction. In Proceedings of natural language processing in biomedicine (BioNLP) NAACL, 2009 Workshop, Colorado, 12 March 2009, 1–9.

Kim, J. D., S. Pyysalo, T. Dhta, R. Bossy, N. Nguyen, and J. Tsujii. 2011. Overview of BioNLP shared task 2011. In Proceedings of the BioNLP shared task 2011 workshop, Portland, Oregon, 24 June 2011, 1–6.

Kit, C., and X. Liu. 2008. Measuring mono-word termhood by rank difference via corpus comparison. *Terminology* 14 (2): 204–229.

Kjellmer, G. 1979. On clause-introductory 'nor' and 'neither'. *English Studies* 60:280–295.

Kjellmer, G. 1980. There is no hiding you in the house: On a modal use of the English gerund. *English Studies* 61:47–60.

Kjellmer, G. 1982. Some problems relating to the study of collocations in the Brown Corpus. In *Computer corpora in English language research,* ed. S. Johansson, 25–33. Bergen: Norwegian Computing Centre for the Humanities.

Kjellmer, G. 1994. *A dictionary of English collocations: Based on the brown corpus*. Oxford: Clarendon Press.

Klein, M., and C. Soria. 1998. Dialogue acts. In *MATE supported coding schemes. MATE project LE4–8370, deliverable D1.1*, ed. M. Klein, N. O. Bernsen, S. Davies, L. Dybkjær, J. Garrido, H. Kasch, A. Mengel, V. Pirrelli, M. Poesio, S. Quazza, and C. Soria.

Kolářik, C., R. Klinger, C. M. Frie-drich, M. Hofmann-Apitius, and J. Fluck. 2008. Chemical names: Terminological resources and corpora annotation. In Proceedings of LREC 2008 workshop: Building and evaluating resources for biomedical text, Marrakesh, 26 May 2008, 51–58.

Kordoni, V. 2013. Annotation and disambiguation of English compound units in the English Deep-Bank. In Proceedings of TLT 2013–12th workshop on treebanks and lingustic theories, Sofia, 13–14 December 2013, 97–108.

Koster, C. H., and M. Seutter. 2003. Taming wild phrases. In Proceedings of ECIR'03, 25th European conference on information retrieval, Pisa, 14–16 April 2003. 161–176. Pisa: Springer Verlag.

Král, P., and C. Cerisara. 2010. Dialogue act recognition approaches. *Computing and Informatics* 29:227–250.

Krogvig, I., and S. Johansson. 1981. Shall, will, should and would in British and American English. *ICAME News* 5:32–56.

Krogvig, I., and S. Johansson. 1984. *Shall and will* in British and American English: A frequency study. *Studia Linguistica* 38:70–87.

Kucera, H., and W. N. Francis. 1967. *Computational analysis of present-day American English*. Providence: Brown University Press.

Kwon, N., M. Fleischman, and E. Hovy. 2004. Senseval automatic labeling of semantic roles using Maximum Entropy models. In Proceedings of the 3rd international workshop on the evaluation of systems for the semantic analysis of text, Barcelona, 25–26 July 2004, 129–132.

Kwong, O. Y. 2001. Word sense disambiguation with an integrated lexical resource. In Proceedings of the NAACL 2001 workshop on WordNet and other lexical resources, Pittsburgh, 3–4 June 2001.

Laar, M. 1998. The Latin component in English medical texts and some of the possibilities it offers for interdisciplinary integrated teaching. In Proceedings of linguistics in estonia and finland: Crossing the fulf symposium, Tallinn, Estonia, 14–15 November 1997, 171–174.

Landis, R. J., and G. G. Koch. 1977. The measurement of observer agreement for categorical data. *Biometrics* 33:159–174.

Lange, C. 2012. *The syntax of spoken Indian English, VEAW G45*. Amsterdam: Benjamins.

Lee, D. 2001. Genres, registers, text types, domains and styles: Clarifying the concepts and navigating a path through the BNC Jungle. *Language Learning and Technology* 5 (3): 37–72.

Leech, G., R. Garside, and M. Bryant. 1994. CLAWS4: The tagging of the British National Corpus. In Proceedings of the 15th international conference on computational linguistics, Kyoto, 5–9 August 1994, 622–628.

Leech, G., P. Rayson, and A. Wilson. 2001. *Word frequencies in written and spoken English: Based on the British National Corpus*. London: Longman.

Leitner, G. 1994. *Begin* and *start* in British, American and Indian English. *Hermes* 13:99–122.

Levine, A. 1977. Syntactic synonymy: Sentences with *for*-infinitival and *that*-clause complements in modern English. PhD Dissertation. Jerusalem: Hebrew University

Li, Z., P. Li, W. Wei, H. Liu, J. He, T. Liu, and X. Du. 2009a. AutoPCS: A phrase-based text categorization system for similar texts. In Proceedings of the joint international conferences on advances in data and web management, Suzhou, 2–4 April 2009, 369–380.

Li, J., Y. Zhao, and B. Liu. 2009b. Fully automatic text categorization by exploiting WordNet. *Information Retrieval Technology* (Lecture Notes in Computer Science, Springer) 5839:1–12.

Lim, C., K. Lee, and G. Kim. 2005. Automatic genre detection of web documents. In Proceedings of natural language processing (IJCNLP' 04), Hainan Island, China, 22–24 March 2004, 310–319.

Liu, X. 1959. *The literary mind and the carving of dragons: A study of thought and pattern in Chinese literature*; translated with an introduction and notes by Vincent Yu-chung Shih. Columbia: Columbia University Press.

Liu, J.-S., P.-C. Hung, and C.-Y., Lee. 2008. A language information retrieval approach to writing assistance. *Computational Linguistics and Chinese Language Processing* 13 (3): 279–306.

Lo, F. 2008. The research of building a semantic category system based on the language characteristic of Chinese poetry. In Proceedings of the 9th cross-strait symposium on library information science. China, Wuhan University, 3–6 July 2008.

Louwerse, M. M., S. A. Crossley, and P. Jeuniaux. 2008. What if? Conditionals in educational registers. *Linguistics and Education* 19:56–69.

Magnini, B., and C. Strapparava. 2001. Using WordNet to improve user modelling in a web document recommender system. In Proceedings of the NAACL 2001 workshop on WordNet and other lexical resources, Pittsburgh, 3–4 June 2001.

Mair, C. 1987. *For/to*-infinitival clauses in contemporary British English—a study based on the material collected in the survey of English usage, University College London. In *English Studies, A Journal of English Language and Literature* 68 (6): 545–559.

Mair, C. 1990. *Infinitival complement clauses in English: A study of syntax in discourse.* Cambridge: Cambridge University Press.

Mair, C., and C. Winkle. 2012. Change from to-infinitive to bare infinitive in specificational cleft sentences: Data from world Englishes. In *Mapping unity and diversity world-wide,* ed. M. Hundt and U. Gut, 243–263. Amsterdam: John Benjamins.

Manning, C. 1993. Automatic acquisition of a large subcategorisation dictionary from corpora. In Proceedings of the 31st annual meeting of the Association for Computational Linguistics, Columbus, 22–26 June 1993, 235–242.

Marcus, Mitchell, Beatrice Santorini, and Mary Ann Marcinkiewicz. 1995. Treebank-2 LDC95T7, Web download. Philadelphia: Linguistic Data Consortium.

Marcus, M., B. Santorini, M. A. Marcinkiewicz, and A. Taylor. 1999. Treebank-3 LDC99T42. Web Download. Philadelphia: Linguistic Data Consortium.

Márquez, M. F. 2007. Renewal of core English vocabulary: A study based on the BNC. *English Studies* 88 (6): 699–723.

Martin, J. R. 2001. Language, register and genre. In *Analysing English in a global context: A reader,* ed. A. Burns and C. Coffin, 149–166. London: Routlege/Macquarie University/The Open University.

Martin, J. R. 2009. Language, register and genre. In *Applied linguistics methods: A reader,* ed. C. Coffin, T. Lillis, and K. O'Halloran, 12–32. London: Routledge.

Mata, J., M. Crespo, and M. J. Maña. 2012. Using MeSH to expand queries in medical image retrieval. *Medical Content-Based Retrieval for Clinical Decision Support* (Lecture Notes in Computer Science, Springer) 7075: 36–46.

McEnery, A. M., R. Z. Xiao, and Y. Tono. 2006. *Corpus-based language studies: An advanced resource book.* London: Routledge.

Meteer, M. and A. Taylor. 1995. *Disfluency annotation stylebook for the switchboard corpus.* ms. Technical report, Department of Computer and Information Science, University of Pennsylvania.

Miangah, T. M. 2011. The effect of exploiting corpus in TEFL classroom: A case study. *Theory and Practice in Language Studies* 1 (4): 370–378.

Mihalcea, R., and D. I. Moldovan. 2001. Word semantics for information retrieval: Moving one step closer to the semantic web. In Proceedings of international conference on tools in artificial intelligence, Dallas, Texas, 7–9 November 2001.

Mihalcea, R., C. Corley, and C. Strapparava. 2006. Corpus-based and knowledge-based measures of text semantic similarity. In Proceedings of the American Association for artificial intelligence (AAAI 2006), Boston, 16–20 July 2006, 775–780.

Miller, G. A. 1995. WordNet: A lexical database for English. *Communications of the ACM* 38 (11): 39–41.

Miller, G. A., and N. Chomsky. 1963. Finitary models of language users. In *Handbook of Mathematical Psychology,* vol. 2, ed. R. D. Luce, R. R. Bush, and E. Galanter, New York: Wiley.

MITRE Corporation. 2009. *SpatialML: Annotation scheme for marking spatial expressions in natural language.* Version 3.0, draft.

Moon, Y.-J., and Y.-T. Kim. 1995. Concept-based verb translation in the Korean-English machine translation system. *Journal of the Korea Information Science Society* 22 (8): 1166–1173.

Moreno, R. 2006. A new approach to register variation: The missing link. *IBÉRICA* 12:89–109.

Mukundan J., and N. Roslim. 2009. Textbook representation of prepositions. *English Language Teaching Journal: Canadian Center of Science and Education* 2 (4): 13–24.

Nakamura, J. 1989. A quantitative study on the use of personal pronouns in the Brown Corpus. *JACET Bulletin* 20:51–71.

Nakamura, J. 1993. Statistical methods and large corpora—A new tool for describing text type. In *Text and technology: In honor of John Sinclair,* ed. M. Baker, G. Francis, and E. Tognini-Bonelli, 291–312, Philadelphia: Benjamins.

Nakamura, J. 2002. A galaxy of words: Structures based upon distributions of verbs, nouns and adjectives in the LOB Corpus. In *Language and computers, English corpus linguistics in Japan,* ed. T. Saito, J. Nakamura, and S. Yamazaki, 19–42, New York: Rodopi B. V.

Nelson, G. 2004. Negation of lexical *have* in conversational English. *World Englishes* 23 (2): 299–308.

Nelson, G., and H. Ren. 2012. Particle verbs in African Englishes: Nativization and innovation, In *Mapping unity and diversity world-wide,* ed. M. Hundt and U. Gut, 197–214. Amsterdam: John Benjamins.

Nenadic, G., I. Spasic, and S. Ananiadou. 2005. Mining biomedical abstracts: What's in a term? In *Natural language processing—IJCNLP 2004 first international joint conference, lecture notes in computer science,* ed. K.-Y. Su, J. Tsujii, J.-H. Lee, and O. Kwong, vol. 3248, 797–806.

Nesi, H. 2009. A multidimensional analysis of student writing across levels and disciplines. In Proceedings of the BAAL annual conference, King's College, London, 8–9 July 2010.

Netzer, Y., D. Gabay, M. Adler, Y. Goldberg, and M. Elhadad. 2009. Ontology evaluation through text classification. *In advances in web and network technologies, and information management,* 210–221.

Newkirk, T. 2003. The learner develops: The high school years. In *Handbook of research on teaching the English language arts,* 2nd ed. ed. J. Flood, D. Lapp, J. R. Squire, and J. M. Jensen, 393–404, NJ: Lawrence Erlbaum.

Nilsson, N. 1996. *Introduction to machine learning,* Draft of incomplete notes. http://robotics.stanford.edu/people/nilsson/mlbook.html. Accessed 9 Dec 2014.

Norrick, N. R. 2009. Interjections as pragmatic markers. *Journals of Pragmatics* 4:866–891.

Ochs, Elinor. 1979. Planned and unplanned discourse. In *Discourse and syntax (Syntax and Semantics, vol. 12),* ed. T. Givón. 51–80, New York: Academic.

Palmer, F. R. 1974. *The English verb.* London: Longman.

Palmer, M., P. Kingsbury, O. Babko-Malaya, S. Cotton, and B. Snyder. 2004. *Proposition Bank I LDC2004T14.* Web download. Philadelphia: Linguistic Data Consortium.

Park, I. 2010. Marking an impasse: The use of anyway as a sequence-closing device. *Journal of Pragmatics* 42:3283–3299.

Passonneau, R., A. Salleb-Aoussi, V. Bhardwaj, and N. Ide. 2010. Word sense annotation of polysemous words by multiple annotators. In Proceedings of the seventh language resources and evaluation conference (LREC 2010), Valletta, Malta, 19–21 May 2010.

Passonneau, R., V. Bhardwaj, A. Salleb-Aouissi, and N. Ide. 2011. Multiplicity and word sense: Evaluating and learning from multiply labeled word sense annotations. *Language Resources and Evaluation* 46:219–252.

Paul, D. B., and J. Baker. 1991. The design for the Wall Street Journal-based corpus. In Proceedings of the workshop on Speech and Natural Language (HLT '91), Pacific Grove, California, 19–22 February 1991, 357–362.

Pestana, O. 2009. Information retrieval in MEDLINE: Searching for literature about critical care. In Proceedings of the 17th annual BOBCATSSS symposium, Porto, Portugal, 28–30 January 2009. 1–5.

Philip, A., J. Mukundan, and V. Nimehchisalem. 2012. Conjunctions in malaysian secondary school English language textbooks. *International Journal of Applied Linguistics & English Literature* 1 (1): 1–11.

Plag, I., C. Dalton-Puffer, and H. Baayen. 1999. Morphological productivity across speech and writing. *English Language and Linguistics* 3 (2): 137–207.

Popescu-Belis, A. 2004. Dialogue act tagsets for meeting understanding: An abstraction based on the DAMSL, switchboard and ICSI-MR tagsets. IM2.MDM report 09 Version 1.2—December 2004. University of Geneva. http://www.issco.unige.ch/en/research/projects/im2/mdm/docs/apb-mdm-report09-v12.pdf. Accessed 9 Dec 2014.

Pound, E. 1916. On 'In a Station of the Metro'. In *A memoir by Ezra Pound,* ed. Gaudier-Brzeska. London: John Lane Company.

Pustejovsky, J., and B. Boguraev. 1994. Lexical knowledge representation and natural language processing. In *Natural language processing,* ed. F. Perira and B. Grosz, 193–223. Massachusetts: MIT Press.

Pustejovsky, J., and A. Stubbs. 2012. *Natural language annotation for machine learning.* Sebastopol: O'Reilly Media, Inc.

Quarteroni, S., G. Riccardi, S. Varges, and A. Bisazza. 2008. An open-domain dialog act taxonomy. August 2008, Technical report # DISI-08-032, University of Trento.

Quirk, R., S. Greenbaum, G. Leech, and J. Svartvik. 1972. *A grammar of contemporary English.* London: Longman.

Quirk, R., S. Greenbaum, G. Leech, and J. Svartvik. 1985. *A comprehensive grammar of the English language.* London: Longman.

Rayson, P., and R. Garside. 2000. Comparing corpora using frequency profiling. In Proceedings of the workshop on comparing corpora, Hong Kong, 7 October 2000. 9:1–6.

Rayson, P., A. Wilson, and G. Leech. 2002. Grammatical word class variation within the british national corpus sampler. In *New frontiers of corpus research,* ed. P. Peters, P. Collins, and A. Smith, 295–306. Amsterdam: Rodopi.

Renouf, A. 2013. 'Hapax Legomena'. The silent majority in text. *Book of Abstracts of ICAME* 34:143.

Renshaw, E., C. J. C. Burges, and R. Gilad-Bachrach. 2014. Selective classifiers for part-of-speech tagging. Technical Report.

Rigau, G., H. Rodriguez, and J. Turmo. 1995. Automatically extracting translation links using a wide coverage semantic taxonomy. In Proceedings of the 15th international conference in language engineering (IA-95), Montpelier, 27–30 June 1995.

Rissanen, M. 2011. On the long history of English adverbial subordinators. In *Connectives in synchrony and diachrony in European languages,* ed. A. Meurman-Solin and U. Lenker, Studies in Variation, Contacts and Change in English 8.

Rissanen, M. 2012. Corpora and the study of English historical syntax. In *English corpus linguistics: Crossing paths,* ed. M. Kytö, 197–220. Amsterdam: Rodopi.

Rittman, R. 2008. *Automatic discrimination of genres: The role of adjectives and adverbs as suggested by linguistics and psychology.* Saarbrücken: Verlag Dr. Müller.

Roberts, H. A. 1965. *A statistical linguistic analysis of American English.* The Hague: Mouton.

Ronan, P., and G. Schneider. 2013. Investigating light verb constructions in contemporary British and Irish English. *In Book of Abstracts of ICAME* 34:146.

Rosset, S., D. Tribout, and L. Lamel. 2008. Multi-level information and automatic dialog act detection in human-human spoken dialogs. *Speech Communication* 50:1–13.

Ruppenhofer, J., and I. Rehbein. 2012. Semantic frames as an anchor representation for sentiment analysis. In Proceedings of the 3rd workshop in computational approaches to subjectivity and sentiment analysis, Jeju, Korea, July 2012. 104–109.

Ruppenhofer, J., C. F. Baker, and C. J. Fillmore. 2002. Collocational information in the framenet database. In Proceedings of the tenth European Association for lexicography, Copenhagen, 13–17 August 2002. vol. 1. 359–369.

Sampson, G. R. 1987. Evidence against the 'Grammatical'/'Ungrammatical' distinction. In *Corpus linguistics and beyond,* ed. W. Meijs, 219–226. Amsterdam: Editions Rodopi B.V.

Sampson, G. 2006. *Love songs of early China.* Donington: Shaun Tyas.

Sand, A. 2004. Shared morpho-syntactic features in contact varieties of English: Article use. *World Englishes* 23 (2): 281–298.

Santini, M. 2004. A shallow approach to syntactic feature extraction for genre classification. In Proceedings of the 7th annual colloquium for the UK special interest group for computational linguistics (CLUK 2004). Birmingham (UK), 6–7 January 2004.

Santorini, B. 1990. Part-of-speech tagging guidelines for the Penn Treebank Project. Technical report MS-CIS-90-47, Department of Computer and Information Science, University of Pennsylvania.

Schilk, M., T. Bernaisch, and J. Mukherjee. 2012. Mapping unity and diversity in South Asian English lexicogrammar: Verb-complementational preferences across varieties, In *Mapping unity and diversity world-wide,* ed. M. Hundt and U. Gut, 137–166. Amsterdam: John Benjamins.

Schmidt, T. 2006. Interfacing lexical and ontological information in a multilingual soccer FrameNet. In Proceedings of OntoLex 2006—Interfacing ontologies and lexical resources for Semantic Web Technologies, Genoa, 27 May 2006.

Schneider, E. W. 2004. How to trace structural nativization: Particle verbs in world Englishes. *World Englishes* 23 (2): 227–249.

Schneider, G., and M. Hundt. 2012. In *"Off with their heads": Profiling TAM in ICE corpora,* ed. M. Hundt and U. Gut, 1–34.

Scott, S., and S. Matwin. 1999. Feature engineering for text classification. In Proceedings of ICML'99, 16th international conference on machine learning, Bled, Slovenia, 27–30 June 1999. Morgan Kaufmann Publishers, San Francisco, US, 379–388.

Sebastiani, F. 2002. Machine learning in automatic text categorization. *ACM Computing Surveys* 34 (1): 1–47.

Sharoff, S. 2007. Classifying web corpora into domain and genre using automatic feature identification. *Cahiers du Cental* 5:1–10.

Shen, D., and M. Lapata. 2007. Using semantic roles to improve question answering. In Proceedings of the 2007 joint conference on empirical methods in natural language processing and computational natural language learning (EMNLP-CoNLL), Prague, 28–30 June 2007, 12–21.

Shriberg, E., R. Dhillon, S. Bhagat, J. Ang, and H. Carvey. 2004. The ICSI Meeting Recorder Dialog Act (MRDA) Corpus. In Proceedings of the Fifth SIGdial workshop on discourse and dialogue, Cambridge, Massachusetts, 30 April–1 May 2004, 97–100.

Sinclair, J. 1991. *Corpus, concordance, collocation.* Oxford: Oxford University Press.

Sinclair, J. 2004. *Trust the text: Language, corpus and discourse.* London: Routledge.

Socher, R., C. C. Lin, A. Y. Ng, and C. D. Manning. 2011. parsing natural scenes and natural language with recursive neural networks. In Proceedings of the 28th international conference on machine learning, Bellevue, Washington, 28 June–2 July 2011.

Sonbul, S., and N. Schmitt. 2013. Explicit and implicit lexical knowledge: Acquisition of collocations under different input conditions. *Language Learning* 63 (1): 121–159.

Stamatatos, E., N. Fakotakis, and G. Kokkinakis. 2000. Text genre detection using common word frequencies. In Proceedings of the 18th conference on computational linguistics (COLING '00), Saarbrucken, 11–15 September 2000, 808–814.

Stehman, S. V. 1997. Selecting and interpreting measures of thematic classification accuracy. *Remote Sensing of Environment* 62 (1): 77–89.

Stein, B., and S. M. Eissen. 2008. Retrieval models for genre classification. *Scandinavian Journal of Information Systems* 20 (1): Article 3.

Stockwell, R., and D. Minkova. 2001. *English words: History and structure.* Cambridge: Cambridge University Press.

Stolcke, A., K. Ries, N. Coccaro, E. Shriberg, R. Bates, D. Jurafsky, P. Taylor, R. Martin, C. V. Ess-Dykema, and M. Meteer. 2000. Dialogue act modeling for automatic tagging and recognition of conversational speech. *Computational Linguistics* 26:339–373.

Svartvik, J., and M. Eeg-Olofsson. 1982. Tagging the London-Lund Corpus of Spoken English. In *Computer corpora in English language research,* ed. S. Johansson, 85–102. Bergen: Norwegian Computing Centre for the Humanities.

Swales, J. M. 1990. *Genre analysis: English in academic and research settings.* Cambridge: Cambridge University Press.

Takahashi, K. 2006. A study of register variation in the British National Corpus. *Literary and Linguistic Computing* 21 (1): 111–126.

Taylor, A., M. Marcus, and B. Santorini. 2003. The Penn Treebank: An overview. In *Treebanks: Building and using parsed corpora,* ed. A. Abeillé, 5–22. Berlin: Springer.

Tesnière, L. 1959. *Éléments de Syntaxe Structural*. Paris: Klincksieck.

The British National Corpus, version 3 (BNC XML Edition). 2007. Distributed by Oxford University Computing Services on behalf of the BNC Consortium. http://www.natcorp.ox.ac.uk/. Accessed 9 Dec 2014.

Thompson, S. 1984. Subordination in formal and informal discourse. In *Meaning, form, and use in context: Linguistic applications*, ed. D. Schffrin, 85–94. Washington DC: Georgetown University Press.

Thompson, C., R. Levy, and C. Manning. 2003. A generative model for FrameNet semantic role labeling. In Proceedings of 14th European conference on machine learning, Cavtat-Dubrovnik, Croatia, 22–26 September 2003. Springer, 2837:397–408.

Thorndike, E. L., and I. Lorge. 1944. *The teacher's word book of 30,000 words*. New York: Teachers College Press. Columbia University Press.

Traum, D. 1999. Speech acts for dialogue agents. In *Foundations of rational agency*, ed. M. Wooldridge and A. Rao, 169–201. Dordrecht: Kluwer.

Ushioda, A., D. Evans, T. Gibson, and A. Waibel. 1993. The automatic acquisition of frequencies of verb subcategorization frames from tagged corpora. In Proceedings of SIGLEX ACL workshop on the acquisition of lexical knowledge from Text, Columbus, Ohio, 21 June 1993. 95–106.

Vadas, D., and J. R. Curran. 2011. Parsing noun phrases in the Penn Treebank. *Computational Linguistics* 37 (4): 753–809.

van Ek J. 1966. *Four complementary structures of complementation in modern English*. Groningen.

van Rooy B., and L. Terblanche. 2009. A multi-dimensional analysis of a learner corpus. In *Language and computers*, ed. A. Renouf and A. Kehoe, 239–254(16). Amsterdam: Rodopi.

Venturi, G., A. Lenci, S. Montemagni, E. M. Vecchi, M. T. Sagri, D. Tiscornia, and T. Agnoloni. 2009. Towards a FrameNet resource for the legal domain. In Proceedings of the third workshop on legal ontologies and artificial intelligence techniques. Barcelona, 8 June 2009.

Vertanen, K. 2006. Baseline WSJ acoustic models for HTK and Sphinx: Training recipes and recognition experiments. Technical report, Cavendish Laboratory.

Ville-Ometz, F., J. Royaute, and A. Zasad-zinski. 2007. Enhancing automatic recognition and extraction of term variants with linguistic features. *Terminology* 13 (1): 35–59.

Vlachos, A., and C. Gasperin. 2006. Boot-strapping and evaluating named entity recognition in the biomedical domain. In Proceedings of BioNLP in HLT-NAACL, New York City, 4–5 June 2006. 138–145.

Wang, S. 2005. Corpus-based approaches and discourse analysis in relation to reduplication and repetition. *Journal of Pragmatics* 37:505–540.

Warren, B. 1978. Semantic patterns of noun-noun compounds. *Gothenburg studies in English 41*. Gothenburg: Acta Universitatis Gothoburgensis.

Westin, I., and C. Geisler. 2002. A Multi-dimensional study of diachronic variation in British newspaper editorials. *ICAME* 26:133–152.

Widdows, D., S. Cederberg, and B. Dorow. 2002. Visualisation techniques for analyzing meaning. In Proceedings of the 5th international conference on text, speech and dialogue (TSD 5), Brno, Czech Republic, 9–12 September 2002. 107–115.

Witten, I. H., and E. Frank. 2005. *Data mining: practical machine learning tools and techniques*, 2nd ed. San Francisco: Morgan Kauf-mann.

Wright, M. 2011. The phonetics-interaction interface in the initiation of closings in everyday English telephone calls. *Journal of Pragmatics* 4:1080–1099.

Xia, J. B., A. C. Fang, and X. Zhang. 2014. A novel feature selection strategy for enhanced biomedical event extraction using the Turku System. *BioMed Research International*, vol. 2014, Article ID 205239, 12 pages, 2014. doi:10.1155/2014/205239.

Xiao, R., and H. Tao. 2007. A corpus-based sociolinguistic study of amplifiers in British English. *Sociolinguistic Studies* 1 (2): 241–273.

Yamazaki, S., and R. Sigley. 2013. Preface: Approaching variation. In *Approaching language variation through corpora: A festschrift in honour of Toshio Saito*, ed. S. Yamazaki and R. Sigley, 17–22. Bern: Peter Lang.

Yeganova, L., D. C. Comeau, K. Won, and W. J. Wilbur. 2011. Text mining techniques for leveraging positively labeled data. In Proceedings of BioNLP 2011 workshop, Portland, 24 June 2011, 155–163.

Yuan, X.-P. 1989. *Research in the art of poetry*. Taiwan: Wunan Book Publishing Co.

Zettersten, A., and H. Kučera. 1978. *A word frequency list based on American press reportage*. Akadmisk Forlag.

Zipp, L., and T. Bernaisch. 2012. Particle verbs across first and second language varieties of English, In *Mapping unity and diversity world-wide,* ed. M. Hundt and U. Gut, 167–196. Amsterdam: John Benjamins.

Index

© Springer-Verlag Berlin Heidelberg 2015
A. C. Fang, J. Cao, *Text Genres and Registers: The Computation of Linguistic Features,*
DOI 10.1007/978-3-662-45100-7